Animal Tracking Basics

JON YOUNG
and
TIFFANY MORGAN

STACKPOLE BOOKS

Published by
Stackpole Books
5067 Ritter Road
Mechanicsburg, PA 17055
www.stackpolebooks.com

Printed in the United States of America

10 9 8 7 6 5 4 3 2 1

First edition

Cover photograph of Grey Wolf Walking in Forest © Corbis
Back cover photograph of Marsh © Laura Flippen
Cover design by Wendy A. Reynolds
Photographs and illustrations by Tiffany Morgan unless otherwise indicated

Library of Congress Cataloging-in-Publication Data

Young, Jon, 1960–
    Animal tracking basics / Jon Young and Tiffany Morgan.
        p. cm.
    ISBN-13: 978-0-8117-3326-7
    ISBN-10: 0-8117-3326-2
    1. Tracking and trailing. 2. Animal tracks. I. Morgan, Tiffany. II. Title.

SK282.Y68 2007
590—dc22
                                                                    2006012166

Contents

Acknowledgments

I have much appreciation for the animals that continue to live in harmony with the earth, particularly the bobcat and gray fox that have taught me much about the realities of their lives. The landscapes I've tracked on have been just as instrumental in my understanding of animals as the animals themselves, so I thank the waters, soils, plants, trees, sun, moon, and stars for shaping and sustaining life.

I would like to thank Tom Brown Jr. and his tracking school for introducing me to tracking and inspiring in me a passion for following footprints—no matter how difficult the substrate. Tremendous thanks to co-author Jon Young and his Kamana Naturalist Training Program and Shikari Tracker Training Program, which taught me the importance of each animal's unique relationship to the landscape—including my personal connection. White Pine Programs was instrumental in providing a community of trackers and naturalists with the shared passion of absorbing themselves, as well as our students, in the mysteries of the natural world; special thanks to Dan Hansche and Dan Gardoqui of White Pine for encouraging me to pursue my goals in tracking and nature studies even in a foreign place. The guidance of Mark Elbroch cemented my knowledge of animal track identification and gait analysis, which opened a pathway for the greater portion of my tracking knowledge to evolve.

Many people contributed to the creation of this book; I am grateful for the knowledge, expertise, and support of the following people: Paul Houghtaling for his dedication to the Shikari Tracker Training Program, which provided much of the inspiration and material for the creation of this book; the Rickes family provided me with a beautiful place to live in San Gregorio with an abundance of wildlife just outside my door; Terril Shorb edited and revised many of my personal tracking stories; Ken Clarkson provided photography and instruction for making soot trays; Doniga Markegard for her support and for sharing her expertise in utilizing camera traps; David Forthoffer for graciously offering his digital camera and photography skills; Karen Dvornich of NatureMapping for providing alternative soot tray instructions; Jonah Evans for his photographs of animal tracks and the tracker evaluation; Barry Martin for his enthusiasm in applying tracking in wildlife research and for his contribution to the chapter on tracking tools; Laura Flippen for offering her photography for the cover and accompanying me on a trip to the desert in the middle of summer; Walker Korby for his interest in how animals move and for offering his animal forms story; Travis Brown for his experience and knowledge related to live trapping small mammals; Louis Leibenberg for his contributions to the field of wildlife tracking and for including me in the first Cyber-Tracker evaluation held in the United States; Wendolyn Bird for her support and for sharing her stories; Maureen McConnell for her encouragement over the years and for permission to use bird language graphics from the Boston Museum of Science bird language exhibit; Cara Burrow for listening and offering help during the editing process and for providing her house as a quiet refuge; Jeff Goldberg for renting me his cherished digital camera at the last minute; and the many people I have tracked with over the years for offering their insights and questions, which have undeniably added to the depth of my knowledge and the quality of my tracking experience.

The following people inspired in me the determination and enthusiasm to see this book through to completion. My father provided moral and financial support, which relieved me of other obligations, so I could meet deadlines. My mother encouraged me throughout the process with phone calls to inquire how the book was coming along. My twin sister, Nicole, continues to share with me an interest in the mysterious lives of animals, which makes tracking that much more gratifying. My sister Alison celebrated my accomplishments with me, which helped me value my work. Lori Damiano, through her friendship and caring, gave me the confidence to tell my stories. Although they've passed on, Ernest Thompson Seton, Olaus Murie, and Ingwe have been constant inspirations for me in tracking as well as naturalist studies. Finally, I offer my deepest gratitude to my loving partner, Thomas Campbell, who helped me in every way possible to realize my dream of passing on this knowledge.

T.M.

1

Mathew and the One-Eyed Cat

It is a wholesome and necessary thing for us to turn again to the earth and in the contemplation of her beauties to know of wonder and humility.

—Rachel Carson

T.M.

Our goose was in the driveway, standing loyally by the side of his reflection in the mirrored surface of the Ford Expedition's bumper. He may have wondered why this other goose insisted on colliding beaks with him, to the exclusion of any other contact. More likely, he didn't wonder about this at all, and that's precisely why the relationship worked. Mathew, as we affectionately called him, flew in one afternoon, became instant chums with the tough-billed bumper goose, and put up with us humans walking back and forth across the driveway.

One day, three months after his arrival, I was working at my computer and could just see Mathew in my peripheral vision through a large window on the north side of the office. He had become like just another object in the yard, and then he made an alarming sound. Mathew was always vocal, to say the least, but this new vocalization was eccentric for him, so it piqued my interest. I lifted my chin and squinted my eyes to focus on the bird. He was taking quick, confused steps away from the car toward the office, as if he couldn't choose which direction to go, or whether to go at all. In hindsight, I wonder whether he was waiting for his imaginary friend to stick by his side. He held his head high and twisted, with one wary eye looking up and to the left while he made rapid squeaking honks. It clearly wasn't the same agitation he exhibited when a human approached; for that encounter, he took on a more defensive posture, hissing and extending his neck for ankles to nip. Gray foxes often visited the garden to eat compost on a nearby hillside, but they hardly got Mathew's attention. Who or what was causing this odd behavior?

The shrill warning calls of Steller's jays began beating down from the trees with an unprecedented intensity. Instinctively rising out of my seat, I scanned the dark areas below the brush and trees surrounding the yard. A predator was moving into the area with the intention to kill. It emerged from behind the office, skirting the periphery down the east side of the driveway, swift and subtle. Moving stealthily into the shadow of a cluster of redwood trees, it crouched into a stalk and slithered up the woodpile to perch. It stood silent, neck outstretched and eyes riveted on the goose, its nub of a tail twitching methodically. It was a bobcat.

I could have pounded on the window or run to the door, shouting words the cat would never know the meaning of, but my curiosity was too great, and my time to react was up. The bobcat glided in on soft padded feet, intent on its target. In an effort to escape, Mathew jumped straight up, giving two quick wing beats and reaching with all his will toward the safety of the sky. The Steller's jays' pleadings were deafening; they cried out as if the victim were one of their own. Ignoring their insults, the cat leaped, its body bowing backward as it stretched with a slight twist, providing just enough leverage for the needled claws to reach in and slice through the feathers, fastening in skin and dragging both of them back down. It seemed to me that the bobcat's mouth was already around the goose's neck when they touched down—such was the speed of this animal. There was hardly a struggle. The only sound was wings brushing the ground, a quiet submission. The goose's body twitched, but the movements didn't seem connected to the listless eye facing me with vacant acceptance.

With its teeth still in the neck, the cat moved to the back of the goose and straddled the kill. It then proceeded to tug with a jarring motion, teetering back and forth, with only three legs touching down at one time, and lugged its quarry onto a wooden walkway in front of the house. Assuming that the cat was going to disappear into the nearest cover, I quickly grabbed my camera. But it surprised me and continued down the walkway, making no protest as I followed. A thin trail of blood stretched behind, soaking into the wood, as the cat dragged the goose to the end of the deck. Dropping down onto the redwood duff and into the shadows of the ancient trees, the cat seemed more at ease. For the first time since I had been following, often at a mere 5-foot distance, it looked back at me, and I saw that one eye was a bulging, bluish-purple orb rippled with veins. I shuddered at the sudden and unexpected sight of this wound, but intrigue held me there.

The cat was small for a male, and immature. A scene played out in my mind: two bobcats fighting over territory, the immature one taking a great risk by pushing past the mature male's boundaries; the larger cat, seeing the smaller one as more of a pest than a threat, attacking without hesitation and slitting the young one's eye with a quick jab.

As my initial amazement subsided, I looked at this creature with more of an investigative eye. If I had learned anything from the young bobcat, it was not to assume. Everything it had done so far had shattered my ideas, from hunting at a residence in the middle of the day to how it carried the carcass. It struck me how thin its torso was, the ribs appearing with each rapid exhalation. Was it near starvation? I had nothing to compare its seemingly emaciated body to, having never been so close to a wild bobcat. I had seen one that hunts in a nearby meadow, but only from a distance. Even so, I could tell that it was bigger and hardier than this one. This cat seemed desperate, taking the risk of coming into the yard and staying with its kill even as I followed. With its eye injury, I imagined that this cat's hunting prowess was seriously hindered. I had heard from many sources that young males or injured animals are most likely to kill livestock; this one was possibly both, adding credence to this premise.

I then wondered whether this cat had come from a great distance, like a pirate seeking new ships. Two days prior to this incident, I had taken notes and sketched fresh bobcat scat at the top of our driveway. I had remarked then that it seemed out of place, abandoned, and I had wondered what a bobcat was doing so near the house. The foxes leave scat all around the garden walkways in conspicuous places, as if to claim the compost there. Now I wondered whether the cat had marked the area in much the same way, with the intention of claiming our goose for its own when the opportunity presented itself.

"One-eye," as I began to think of him, began his descent on a wide trail beyond the house into a grove of redwoods; an entourage of scolding Steller's jays followed, as if to point out the escape route of the murderer. With the goose still laced between his legs, One-eye arrived at the first of two rivulets that feed into Corte de Madera Creek. He didn't hesitate to pour his thin frame down into the water, and the lifeless goose followed like an appendage. One-eye tried to pull Mathew's weight up the other side of the narrow crevice but lost the battle; both tumbled back into the water, the goose landing squarely atop the spread-out cat, and I couldn't help but laugh. Still, it was thrilling to have a close-up look at a wild animal involved in its everyday life—its triumphs, struggles, and limitations. It was an opportunity to rub away the fantasy and get a glimpse of the animal as it truly is.

One-eye didn't have much of a choice. The banks were too steep, so he left the goose in a shallow pool and crawled up on shore. This brought the two of us even closer. I could see that he was out of breath, his sides moving in and out spastically. He glared at me with that creepy eye, and I realized that I had crossed the creek and that the bobcat was between me and the house. Although it was unlikely, I was fearful of a savage attack like the one I had just witnessed. I made a large arc around the cat, crossing back over the rivulet where it meets Corte de Madera Creek. The cat's good eye followed me the whole way, his head swiveling around on a slinky neck to examine me on the other side of interfering trees. Coincidently, the jays had the same inclination to return to their previous activities, and we retreated to our respective territories, leaving the cat alone for the time being.

After alerting the others in my household about the loss of Mathew, I returned to investigate the scene. The jays continued building their nests and foraging overhead while I looked for clues that would lead a tracker to the story behind the missing goose. There was no obvious drag mark through the redwood duff, just a few downy feathers spaced 20 to 30 feet apart along the trail. And these were difficult to spot, even though I knew where to look. The blood tracks on the deck were already fading to a faint smell of death. There were no apparent marks of a struggle in the dirt on the driveway; the few feathers that remained were rapidly blowing away. I was astonished by the patience and the skillful observation it would take to piece this event together had I not been there to see it firsthand, but more important, I realized that it was entirely possible to do so.

I returned to where the bobcat was now feeding. He had resorted to pulling the kill up between two half-submerged rocks wedged with redwood duff and other debris, forming a leaky little dam that dripped under the goose's back. Wasting no time, One-eye pulled out mouthfuls of downy feathers from the stomach until he had made a bald spot. The more he ate, the less he tolerated my presence; twice he hissed and growled at me. The jays returned with an occasional reprimand. The cat fed for five hours, until all that was left was a pile of feathers and bones.

It rained lightly that evening, and a gray fox appeared in the garden looking suspicious, sensing something in the air. When I returned to the creek in the morning, the kill had been covered with debris scraped up from the banks. I'm not sure whether the cat planned to return, but it seemed that there wasn't much to return to. Most of the feathers had washed downstream, and all that was left was one of Mathew's bright orange feet. I recalled with fondness the rhythmic slapping sound his feet had made as he walked across the driveway. It's strange how weeks after the incident I still think I hear Mathew honking, only to remember that he's dead and that the bobcat lives on, if only for another day.

J.Y./T.M.

Anyone who tracks animals knows that tracking involves more than just footprints. It's about paying attention to the language of birds, such as the alarm calls and mobbing behavior of Steller's jays. It requires searching for sign, such as bobcat scat, and knowing that it's not fox. It's about piecing together subtle clues, such as feathers, drag marks, and bloodstains. And it's also about reaching for the highest level of perceptual training.

In the modern world, we have been trained to accept a much lower degree of perception than our ancestors could afford, especially when they depended on their hunting and gathering skills to live. However, our modern brains and bodies can still rise to these challenges—we were designed for them. We believe our indigenous ancestors, whose skills were refined by real need, likely represent the pinnacle of skill in every category of tracking: human tracking, big-game tracking, law-enforcement tracking, inner tracking, spiritual tracking, search-and-rescue tracking, and wildlife tracking. Today most of us, however, typically choose only one or two of these categories and develop the requisite skill sets; although these are valuable for specific jobs and tasks, they are often one-dimensional. Our intention with this book is to help you get the most from your tracking experience. This doesn't necessarily require a lot of effort; it can be as simple as paying more attention.

We believe our indigenous ancestors, by their very nature, were constantly aware of multiple aspects of tracking. They had access to a vast store of memories, skills, and knowledge in their minds and bodies. In this way, they were able to reach well beyond the boundaries of many current tracking applications and practice a multidisciplinary approach. We call this holistic tracking.

Holistic tracking relies on the development of the senses, combined with knowledge of the local environment. Let's start with the development of vision, because this is our most dominant sense. In holistic wildlife tracking, the eyes are utilized to their fullest potential. The ability to scrutinize subtle patterns and tiny details is but one aspect of how we see the world. We experience many hours of this perceptual training: we learn to recognize letters, words, and numbers on black and white pages; faces, roads, houses, and other places of regular visitation; and images projected onto screens. Although all these aspects of vision are useful and practical, they do not compare with the visual challenges provided by nature.

In nature, the opportunity to focus on detail and complexity, on color and beauty, on pattern and mystery is unlimited. Sometimes I fall into the trap of seeing the man-made world and its writings and workings as complex; then my eyes fall onto nature and I remember that nothing humans have constructed can compare with the pure infinite of nature. When I use my eyes to scrutinize and recognize nature, it is an entirely different process from using my eyes to read or to find my way in a city or to identify something I need in a store. Nature has a way of adding multiple dimensions and awakening a part of my perception that seems to model or mirror the patterns of nature. My eyes, trained by countless hours of observation, feel like fine instruments in an orchestra when I am studying the tracks of a deer or a mouse or a deer mouse. I am awakening to something, not just identifying it.

Tracking involves so much more than using the eyesight to study a pattern in the mud. It also draws on the power of peripheral vision—the ability, after years of practice, to see and recognize the flick of a sparrow's tail at 100 yards and know that it means a cat is hidden just beyond view. There is a context to what the eyes see—both the focused vision that recognizes and interprets detail and the peripheral sense that recognizes the larger patterns all around. This cannot be gleaned from a book or from a set of footprints.

This holistic sense of orchestrated visual perception comes from years of relating to a particular landscape and its inhabitants. This holistic sense of observation with the eyes alone is derived from countless hours of living on and loving the land. The eyes are trained on the patterns of distant and close trees: their leaves, bark, fruit, seeds, and overall shapes at all ages. The same is true for the small herbaceous plants. The eyes are trained on the hundreds of species of plants in all seasons that become a living, interwoven context in which insects, spiders, and other invertebrates move and crawl, seemingly without end. This level of complexity involves the moving images of sun, shadow, cloud, and snow and the tapestry of stars and moonlight. This provides a visual framework for the lives of four-legged or no-legged or swimming creatures. Their patterns and motions mark the landscape over time in subtle layers of evidence. Unconsciously and consciously, the mind asks questions of the eyes, based on the landscape's subtle and obvious cues in all realms of study: ecology, botany, geology, meteorology, astronomy, zoology, psychology.

Vision alone provides infinite potential in tracking, but humans also possess a remarkable ability to glean terabytes of information from a split-second glance at body language. Perhaps this is a holdover from our need to understand the intentions of our enemies and predators ages ago. Birds and mammals can clearly do this, and they need to do it to conserve energy and make sound choices throughout their wild and risky lives. Nothing in our modern world awakens this ability like living close to nature, as part of nature.

The holistic tracker seeks to simulate that wild world in as many ways as possible, deriving power from the challenge of discerning endless diversity in a split second. Move through the forest and allow yourself to believe that there are good reasons to stop, look behind, and look above while moving through the landscape, as if you're living in a constant game of predator and prey. Your instincts and behaviors will reflect the training that your eyes have experienced.

This same quality of experience is provided to the senses of hearing, smell, taste, and touch. With the highly refined ability to visualize, you can mentally relive or physically re-create the experiences of the other senses.

Holistic tracking is also about mental processes. It is about unbridled imagination and curiosity about absolutely everything—from the greatest to the tiniest aspects of this endless creation. It is about asking questions and remembering the answers. It is about taking those answers and linking them to other questions. It is about linking the moon to the tides, the tides to the mud, the mud to the algae to the shrimp to the curlew to the fox. It is about finding a fox hair caught on a thorn 2 miles from the marsh and knowing that it was on the marsh that morning.

You wander through the forest, carrying all your questions, and your senses are piqued to find the answers. Yet, you have no thought in your mind as you move. Your instincts guide you. You are quiet inside, poised and ready. You have the wariness of the deer, the nose of the fox, the movements of the cat. You are nature. You are wild. You are fully alive and expressed.

Now you are beginning to sense the world of the holistic tracker. You are experiencing a blending of absolutely all aspects of the universe, yet you are silent inside and out. You have tracked the world around you. You have tracked the world within. You know why people move the way they do, because you know why you do this yourself.

When you weave together all aspects of creation, you are practicing integral awareness. When you take your perceptual ability and see through the eyes of the wildlife you study, when you go forward with all your curiosity and all your questions about the world of the animals, you are tracking holistically.

To reach for the singular goal of being a wildlife tracker is to drop the tail of a powerful, mythical being whose tracks lie in your very soul. Instead, challenge yourself to reach for the whole of creation when practicing this extraordinary activity, which encompasses all of nature and the nature of humans, external and internal, tangible and intangible. Take a risk. Stretch beyond your current limits of perception and delve into the great mystery of creation. Wildlife tracking will then come naturally.

2

Getting Started

Climb the mountains and get their good tidings. Nature's
peace will flow into you as sunshine flows into trees. The
winds will blow their own freshness into you and the storms
their energy, while cares will drop off like autumn leaves.
— John Muir (1901)

BECOMING A TRACKER:
THE STAGES OF DEVELOPMENT

The process of becoming a tracker follows an ancient, natural flow. Stage 1 consists of basic naturalist training, a time of exploration, hiking, reading, and lots of fun. Fledgling naturalists know that they have much to learn and are eager to do so.

Stage 2 is what we call the time of the focused naturalist. These students are much more focused in their studies than beginners are. They are uncomfortable with tracks and sign they can't identify. They journal and draw everything they find in the wilderness, and spending time in the woods becomes more like studying and less like playing. They are never caught without their binoculars, field guides, tape measures, journals, and magnifying glasses in their backpacks. This is a time of intense learning. Those who stay in stage 2 for a while know that they want to be trackers. Time and again, they discover that they will never master nature and that there will always be more to learn—and that thought drives them nuts.

Stage 3 is what we call the tracker. Something subtle but dramatic happens between stages 2 and 3. Studying once again turns into playing. Trackers still carry tape measures and field guides, but they laugh a lot more than focused naturalists do. They are again comfortable with the fact that they will never know all that can be known in nature, and they find joy in that humility.

Bruce Lee, the famous martial artist and actor, called the three stages of a martial artist "the stages of cultivation." He wrote: "Before I learned martial art, a punch was just like a punch, a kick just like a kick. After I learned martial art, a punch was no longer a punch, a kick no longer a kick. Finally, after I understood martial art, a punch is just like a punch, a kick just like a kick." This analogy is perfect for tracking and nature observation.

The key is that every step in the process is important. There is no shortcut around the focused naturalist stage, and trying to skip it will only set you back. Let yourself get into it and enjoy the whole process, even if it drives you crazy.

This guide is designed to be used by the readers at any stage—from beginning naturalists to experienced trackers. It is a reference guide for teachers, students, and tracking enthusiasts. This chapter lays the foundation for all the tracking exercises that follow. Some of the practices detailed in this chapter may not seem to be related to tracking, but they have been tried and tested by students of Jon Young's Kamana Naturalist Training Program. We've seen the profound influence that these routines can have on students' tracking ability—often without the students realizing that any training in tracking had taken place. These practices are also enjoyable, so have fun with them to derive the greatest benefit.

LESSONS FROM A SIT SPOT

A sit spot is simply a place on the landscape that you feel connected to and are drawn to visit. It is a place of solitude and stillness where your senses are activated and your mind is engaged in processing the nuances and rhythms of nature. The routine of frequently visiting your sit spot can sharpen your tracking skills like nothing else. With time, your chosen place will become as familiar as your own bedroom. A recent dig or a broken limb will grab your attention as if someone had moved the furniture in your bedroom during your absence. As you seek to discover exactly what occurred, layers of learning will unfold to reveal the intricacies of the lives of animals and their relationship to the landscape, one another, and you. Visiting one place repeatedly over time will expand your awareness to include a greater knowledge of all places. This spot will create a context for all your studies, no matter how far they take you; the observations you make at your sit spot will build on your knowledge of natural systems. This knowledge can be applied to any ecosystem, whether you're in Africa, Australia, or the middle of the ocean. Wherever you travel, you will already have a basic understanding of the rhythms of the animals there.

T.M.

I grew up loving nature and spending every possible moment outside, yet the idea of animal tracking never crossed my mind. Perhaps it was the lack of snow in San Diego, but I never consciously thought about tracks. Sure, I must have seen tracks: dog tracks on the beach, or the humanlike fingers and toes of a raccoon track in a mud puddle. However, the usefulness of this information was lost to me. Studying or attempting to categorize animal tracks seemed akin to counting sidewalk cracks or looking for images in wall plaster. Then I attended Tom Brown's tracker school in New Jersey, where tracking was intro-

Raccoon tracks.

duced not only as a legitimate pastime but also as a gateway to spiritual enlightenment. Brown (1999) wrote, "Yet awareness and tracking go beyond the physical. Grandfather once said, 'Awareness is the doorway to the spirit.' A track is not only a window to the past but a doorway to an animal's very soul. The challenge is to step through that doorway." I'm not sure that I stepped through that doorway on my first day at the tracker farm, but I did make the physical connection: animal tracks *are* an animal's story. Those stories aren't locked away in books or accessible only through chance meetings with wild animals. Tracks, I learned, are everywhere: mud puddles, dirt roads, dusty barns, grass, sand, snow, and trees. One need only look for them.

After completing Brown's course, I was thoroughly intrigued by tracking but unsure how to apply my new interest and knowledge. Then my friend Wil Daniel told me about the Kamana Naturalist Training Program developed by Jon Young. Wil told me intriguing stories about his sit spot, but what stood out was the connection he felt to his place and the sense of peace it brought him. I didn't need any convincing. Upon my arrival back home in San Diego, I set out immediately to find this unique place where I would learn to be a naturalist. I lived in a suburban neighborhood that wrapped around a chaparral canyon, and there was a small opening at the southwest end where a mostly dry river emptied into the Pacific Ocean. The canyon was like an island: if an animal wanted to leave, it had to cross a sea of houses and buildings to get to the next natural area. These limitations may have made life difficult for the animals, but it was the ideal location for me to begin my studies. There was just enough variety to hold my interest; any more would have been overwhelming.

I had been in the canyon only once before, so my search for a sit spot started out as more of a wander. I meandered down to the river, which was really just a stagnant pool in the hot, dry days of late summer. It wasn't very appealing, so I perused the far edge of the canyon, where few people roamed. In the distance, I saw the green of what I would later learn was an ash tree. It beckoned to me. The air felt cool and fragrant as I weaseled through the coyote brush. When I neared the tree's trunk, the brush became sparse and revealed a hidden rivulet. So this was why the ash tree had spread its roots here. I reached for the closest branch, hoisted myself up, and climbed to the highest sturdy limb. A light wind rustled the leaves; dampness wafted up through the branches—a welcome smell in this scorched landscape. The branches gently swayed and shifted the leaf shadows that dappled my legs. I was settling in nicely and entertaining the idea of a sit spot in a tree when I spied a small, flat mark on the sloping wall of the canyon. It was right at my eye level, and I wondered whether it had an equally sparkling view of the valley below. I imagined myself sitting there, and knew immediately, without having been there physically that it would be the perfect spot. I went home and reread the guidelines for finding a sit spot, and it seemed that my choice didn't meet all the requirements. I spent three days searching for another one, but my first instinct pulled me back to that small, inconspicuous spot behind a bush on the west face of the canyon with a clear view of the valley floor.

I had lived in San Diego for twenty years, but it was there in the canyon that I made a profound discovery: San Diego *did* have seasons—spectacular seasons made all the more so by their subtlety and illusive nature. By just sitting still, I saw things that had been right under my nose my entire life. Up until that time, I had been looking at nature from a distance, even when I was surrounded by it. The alienation had been profound, yet I had been unconscious of its effects.

After three months of sitting, I was used to seeing coyotes, alone or in pairs, ambling through the valley in the afternoons, hunting for voles and mice or just stretching out in the sun. On a golden autumn afternoon, one of the coyotes stopped in its tracks, looked right at me, and started barking. I was intrigued. What was causing this outburst? I had never heard one of them bark so insistently. I looked down the canyon to either side of me and saw nothing offensive or strange, yet the reaction was so pointed, it was surely something obvious. It took a considerable (and embarrassing) amount of time for me to realize that I was the cause. Up to that point, I had thought of myself only as an observer, a ghost on the landscape, affected by but unable to influence my surroundings. The sudden recognition was surprising, and I wasn't sure how to respond. A hummingbird hovered just in front of my face and then took off behind me. I took this as an invitation, so I jumped up and ran in the same direction. Scrambling up the face of the canyon in an awkward panic, I felt a sharp pain in my leg that dropped me to my knees. A cholla, also known as the jumping cactus for its ability to seemingly leap off its stalk and onto your body, had burrowed its crisscrossing, needlelike thorns into my thigh. The coyote continued to bark, as if to mock me. She seemed to be saying, "So you thought we weren't connected. Well, look at you now with a cactus lodged in your

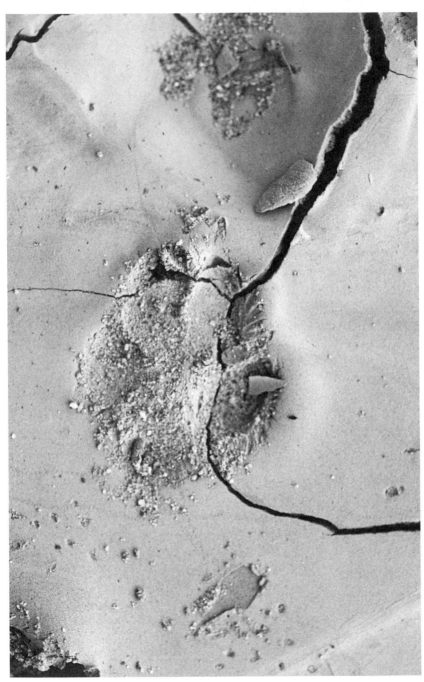

Coyote tracks.

leg." I stared in awe at the depth of the needles in my skin, caught my breath, and began the painstaking process of pulling them out. Once the cactus was out of my leg, I ran home, elated and eager to tell someone that a coyote had barked at me. It was like finally capturing the attention of someone I deeply admired. It didn't matter that the recognition was negative, because to the coyote, I finally existed.

I set out early the next morning with a new sense of how I might be influencing the wildlife in my sit area. As if to confirm this revelation, I found a cluster of doglike tracks in the dust at my sit spot, right where the print of my back end would be. Were these the tracks of the coyote that had barked at me? I needed to know. I found a string of clear tracks following my own from the previous day. I pursued them for a few yards, but the soil hardened and the tracks became unclear. My eyes weren't trained to see the minute details of a single nail mark or a shiny patch on the soil's surface. I decided to backtrack, but the story was the same. The tracks seemed to be coming from the valley where I had seen the coyote barking at me, but I couldn't be certain. I knelt down next to one of the clearer tracks and attempted to decipher who the maker was. It had four toes and obvious nail marks in front of every track, so I was fairly certain that it was canine. But was it wild or domestic? There were also foxes in the canyon—another confounding variable. Because I had seen only coyotes, and because the domestic dogs were mostly on the opposite side of the river, where their owners walked them on a wide dirt road, it was pretty safe to assume that these were coyote tracks. But it bothered me not to know for certain. The desire to identify those tracks marked the beginning of my tracking journey. From that day forward, I couldn't pass up any animal track without a dozen questions racing through my mind, trying to fit it into the context of the whole of nature.

After a year of tracking, questioning, and sitting in quiet contemplation, I discovered that I had gained a considerable amount of knowledge about the wildlife in the canyon. Unlike school, where I expected to learn something, this knowledge just sort of sneaked up on me. Jon Young in his Kamana Naturalist Training Program suggested that I never take the same route to or from my sit spot, but I was running out of new ways to get there. So on a warm afternoon in late winter, I decided to take a new trail that went in a large loop around my spot and eventually came back to it. I started out on a wide path that ended in a small clearing on the valley floor. As I neared the clearing, a Great

Blue Heron flew overhead, and I admired its elegance. Then a coyote emerged from the brush on the opposite side of the clearing. His head was swathed in sunlight; his flanks were in shadow. Another coyote soon entered the clearing, a female. They slowly approached each other; it had the feeling of a shoot-out, and I waited in anticipation. The obligatory sniffing of each other began, which developed into nuzzling. A playful wrestling match ensued for several minutes before the male mounted the female. He then turned away, as if to leave, but they were stuck end to end. A tug-of-war began, with each trying to go the opposite way, and eventually they were able to disengage themselves. The female nuzzled up to the male, and he nudged her with his nose. She sat back on her haunches with her front legs outstretched, tempting him into another wrestling match. As they frolicked, I was struck by the intimacy and playfulness of their interaction. When they left the clearing, I stood up stiffly from my crouched position, grateful that the coyotes had allowed me to observe their private encounter.

The trail narrowed and meandered out to the dirt road on the opposite side of the river. I expected the road to be busy with human traffic, but it was empty except for the ranger truck that was rolling slowly toward me. I had become friendly with the ranger who patrolled the canyon, and he pulled over when he saw me.

"Nice to see you out here," he said.

"It's nice to see you too, it's been a while." I was eager to tell him about the coyotes, and I thought he might have some stories of his own to share or some information about coyote habits.

"I was hoping to find you sooner," he said excitedly. "I saw a coyote crossing the road here a couple of weeks ago, so keep your eyes open."

A couple of weeks ago? I was confused. He patrolled the canyon daily. Surely he had seen coyotes more recently than two weeks ago. I wondered whether he had been on vacation but didn't linger on that thought.

"I saw them too," I blurted out, "just a few minutes ago. There were two of them mating on the other side of the river." I waited in naïve anticipation for his response, but he only looked at me with a perplexed expression. The wind rustled the giant dry leaves that still remained on the sycamore trees; I brushed a loose hair away from my face.

"Hmmm," was all he said. His mouth had become a confused frown, and the wrinkle in his brow deepened. "Yeah, well, you keep an eye out for those coyotes," he finally said. The dust from his tires lingered in the air a long time after he left.

It wasn't until I was seated comfortably at my sit spot that I realized that he didn't believe me. And why should he? He had no chance of seeing coyotes mating while driving a truck up and down the valley, even if he drove the road on a daily basis. I realized, with some sadness, that he didn't even know that the coyotes hunted in the large field nearly every afternoon. He couldn't have known that where we had stood on the road was less than half a mile from the coyote's den. When I had discovered it, there wasn't a single human track up that finger of the canyon. Why didn't it occur to me then that no one else was looking for it? There was probably no other visitor to that canyon who would sit in silence for over an hour just to see a coyote relaxed and stretched out in a patch of sunlight on a dusty trail. I was baffled by others' disregard for something that was my greatest pleasure. Yet their lack of interest was easy to understand. There's no training for the kind of experiences I was having. Rarely are we encouraged to commune with wildlife, especially as adults. As a result, you will find very few people who can relate to your interest in tracking, and even fewer tracking teachers. This may be discouraging, but if you maintain the routine of visiting a sit spot, your place could very well become your greatest tracking teacher.

CHOOSING A SIT SPOT

J.Y./T.M.

You will be investing a lot of time and energy at your sit spot (also called an anchor point), so choose it carefully. The following guidelines should be considered and balanced against your personal needs, such as your physical condition, daily schedule, and preferences.

Convenience

Your sit spot should be somewhere that you can walk to easily. If you must drive, it should be no more than a few minutes away. This is important, because you are going to be visiting this place for 5 to 105 minutes as often as possible—every day, if you can. Students who select convenient sit spots are more likely to actually use them, which can make a huge difference in their development. You can track at any of your favorite places anytime, but you should visit your sit spot every day.

Access and Safety

Ideally, you should have access to your sit spot twenty-four hours a day, seven days a week. At some point, you may want to visit it in the middle of the night. If you visit only during the day, you'll miss out on the nighttime rhythms of your place. You are encouraged to spend nights there on a regular basis; enjoy a campfire and relax.

Feeling secure and comfortable is also important. Your place may actually come to symbolize peace of mind as you train your awareness there. Therefore, it should provide you with true security. There are many commonsense things to avoid when choosing your location. One good rule of thumb is that if it feels unsafe or dangerous, it probably is. Pay attention to your gut feelings.

Other areas to avoid are power line rights-of-way, which are often sprayed with toxic chemicals, as are railroad grades. Both can also be a source of electromagnetic energy. Floodplains are called that for a reason. In some seasons and during certain weather patterns, if your anchor point is in a floodplain, you may need an anchor to keep from washing away. Study the landscape for clues to water levels, and check with the locals if you're not sure. Places close to highways and airports can cause distractions due to the noise. Also avoid "party areas" where there is evidence of frequent and disrespectful use of the land, such as litter, cans and bottles, broken glass, junk piles, and spent ammunition shells. Later on, you may choose to adopt such an area and do a little "native reeducation" of your own, but for now, you are looking for serenity, not confrontation.

Avoid natural areas that are known to harbor poison ivy, poison oak, or poison sumac until you really get to know the local variety. Your quiet sit will be a good deal more peaceful if you aren't scratching.

Size and Location

How big is big enough? Two acres would start to feel really small after a few visits, but it would do in a pinch. One hundred acres with your anchor point near the middle is ideal. A routine visit to your anchor point includes an exploratory walk through the natural area surrounding your spot and then an extended visit at your one chosen place.

When looking around your neighborhood for this place, get your hands on some maps of the county and do an "aerial" search. You will be surprised at the number of little parks and out-of-the-way places that don't get much attention. You may discover the perfect place in a school yard, a "green acres" easement, a pipeline right-of-way, or other undeveloped area right in your own neighborhood that you never knew existed. The maps should include waterways, wetlands, natural features, parks, and settlements. Most county maps, especially those used by real estate agents, are perfect for this purpose.

Diversity

Your study area should contain certain key features.

Water. This could be a stream, a pond, or wetlands. A stream or a pond is best. Streams are a great resource for many life-forms, as they represent a transition zone between wet and dry environments. Wetlands are fine, if it's all you have. Even puddles will do in a pinch.

If you live in the desert, look for a hidden watershed somewhere in the hills or among craggy rocks where water accumulates at least several times a year. In seashore environments, fresh water is also at a premium. Freshwater pools and wetlands are oases in both dry and salty environs.

Meadow. Find a meadow or grassy area, such as a naturally treated lawn or a not-so-busy roadside. Lawns, if they are mowed but fertilized with natural products and pesticide-free, can be highly productive locations. This is especially true when all kinds of wild plants are allowed to coexist with the grasses. When such a lawn is up against a border of thicket or forest, it can make an amazing sit spot.

Forest. Look at the age of trees, their sizes, and the varieties. Try to select an area where old trees are mixed with younger ones. Shrubs, thickets, and a variety of different species, including both evergreens and deciduous, make an ideal combination. A lone tree in the midst of a meadow can also be a great site, but it's best to have a varied forest surrounding your spot.

Privacy

Choose a place that affords you time away from the busy pace of modern life, somewhere away from the flow of human traffic. Follow a creek bed, forest edge, or game trail when searching for your spot (keep in mind that you should tread lightly and move gently through these sensitive environments). Your ultimate anchor point should offer you an "invisible advantage." This means that if you were dressed in natural or dark blending colors and sitting relatively still, other people on the trails would not be likely to see you. It's okay if you can see them, however, because you'll probably feel safer if you can see approaching or passing people from a distance without being seen.

Ambience

The final characteristic of your sit spot is that it must feel good to you. After you have considered all the requirements, used your instincts to guide you, and finally found a potential anchor point, do the final test: sit at your chosen spot quietly for a while and see how it feels. Look around; introduce yourself to the place. Tell the trees and the grasses, the birds and the waters why you are there, and ask them whether this is the right spot for you. Be aware of your surroundings and the feelings that arise in your heart. It is important that you feel comfortable and welcome.

Managing Two Locations

Sometimes there's just no way to cover all the bases at one place, or you may be too busy to get to the best spot often enough. Although it's not the ideal situation, you can use two locations—a convenient local spot and an ideal chosen spot—and divide your priorities into two basic categories: sensory development and naturalist awareness. You will practice both priorities at both locations, but your expectations will be different at each place. This has worked well for people with time or setting challenges.

At your local place, focus on sensory development. Choose a spot that you can walk or drive to on a moment's notice, feeling safe and comfortable. A local park, your backyard, a small greenbelt, a school yard, a riverbank, or any other small slice of nature with a view or some other natural feature is all that is needed. It might even be a particular stretch of freeway where a hawk hangs out.

Your chosen spot may be an hour or more away on foot or by car, but it has all the parameters listed earlier. At this location you will work on various naturalist training skills and emphasize the study of things that were missing at your local spot.

When visiting your chosen spot, do the following:

1. Arrive by a different route each time you visit.
2. Visit your sit spot each time you go to the area.
3. Sit there for as long as is practical and practice sensory exercises.

4. Work on naturalist awareness skills, such as tuning into bird language.
5. Relax.
6. Get to know the trees, plants, insects, birds, and other natural and unnatural neighbors, and allow them to get to know you.
7. Dream.
8. Eventually, quietly leave.

SETTING UP AN INDOOR SIT SPOT

J.Y.

You're going to be spending considerable time at your indoor sit spot reading, journaling, and sketching, so you might as well be comfortable. A good desk or table at the right height, a comfortable chair, and a good reading lamp will make your studies a lot more enjoyable. If you have a permanent area that can be devoted to your tracking studies, this is ideal. Set up your study area in a way that will inspire you to learn and discover new and exciting things about the world of nature. Suggestions include photographs, paintings, or your own drawings; animal skulls, bird feathers, seashells, or other objects that remind you of the natural world; and anything else that has special meaning for you. Consider hanging pictures of nature on your refrigerator or posters throughout the house to catch your eye and make you briefly aware of the natural world.

Remember to leave room for your growing nature museum. If you track frequently, you will likely begin to develop a collection of curious and beautiful things you find in the woods. Your nature museum will also serve as a tangible demonstration of what tracking means to you, which may help your friends and loved ones better understand your interest in tracking.

I will always remember the nature museum of my mentor. For a young amateur naturalist, seeing Tom's collection for the first time was an incredible inspiration. I felt as if I were walking into a magical place. All the specimens were neatly arranged in rows on shelves, carefully placed and lovingly tended. In a few words, Tom could take me on a journey to the time and place where he had found an object. He painted a picture so real that I could feel the wind blowing on my face, hear the birds singing from the treetops, and see how a skull had been lying when he found it.

Objects to inspire the tracker.

Another vivid memory of Tom's nature museum is that his nature journal was always lying open on his desk, as if awaiting his next entry. Tom's observations included animal tracks, plants, trees, and birds, but his notes always began with the weather for that day.

A notebook may hardly seem worthy of mention, but your journal can be the focal point of your indoor sit spot. You can pick up a field guide and read it, but if you're like most people, in a week you will have forgotten most of what you read. However, if you take excellent notes, including drawings, on a subject of interest, you will remember most of what you write down. Just the physical act of your hand making the letters on the page patterns this material into your brain.

A GUIDE TO FIELD GUIDES

On the way to your sit spot early one morning, you see a small brown animal with glistening wet fur and a sleek, slinky body dart across your path. You catch only a glimpse of it, but you're certain you'll be able to identify it from the pictures in your mammal guide when you get home. But when you open the field guide a couple hours later, you start to think that the animal had to have been four feet long with black fuzzy hair, because that's the closest thing you can find to it in the pictures. Something's wrong here, but with a little help, you can avoid this frustrating foray into field guides.

Doug Gaulke wrote, "Books cut the tracker's interpretation time in half, enabling her to understand what was observed during a particular outing. However, beware the trap books can set. Relying on books too heavily, or as a primary source of knowledge, will retard the tracker's growth, making her believe she knows a lot, when in fact she knows very little. The authors of the first field guides were themselves awesome observers and naturalists. Using their experience to highlight one's own is wise, but using their experience in place of one's own is the act of a fool."

In a real sense, the field guides are your village elders, your herbal medicine women, your experienced trackers and successful hunters. These books have many lifetimes of knowledge right there on every page, just waiting to be extracted. But for the most part, today's field guides are written for people who already know quite a bit about the subject and who already know how to use them.

In contrast, Roger Tory Peterson's early version of *Peterson's Field Guide to the Birds* was filled with personal stories of time spent with a chickadee or a nuthatch. The stories really brought the birds to life for me, and I longed to have such experiences myself. I often fell asleep at night while reading it, the musty scent of the old book like perfume to my nostrils. My dreams picked up where the book left off, and I would be on the trail of a flycatcher darting over the lake or an owl winging its silent way through the forest by moonlight. The next day after school I would be off again with my tattered guide and my binoculars for an afternoon of real adventure that often lasted beyond the twilight and into the night, filled with the magic of my own experiences.

Today's field guides don't offer much in the way of inspiration. Paintings, photos, and line drawings, though expertly done and eminently helpful as identification keys, are designed for speedy and accurate reference. This is good and necessary, but I really miss my old Peterson's guide. You, as a student, need to put the inspiration in your studies by using your mind's eye and your experiences to create stories and lore and allowing curiosity to surface.

You will notice that most field guides are organized in much the same way, reflecting phylogenetic order and the Linnaean system of classification (see the section on taxonomy later). Many field guides are like a journey through time. They begin with the most primitive mammals—the ones that have survived, pretty much unchanged, over eons.

For example, the most ancient character in mammal guides is the opossum (order Marsupialia). There's only one listed for North America, but in New Zealand, there are lots of them. Female marsupials have a fur-lined pouch on the abdomen that the babies crawl into immediately after birth. They weigh only about $\frac{1}{15}$ of an ounce when they emerge from the birth canal, and the whole litter could fit in a teaspoon. They are basically born very prematurely and most claw their way through the mother's fur into the pouch, where they bite into the mother's skin, from which milk is excreted. Opossums' brains are very small, just slightly bigger than a lizard's. They're solitary animals with poor eyesight and unremarkable hearing, and they spend most of their lives seemingly blundering about in an aimless search for food. They also have a repulsive nature that wards off predation and increases their likelihood of survival and evolutionary success.

In contrast, toward the back of field guides are members of the deer family and their close kin. Their brains are larger in proportion to body size compared with opossums, and they exhibit a strategic method of territory memorization and defense and have a good understanding of the language of the birds around them. "Wise" bucks depend on an accumulated knowledge of food sources within their territories, and they simultaneously develop a strategy that helps them remain invisible to all but the most skilled and experienced naturalists, natives, and hunters. This takes a high degree of sophistication, sensory awareness, and site fidelity. The members of this order communicate to one another via scent signals that constitute a simple "language."

Field guides are also arranged by families, which consist of groups of living organisms that share basic outward characteristics—in other words, there is an identifiable family resemblance.

For example, consider the red fox, *Vulpes vulpes*. The members of its family, Canidae, include dogs, coyotes, and wolves, all of which are easily recognizable as being related in some way. All have the familiar doglike appearance with a long nose (some domestic dog breeds with pushed-in noses are the exception), large ears on top of the head, five toes on the front feet and four on the back, prominent canine teeth, and a weight distribution that strongly favors the front half of the animal. It's fairly easy to look at a wolf and see that it's related to Fido and to that coyote you saw slinking out of your chicken coop with a mouthful of feathers.

Another useful aspect of field guides is the range map, which shows where a particular species is supposed to be found. Range maps can save you the trouble of going through all the possible species after you have narrowed the candidates down to one family. Just skim the

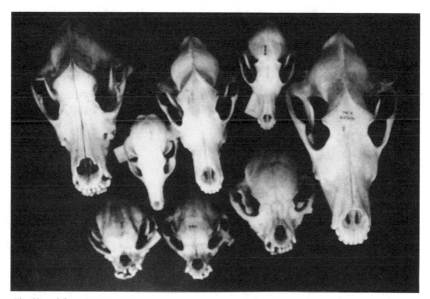

Skulls of family Canidae. MUSEUM OF COMPARATIVE ZOOLOGY, HARVARD UNIVERSITY

pages with the maps and ignore any that aren't near you. However, remember that animals move and are adaptable; clever animals such as wolves, coyotes, and cougars are all a bit elusive and are often found in places where they're not supposed to be.

Good field guides, such as the Peterson guides, also use field marks—little arrows that point to important features that can help you distinguish a specimen from its close relatives. To save time when trying to identify an animal, check the field marks first, and then go to the text for an explanation.

TAXONOMY

Taxonomy is the science of naming and classifying organisms, often according to structure and form. Eighteenth-century Swedish botanist Carolus Linnaeus is the originator of the binomial system of scientific classification (that is, genus and species). The purpose of having scientific or Latin names is to avoid confusion and to create a common language that allows communication with others. This is necessary because the common names used to describe organisms vary from place to place, or the same name may be used to describe two entirely different organisms. An example of the latter is the American Robin and the European Robin. The American version, *Turdus migratorius,* is about 10 inches long with a brick-orange breast, blackish gray upper parts, and a bold white eye ring. Its European counterpart, *Erithacus rubecula,* is about half that size with a brownish orange breast and forehead and brownish olive upper parts. Likewise, poison hemlock, *Conium maculatum,* is a medium-sized member of the parsley family that closely resembles wild carrot; it is one of the deadliest plants found in North America. In contrast, the North American hemlock is actually a coniferous tree, *Tsuga heterophylla,* that inhabits much of the Pacific Northwest; parts of this tree can actually be a valuable food source in survival situations.

It is helpful to know the meaning of Latin or Greek scientific names, because they often reveal something about the nature of an organism. For example, the honey locust is *Gleditsia triacanthos; triacanthos* refers to the three-pronged cluster of thorns common on this tree. The Mockingbird, *Mimus polyglottos,* is part of a family of birds that mimic *(Mimus)* other bird calls, and indeed it is the master of many voices *(polyglottos).* The spring peeper, *Hyla crucifer,* is a tree frog that has a brown cross, or cruciform shape, on its back.

It isn't necessary to take a class in Latin or Greek to gain some understanding of scientific names. A good college dictionary gives many of the classic roots of words, or you may find it useful to consult a book on etymology (the origins and derivations of words).

Definition of Terms

Scientific terms can be intimidating at first, but they can be useful.

Phylogeny refers to the evolutionary development of an organism over the entire history of its existence on earth. A phylogenetic tree is simply a family tree. Most phylogenetic trees are combinations of the fossil record and structural relationships and are useful graphic expressions of the system of classification. Phylogenetic order is the basis of the organization of most field guides, going from the most primitive and ancient to the most modern and complex.

Ontogeny is a combination of the Greek term *onto,* or "existence," and *genesis,* which means "creation," "formation," or "evolution." Thus *ontogeny* refers to the embryonic history of an organism from the union of egg and sperm through the completion of the maturation process. Some scientists believe that the ontogeny of an organism is a recapitulation of its evolutionary history or phylogeny. If this is true, through the study of embryology, we can peek through a virtual keyhole into the past.

Homologous and Analogous Structures. One of the most interesting aspects of taxonomy is the study of the origins and functions of physical structures. Structures in living things can resemble each other in one of two ways: having the same roots in evolution (homologous) or serving the same purpose (analogous).

When structures have the same evolutionary ancestry, such as the leg of a human and the leg of a horse, the structures are said to be homologous because they are technically the same structure. Human fingers and those of a lizard have the same fossil ancestry and contain the same bones. Likewise, a human forearm has two bones in it, as does that of a mouse or a lizard. These are all homologous structures that originate from the same embryonic tissues and initially develop in a similar manner.

In contrast, analogous structures are used in the same way but may not have the same origin. A housefly's wing and a robin's wing are good examples of analogous structures. A casual study of these two appendages quickly reveals that they have no common ancestry in recent evolutionary history. The fly's wings were "constructed" from a completely different set of blueprints than were those of the robin. The development of wings was simply a good way to inhabit a different environmental niche, and both the housefly and the robin picked up on it, but independently of each other from an evolutionary standpoint. Therefore, we can say with some certainty that the housefly and the robin were not sitting on the same branch of the evolutionary tree. When classifying organisms, we have to be careful not to lump things together simply because they have certain features in common. Instead, we need to pay careful attention to the evolutionary history of living things.

The Five-Kingdom System of Classification

The current system of classification is based on the five-kingdoms: Animalia (animals), Plantae (plants), Protista (protozoans and unicellular algae), Monera (bacteria and blue-green algae), and Fungi. There was a time when scientists recognized only two kingdoms: plant and animal. Today, however, we recognize these five distinct divisions in the world of living things based on similarities of structure, evolutionary history, and biochemistry. In the process of classifying a species, determining its kingdom is the first major decision to be made.

There are some organisms that seem to make up their own rules: lichens that are half fungus and half algae, slime molds that are half protozoan and half fungus, and viruses that seem to march to a completely different drummer. As these organisms prove, Mother Nature doesn't like sterile uniformity; she delights in experimenting with new and interesting combinations and variations on old themes. We simply have to accept nature's exceptions to our human rules.

After kingdom, organisms are divided into phylum, class, order, family, genus, and species (and sometimes variety). Biology students typically use a mnemonic device, such as "King Philip Came Over From Great Spain," to help them remember the order of these divisions.

Kingdom is the highest and most encompassing group in biological taxonomy.

Phylum. Under kingdoms are divisions called phyla. For example, under the kingdom Animalia, creatures that have central nerve cords along their backs are known as Chordates, the group to which people, birds, and sharks belong. Note that when referring to plants, botanists call this level a division rather than a phylum.

Cladistics

Maureen McConnell

In biology, classification is the process of organizing the fantastic array of living things into categories based on their similarities. Ideally, biologists strive to make their classification system mimic the way that evolution actually happened. The classification of organisms has been turned upside down due to recent breakthroughs in genetic research. Rather than using outward inspection and similar physical characteristics, we are now grouping species based on their similarities at the genetic level. Thus, phylogeny has been rearranged dramatically, along with our understanding of how animals evolved.

The newest system of classification is called cladistics. Two big scientific breakthroughs have revolutionized the study of phylogeny and opened the door for the age of cladistic analysis. The first breakthrough was the rapid advancement in the power and availability of computers. Cladistic analysis takes into account a multitude of observed characteristics of living things and groups organisms statistically according to their similarities. Without computers, we would not be able to analyze all possible characteristics at once.

The second breakthrough was the molecular sequencing of genes. In the race to decode the DNA of the human genome, machines were invented that could quickly sequence a creature's DNA, and these sequences can be compared with the DNA of other living things. This has resulted in many classification surprises (it's still going on), and as everything is sorted out, terms such as *reptile* fall out of favor as biologists realize that not all animals in the reptile group are close relatives.

Other interesting surprises include the fact that chimpanzees are our closest relatives, with about 98 percent of their DNA sequences identical to ours. And of the races of human beings, the Bushmen of Africa are the oldest people on earth. Their DNA sequence has significant differences that predate all other races, making them the ancestors of us all.

A mini-course on cladistics is presented in a book and CD produced by the London Natural History Museum: *Cladistics: A Practical Primer on CD-ROM*, by Peter Skelton and Andrew Smith, published by Cambridge University Press.

Class. Mammals are an entirely separate class from birds, as are reptiles, amphibians, and the bony fish (as opposed to sharks). Birds, for example, belong to class Aves, phylum Chordata, kingdom Animalia.

Order. Members of an order generally share some fairly obvious characteristics. For example, under the class Aves is the order Falconiformes, which includes the broad-winged hawks such as the Red-tailed Hawk, forest hawks such as the Sharp-shinned and Cooper's Hawks, vultures, eagles, and the fast-flying falcons. These birds have many features in common, such as powerfully muscular feet armed with lethal talons and hooked bills used to tear flesh. However, there are also many differences among these birds, necessitating a smaller division.

Family. Each of the different types of birds mentioned above in the order Falconiformes is more or less a distinct family of birds (some of them are grouped together, such as broad-winged hawks, forest hawks, and eagles, because they are still fairly similar). Although some families may have only a handful of species—or even just one species—in it, others have hundreds. For example, family Emberizidae includes birds as seemingly diverse as warblers, blackbirds, sparrows, tanagers, and grosbeaks.

Genus is the first part of an organism's Latin name (it is always capitalized and italicized). Individuals with similar characteristics share that same genus name. For example, the wolf, coyote, and dog are all in the genus *Canis.*

Species. The accepted definition of a species is "a group of similar beings whose members can interbreed freely with one another, but not with members of any other taxonomic group." Basically, this means that wolves don't ordinarily breed with coyotes, and that neither of them breeds with dogs. This is a bit hazy, however, because it is surmised that all the possible combinations—wolf-dog, dog-coyote, coyote-wolf—have taken place, but usually with the aid of breeders who purposely hybridize these animals. Throughout nature there are also examples of species occasionally mixing with one another, causing some taxonomic confusion. For the most part, however, you can consider each species to be separate. The species constitutes the second half of an organism's Latin name (it too is italicized). The dog is *Canis familiaris;* the wolf, *Canis lupus;* and the coyote, *Canis latrans.*

Variety. For most purposes, species is the end of the line in terms of classification. There are, however, distinctions that go beyond that level. A variety, or subspecies, is usually a group of individuals from one species found in a particular area with certain minor adaptations that give them an advantage in their unique setting. The gray wolf is an excellent example. There was once a Great Plains wolf, *Canis lupus nubilis,* a unique variety of gray wolf that had slightly longer legs. This gave it a greater ability to move through and see over tall grasses. In addition, the Great Plains wolf fed primarily on bison and had some unique behaviors that enabled it to hunt successfully. However, the Great Plains wolf could still freely mate with other varieties of wolves found in other places. It is thought that these minor adaptations may be the basis from which new species are created over time.

Using Taxonomy Wisely

Recognizing that all members of a family possess similar physiological characteristics can make life much easier. For example, if you know that all members of the deer family have cloven hooves, chew their cud, have no upper front teeth, and shed their antlers every year, it is much more efficient than learning these characteristics for elk, mule deer, white-tailed deer, moose, woodland caribou, barren ground caribou, and Greenland caribou individually. But beyond this, scientific names and classification teach us *how* to look at animals and their tracks. If you know which species belong to the mustelidae, or weasel, family you can learn to recognize a weasel track or track pattern without knowing exactly which species of weasel it is just by knowing the characteristics of that particular family. For instance, members of the mustelidae family all have five toes on the front and back feet. Because their bodies are long and slender with short legs, they typically move in a bounding or loping pattern that enables them to make sharp turns. It is useful to know that for many species in this family, the male is noticeably larger than the female. They tend to be crepuscular and nocturnal, although they do move at anytime day or night. With this information you will be able to rule out many other families, such as felidae and canidae, whose members show four toes on front and rear and move mostly in walking or trotting patterns.

STARTING A MASTER LIST

Using a field guide to mammals, check the range map for every animal to determine whether it exists in your area, and make a list of all those that do. If you are right on the edge of an animal's range, include it. If animals such as cougars once lived in your area but the prevailing wisdom is that they have been exterminated, include those species as well. Become familiar with this list. If you'd like to include a bit more information, you can place the mammals in phylogenic order and add descriptions of habitat preferences, food preferences, and common predators.

Using the most recent edition of National Geographic's *Guide to North American Birds* or *The Sibley Guide to Birds* by David Allen Sibley, do the same for birds, and note in which season they are present. Again, a brief description of habitat, food preferences, and common predators is recommended.

Post your mammal and bird lists conspicuously on the wall above your desk. These are the animals on which you are now focusing.

3

The Art of Journaling

The important thing is not to stop questioning.
—Albert Einstein

J.Y.

Beginning students often believe that journaling and questioning are *not* the way native people learned, and in a narrow regard, they are right. The system is not exactly the same, but all the core concepts of original native learning systems are here.

The real adversaries of learning are those common to everyday life: distraction, busyness, the need to make a living, laziness, and lack of focus. However, with commitment, anyone can discover the all-important key to the journey—passion. As my mentor, Tom Brown, was fond of saying, "I can give you the tools, but I cannot give you the passion." A look at my own life story can provide some perspective on where that passion comes from.

When I was ten, I went on a camping trip with Tom and had an amazing time. On the way home, I couldn't stop thinking and talking about how incredible it had been.

When he asked, "Do you want to go again?" my answer was, "Of course." He smiled at my excitement as we sat in my parents' driveway. "If you want to go again," he said in a serious tone, "you'll have to practice 'camping' by setting up a sit area in the woods and going there each day—alone. You can build a fire or just sit in the stillness." He told me that I should wander into my place using a different route as often as possible to avoid making trails. The place I chose should be a strategic point—a lookout in all directions—because I would never know when someone might be sneaking up on me. In retrospect, these things didn't have much to do with camping in the usual sense, but at the time, I was eager to follow any instructions that would guarantee another camping trip.

When I first began visiting my place, it was outright boring. It was difficult for me to just sit still and not go fishing or exploring. Sitting idly in the woods was not my idea of a fun way to spend an hour, but the carrot was there: to go camping and fishing again—the real adventure!

Tom called me on the phone to check on my progress. Our conversation went like this:

Tom: Hey Jon. Did you find that place?

Jon: Yep. Right in Drucker's Woods on the first hill when you walk in off of the cul-de-sac. There's a big tree that I lean against.

Tom: How long does it take to get there?

Jon: A few minutes. It's not that far.

Tom: Which way are you facing when you sit against the tree?

Jon: Uh. I don't know. I'm not sure. How can I tell?

Tom: Find out where the sun rises. What direction does the sunrise in?

Jon: East?

Tom: Yeah. Just figure out where it rises from your tree, then you'll know where east is. . . . By the way, what kind of tree is it that you're leaning against? Describe it to me.

Jon: Wow. I don't know what kind of tree it is. It's tall and pretty straight. It's fat around the base.

He continued for a few minutes asking me questions that I could answer, followed always by a question or two that I couldn't. He let me know that he expected me to figure out those answers, and he reminded me that this was the work I had to do if I wanted to go camping again.

After three years, Tom's questions became quite advanced. The kinds of things he asked me when I was thirteen and fourteen are questions that most adults couldn't answer about tracking, bird language, survival, plants, and awareness in general. But because he held my feet to the fire—asking questions and making me discover the answers on my own—I eventually learned to ask questions on my own.

When I was about twelve, I began journaling, because I always saw Tom doing this. When we journal, we make connections that we otherwise wouldn't make, just as, in the native learning system, an elder would help us to do. But because there are so few elders around today who know about tracking and awareness skills, we each have to find the passion inside. Interestingly, the key to uncovering my passion didn't happen while fishing or camping or even during the time spent at my sit spot. The passion actually emerged over time through the journaling and questioning process. It began slowly, but soon took on real power, the source of which was twofold. The first was my discovery of the abounding mysteries in tracking and bird language and the challenge of solving them. The second was my discovery that I could learn to solve these mysteries myself—though not immediately, and not without a struggle. But this gave me self-confidence and helped me appreciate the value of learning according to my own style and way of inquiry. Through this, I learned that with enough focus, time, patience, and true desire for knowledge, I could eventually answer the questions myself.

You can unlock that passion through the research process. Get out in the field and struggle with your journals, play the role of elder to yourself through the art of questioning, and you will eventually begin to uncover the light of your own passion. Unlike the natives, you won't get to sit by the fire and tell your stories of the day. But remember that it is still just as vital as it always was to ask the questions and to tell the stories. You just have it do it with paper, pen, and books. These things are a gift to all trackers.

We refer to the questions Who? What? When? Why? Where? and How? as the elders of tracking. These questions are deceptively simple, but they can be the basis of your growth as a tracker. Let these elders of tracking take shape in your mind, and allow your quest for answers to guide you. The subconscious need to know, connected with good habits of sensory awareness and good routines of research and journaling, will eventually cause the passion within you to rise. Commitment to this journey of asking questions, even when you think you have the answers, is what creates the tracker within.

ELDERS OF TRACKING
Who? The Question of Identification

J.Y./T.M.

Who has left the track? The questions start out generally and become more specific: Is it a cat or a dog? Is it wild or domestic? Male or female? Young or old? Healthy or sick? Pregnant? With time and experience, you will know not only the species but also the individual animal, like you would a good friend. The "who" elder of tracking also covers the identification of sign such as scat, feeding sign, bedding areas, and dens.

What? The Question of Interpretation

What was the animal doing when it made the tracks? Again, your questions begin simply: Was it walking or running? and progress to deeper questions: Was it looking straight ahead or to the right or left, and what caused it to look in that direction? The question of "what" begins with interpreting track patterns created by placement of the animal's four feet and leads to interpreting animal behavior, such as whether the animal was searching for food or escaping predation.

When? The Question of Aging

When was this animal here? You ask, Is this track fresh or old? More specifically, Was this animal here before or after the last rain? Was the ground moist when the animal passed by? Careful observations of the weather and its impact on different substrates can tell you not only the day the animal passed by but sometimes even the hour or minute.

Why? The Question of Ecology

Why was this animal here? The "why" question asks you to consider the vast world of nature and observe how things are related to and influence one another. Why are the deer always in a particular field come summer? Why does the cougar travel along the creek? What begins as disparate observations of insect activity, ripening fruit, vegetative cover, and terrain eventually leads to the ability to predict where animals will move on the landscape and why, based on their nutritional needs, safety, preferences, and territories. Focusing on this elder of tracking can significantly cut the amount of time you spend looking for specific animals. It's easier to find the fruiting trees an animal eats from in the fall (and thus the animal) than to search for the animal over a vast landscape without knowing the animal's preferences and needs.

Where? The Question of Trailing

Where is the animal now? To determine where a particular animal has gone, you have to find the next track. With deeper understanding, you may be able to answer the question, Where is this animal going? With the guidance of this elder, you will be able to follow tracks right to the animal that made them, even in difficult substrates.

How? The Question of Empathy

How did this animal feel? Did it feel pain or hunger? Through this elder of tracking, you will develop a greater empathy for the animals you track, perhaps even to the point where you can see through their eyes. Of course, when it comes to animals' feelings, we are dealing largely with conjecture. There are no absolutes and very few certainties, but the question of "how" opens our minds and hearts to greater possibilities.

MIND'S-EYE JOURNALING AND SKETCHING

Any memory created through strong sensory and emotional experience tends to stick. Sketching and journaling are your strong sensory experiences that anchor your studies of natural history firmly in your memory. Fredrick Frank, in *The Zen of Seeing,* noted, "I have learned that what I have not drawn, I have never really seen, and when I start drawing an ordinary thing, I realize how extraordinary it is, sheer miracle." Build on your emotional side with some imagination and some real bonding while studying. Allow yourself the quality time necessary to create strong mental pictures and imagery linked to the subject under study. Imagine, for instance, that you have to make up a story to teach a child about an animal. What things would you focus on in the animal's natural history? What features in the drawing of that animal would you focus on? Develop memories of all senses and feelings along with images.

If you do your sketching and journaling according to the directions that follow, you will create a good set of mental file cards. Then, when you go into the field, the images and information from these file cards will pop into your awareness when you encounter something that triggers the memory of the sensory experience you created while drawing and writing about it. Not only that, but the process will be much more fun.

You don't have to draw a detailed, perfect sketch of the animal or track or write in detail about its features. This would result in learning, but it is not the kind of learning that most students of nature enjoy. Digest first, extract the jewels for yourself, and then express yourself like a storyteller.

INSTRUCTIONS FOR MIND'S-EYE SKETCHING

1. Open your field guide and choose an illustration or photograph to sketch. Quiet your mind for a moment or two. Then shift your attention to the illustration and study it carefully for about 15 seconds, noting important details.
2. Close your eyes and picture the illustration in your mind's eye as precisely as possible. Hold this image for a few seconds, then

open your eyes and check the illustration against what you visualized.

3. Really look at the illustration and practice the art of questioning. Pretend that you have a real, live specimen before you and spend a minute or so doing the following, using your imagination:

   • Look at it closely; notice the overall pattern and structure, the shadings and coloration. Notice any field mark details.

   • Pick it up and see how it feels in your hands, how the weight is distributed, what its mass is compared to its size. Is it heavy or light? What is the texture of its skin? What do its claws, foot pads, and hooves feel like?

   • Sniff it. Does it have the aroma of earth clinging to it, or does it have the smell of something that lives in the water?

   • Listen to it. What sound does it make as it moves through its normal habitat? What is its song or cry?

   • Think of its strategies. How would you tell a story of this being? What is its essence? There is no right or wrong answer. Just use your instincts.

   • What are the structures that can help you identify it? How is it different from other closely related animals on the same page?

4. Close your eyes and visualize the animal or track in the illustration again. Repeat this process, noting new details each time.

5. Allow your mind to clear. Close your eyes and ask the animal or track to appear in your mind's eye in whatever form it would like to take. Observe the image that takes shape for about 15 seconds, then open your eyes.

6. Study the illustration one more time and then close the guide and to sketch the animal or track exactly as it appears in your mind's eye. Think of time efficiency—detailed, beautiful masterpieces are not called for. Aim for something that captures the structure, strategy, and field marks of the animal or track.

This whole process should take only a couple of minutes. As you progress, you'll improve in capturing the essential details of the illustration in a surprisingly short time. If you laboriously draw every vertebrae in the mountain lion's back and carefully pen in every whisker on its chin, you've missed the point. Quick, efficient, effective capturing of the essentials is the goal.

MAKING ENTRIES IN YOUR
ORIENTATION TRACKING JOURNAL

With the tools of mind's eye sketching and journaling at your disposal, you are now ready to begin the tremendous growth period of journaling your observations and researching questions. The orientation track journal has been developed over years of trial and error to create a journal template that asks dynamic questions and inspires you to seek the answers that will lead to the greatest success in your learning. The orientation tracking journal consists of four pages of questions related to tracks with spaces to fill in your answers. Your assignment is to complete twenty-seven orientation tracking journals of twenty-five different mammals, one bird, and additional track made by anything other than a mammal or bird. Completing these journals will orient you in your place and provide you with a foundation of knowledge that will guide your growth as a tracker in profound ways.

Depending on where you live, locating the tracks of twenty-five different mammals may be easy or difficult. Therefore, your twenty-five different mammal tracks can come from anywhere. It doesn't matter how or where you find the tracks. If a friend knows that you're studying tracking and tells you about some tracks he found, go and take a look. We encourage you to explore as many new and different places in your local environment as you can. One of the broader goals

Raccoons are found in most areas and are relatively easy to find.

is to familiarize yourself with the area you live in, because in the long run, it is your experience in one place that will make you a master tracker. As you make your field notes, look around at the landscape. Also study some maps. Get to know the creeks, lakeshores, dirt roads, fields, sandy areas, and other tracking hot spots that surround you.

When tracking, take your field notebook and tape measure with you, but leave your orientation tracking journal at home. When you return home at night, that's when you fill out an entry based on the notes you made in the field. When recording your experiences in your orientation tracking journal, use your field notebook only as a prompt for your memory. Don't just copy from it.

In the orientation tracking journal, we don't want you to come to any definite conclusions about the tracks you've found. You may see a track on the ground and know with all your being that it was made by a coyote. Why have you ruled out a dog? Why have you ruled out a small wolf or a large red fox? Could it be a cat with its claws exposed? Does avoiding a definite conclusion seem contrary to the point of tracking?

Tracks are like snowflakes—no two are exactly alike, and there is something to learn from every track, no matter how many times you may have seen tracks that look "just like it." How a track appears at the time you find it depends on a number of variables—variables that the elders of tracking can help you understand. In the end, however, there are an infinite number of forms that any animal's tracks can take, and some of them end up looking like the tracks of other animals. One of the things you have to be comfortable with is the possibility of being wrong. And the more you allow yourself to be wrong, the more you learn as a tracker. If you go through the entire deduction process and come up with a conclusion that turns out to be wrong, that's fine. It is more important that you can say with confidence what did *not* leave a track, as opposed to what did leave it and why. The process is most important.

Following are page-by-page instructions for making entries in your orientation tracking journal.

Page I:
Assessing the Possibilities
Make a quick sketch of the general area where the tracks are, as if you were a bird looking down on the scene from above—in other words, from a bird's-eye view. On this map, show major details such

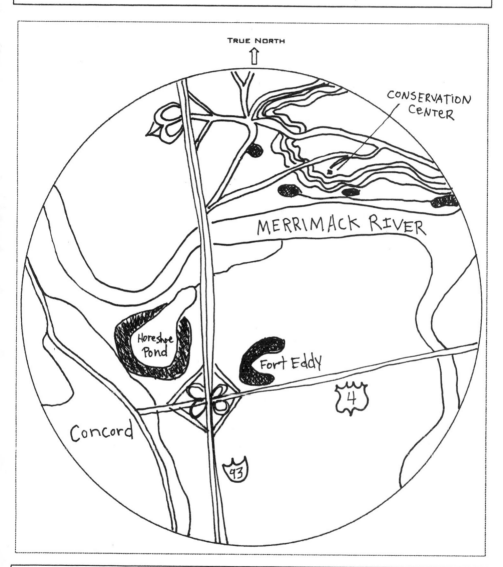

TRUE NORTH

CONSERVATION
CENTER

MERRIMACK RIVER

Horeshoe
Pond

Fort Eddy

4

Concord

93

NAME: Tiffany Morgan   DATE: 3/21/02

DIRECTIONS TO LOCATION: Conservation Center Concord, NH
From visitor center take main trail SE cross over small foot bridge
to Merrimack River.

as streets, highways, dirt roads, human paths, fields, forests, waterways, lakes, swamps, and the like to give a sense of the location of the tracks and what animals might have access to such a place. Don't make these drawings overly complex: simple shading and quick notes will suffice for detail. Orient your drawing to true north; a compass may be helpful.

If you have multiple journal entries from the same day from one site, you don't need to re-create this first page for each entry. Draw just one map, but be sure to indicate the location of each of your entries.

In addition to the map, at the bottom of the page is a section labeled "Directions to Location." Here, write some short directions that would enable you or somebody else to find this site again.

And don't forget to include your name and the date that you studied the tracks.

Page 2:
Perspectives

Local Landscape Context (top). How do the patterns of vegetation and the tracks you are journaling relate to each other? Looking again from a bird's-eye view, sketch the terrain in the immediate area around the tracks you found relative to the animal's size. The features of the environment that influence a cougar won't necessarily be the same as those that impact a mouse. Thus, the scale of your map should reflect the size of the animal, and this map should be drawn to a smaller scale than the one you drew on the first page. Include features such as plants, shrubs, trees, water sources, trails, and other prominent features around the tracks that would influence the actions of the animal.

In the corner of the local landscape context box is a smaller box labeled "Approximate Scale." This is simply an approximation of the size of the area you've drawn. The first measurement in the box is the number of paces it would take to cross the area; the second is the same distance in feet.

Also, consider how the tracks relate to the larger view you sketched on page 1. Indicating where true north lies will help you to put this map into the context of that larger map.

Weather (bottom left). Most of these sections are self-explanatory—just fill in the information about the weather conditions in the field. Under the section labeled "Weather Trends," write some general notes about the weather over the past two or three days. For example: "It

LOCAL LANDSCAPE CONTEXT

Grassy Field

Human Trail

steep River Bank

Track on River Bank

Mink Slide

Tracks under water

Merrimack River

APPROXIMATE SCALE	
25 PACES X	25 PACES
___ FEET X	___ FEET

WEATHER

TIME: 9:15 AM   TEMP: 38°

WIND DIRECTION: NW   SPEED: 5 MPH

PRECIPITATION: None

CLOUDS: Partial cover

SUN RISE: 6:30 am   SUN SET: 5:30 pm

LUNAR PHASE: ◐

WEATHER TRENDS:
(WHAT WERE THE LAST FEW DAYS LIKE?)

It started snowing yesterday
at 2:15 pm and snowed until
1 am last night when it
stopped.

OBSERVATIONS OF NATURE AND ECOLOGY

BIRDS: Robins, Ducks, Jays, chickadees

INSECTS: Stone Flies

OTHER MAMMALS: Coyote Raccoon

HUMAN INFLUENCE: Human Trail 20 feet
from mink tracks. Hwy bridge
accross river.

HUMAN ACTIVITY:
A Man walking his dog.

PLANTS:
Mostly grasses

TREES:
Pine and Oak

WATER:
Merrimack River

OTHER:
Tracks are clear-even registering
under water.

NAME: Tiffany Morgan   DATE: 3/21/02

rained hard yesterday and was very windy. Dry and cold, but sunny for the two days before that."

Observations of Nature and Ecology (bottom right). This is the place to record some of the feeding opportunities for wildlife in your tracking area, as well as the general activity going on while you were there. A word or two of description for each category is sufficient. For instance, if there were plenty of ripe blackberries on a hot, late summer day, under "Fruits" you might write, "many ripe blackberries; strong smell in the air." Everything categorized here contributes to the unfolding story of your journal. Even if something seems trivial to you, it might be very important to the animal that you're tracking.

Page 3:
Tracks and Patterns

Master List of Possible Animals (top left). Study the range maps for each mammal in the region and begin to consider the possibilities. When doing this, consider the size of the animal as it relates to the tracks. Try "air sculpting" the animal with your hands to approximate the size. Repeat this process for every mammal whose range map coincides with your tracking area and whose body size corresponds with the tracks you're journaling. List all the animals that fit these criteria, and use common sense. For instance, if the tracks measure 3 inches across, a mouse would not be included on your list of possible mammals.

Sketch a Group of Four Tracks (bottom left). Make a sketch of the four-track pattern observed in the field. This pattern is likely to be either a small cluster or a series of tracks in a line or gait pattern. Transfer this sketch from your field notebook, and include all the appropriate measurements (discussed later).

Sketch the Larger Print (top right). If the tracks you studied are different sizes, sketch the larger print. Use the whole space and make your drawing as detailed as you wish. For instance, note the presence of spider webs in the track, or find some way to show how large grains of sand seem to have collected in the floor of the track. Balance the amount of detail, however, with efficiency, and include the appropriate measurements.

Sketch the Smaller Print (bottom right). Sketch the smaller print, following the same procedures as for the larger track. Again, include all measurements.

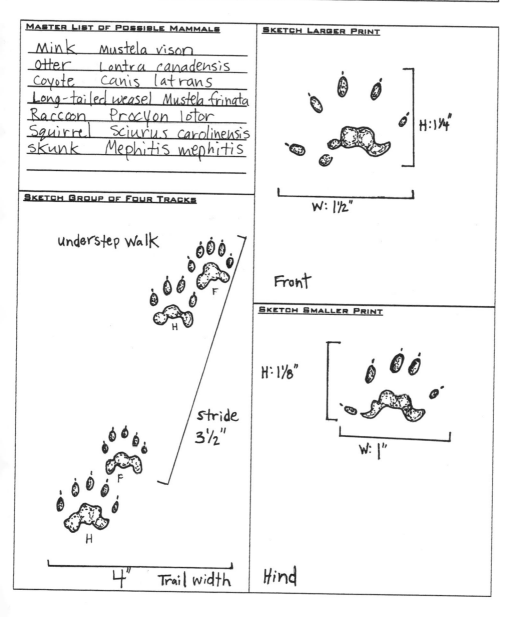

MASTER LIST OF POSSIBLE MAMMALS

Mink   Mustela vison
Otter   Lontra canadensis
Coyote   Canis latrans
Long-tailed weasel   Mustela frinata
Raccoon   Procyon lotor
Squirrel   Sciurus carolinensis
Skunk   Mephitis mephitis

SKETCH LARGER PRINT

H: 1¼"
W: 1½"
Front

SKETCH GROUP OF FOUR TRACKS

understep walk

F
H

stride 3½"

F
H

4" Trail width

SKETCH SMALLER PRINT

H: 1⅛"
W: 1"
Hind

NAME: Tiffany Morgan   DATE: 3/21/02

Page 4:
Reflections

Three Best Possible Animals (top left). Even if you saw the animal make the tracks, go through the process of comparing the tracks with those of other animals that could have left something similar. Start with *Mammal Tracks and Sign (MTS)* by Mark Elbroch and the master list of possible mammals from page 3 of your journal entry. Using *MTS*, study the tracks of each of the mammals on your list and compare their tracks with the ones you drew on page 3. The goal here is to narrow the possibilities to the three mammals in your area whose tracks and body size most closely match the tracks you found. Once you have identified the best options, briefly describe why each animal could have made the tracks, as well as why it might not have made them.

Draw the Best Match (middle right). From the list of three possibilities, choose the one that you believe is your best bet. Draw a picture of the tracks from the field guide, and include the measurements given in the guide. List the animal's name in the appropriate space, and give appropriate credit to the author you referenced by naming the book and page number.

Describe or Draw What You Saw from the Animal's Perspective (bottom right). Using words, pictures, or both, describe what you saw when you viewed the area around the tracks as the animal would have—looking from the same height as the animal and using its senses. Describe what you believe the animal may have smelled, saw, heard, and felt. In addition, if the animal was on a trail, sketch the view looking down the trail, including measurements of width and height. Vital pieces of the story can be gleaned from this perspective.

Survival (bottom left). *Where were the tracks coming from?* This is an opportunity to backtrack and find out where the animal was coming from, which often provides clues to why it ended up where it did. If you can't see the tracks to backtrack the animal, make some educated guesses as to where the animal may have come from. Take clues from the landscape: If there's a trail nearby, was your animal using it? Is there a water or feeding source where your animal could have come from? Investigating in the area might even turn up some more tracks that will help piece the story together.

Where were the tracks going to? If you can see the tracks, follow them for as far as you can or have time for. Include in your journal details

THREE BEST POSSIBLE ANIMALS (USE MASTER LIST FROM PAGE 2)

1. NAME	WHY?	WHY NOT?
Mink	Double bounding pattern. slide down bank into water	Prints registered under water - if mink why wouldn't it swim in water.
2. NAME	WHY?	WHY NOT?
Otter	In and out of water. slide into water. Bounding pattern	Tracks and width of slide too small for otter
3. NAME	WHY?	WHY NOT?
Coyote	Coyote tracks overlapped the tracks, confusing the trails.	Tracks too small, obviously not coyote when clear track found. Coyote trail went North across Human Trail.

SURVIVAL

WHERE WERE THE TRACKS COMING FROM?

From the east parallel the river, at least 100 yds

WHERE WERE THEY GOING TO?

Moving in and out of water repeatedly, going West toward HWY 93

WHERE DO YOU BELIEVE THE ANIMAL WAS DURING THE TIME THAT YOU WERE TRACKING IT?

Hiding in its riverside den, perhaps sleeping or munching on caught prey.

WHAT WOULD YOU DO IF YOU WANTED TO SEE THE ANIMAL THAT MADE THESE TRACKS?

I would wait on the river bank 1 hour prior to dawn + 1 hour after in a place of dense cover.

WHAT DO YOU BELIEVE THE STORY OF THESE TRACKS TO BE?

I believe the mink was traveling along the river - pre-dawn - in search of frogs, crustaceans or other river food.

DRAW YOUR BEST MATCH FROM A FIELD GUIDE BELOW! (INCLUDE MEASUREMENTS)

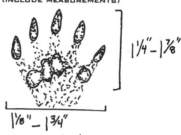

$1\frac{1}{4}" - 1\frac{7}{8}"$

$1\frac{1}{8}" - 1\frac{3}{4}"$

NAME OF BEST MATCH: Mink

SOURCE: Rezendes   PAGE: 120

PERSPECTIVE

DESCRIBE OR DRAW WHAT YOU SAW FROM THE ANIMALS PERSPECTIVE:

I saw the steep bank of the river from the water and climbed up for a perch and view into the river water from above. From that vantage point, I saw the river below, a possible meal, and a smooth decline to slide on.

NAME: Tiffany Morgan   DATE: 3/21/02

about the trail: where the animal stops, what it investigates, scat, change in direction, feeding sign. Make a guess as to where the animal was going and why it was going there.

Where do you believe the animal was while you were tracking it? Take a moment to envision the animal in your mind's eye. Where is it now? There's usually no way to be certain if you can't see or hear it, so this is an opportunity to think about the animal's survival needs relative to the time of day. Does the animal sleep during the day? Is it active at dawn and dusk? Where would it rest—a shady spot or a sunny slope? Could it be in a tree or burrowed safely underground? Research the animals that you suspect made the tracks and find out their habits and habitats to answer the question of where the animal might be.

What would you do if you wanted to see the animal that made these tracks? What strategy would you use if you wanted to see this animal? Where is a likely place to look for it? What time would you go? Where would you hide? How can you use what you've learned about the animal's life to observe it?

What do you believe the story of these tracks to be? Here, you can speculate about what might have happened. Be as detailed or as general as you would like, but don't spend too much time. This is also where you can note questions to yourself for future reference.

MEASURING TRACKS AND TRAILS

In the beginning, the best way to positively identify tracks is to accurately measure them and then consult a trusted field guide. (We recommend *Mammal Tracks and Sign: A Guide to North American Species* by Mark Elbroch [2003] and *Bird Tracks and Sign: A Guide to North American Species,* also by Elbroch [2001]. Others that we recommend are *Tracking and the Art of Seeing: How to Read Animal Tracks and Sign* [Rezendes, 1999], and the Peterson field guide *Animal Tracks* [Murie, 1954], or look for the revised edition with Mark Elbroch.) As with any new skill, when you are first attempting to identify animal tracks, it's important to learn to do it the right way. This is especially true with tracking, because you will most likely be learning on your own, and there will be no one to correct you if you're wrong. Your field guides may be the only thing that keep you in check.

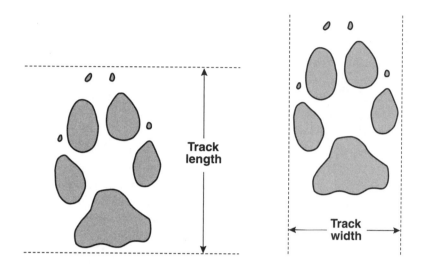

Measuring Tracks

Measure several front and rear tracks of each individual animal you find, because there can be great size differences in the tracks of a single animal, depending on it's speed and substrate variation.

Track Length. To find the length of a track, measure the longest section stretching from the back edge of the heel pad in the rear to the tips of the leading toenails in front. (If you're not including nails, measure from back edge of the heel pad to the leading edge of the toes in front.) It is important to note that some field guides include the nails in the measurement and some do not. The books we recommend include nail measurements because certain mammal species, including porcupines and pocket mice, rarely register toes, making it impossible to measure their track length without including the nails. Make sure to find out which method your field guide uses for track length measurement. If you want to play it safe or are cross-referencing field guides, simply take two measurements: one with nails and one without.

Track Width. To find the width of a track, measure the widest part. Note that tracks are not always longer than they are wide.

How Big Is That Track?

Jim Halfpenny

Central to tracking is knowing how large a footprint is. This is a simple question until you think about it. One animal moving on a progressively softer surface will leave progressively larger tracks. What is the size of the animal's track?

Try this experiment. Place your hand on a hard surface, a table for instance. Feel the contact area with your hand with that surface. Imagine that contact area as your first contact with a mud surface. As your hand goes deeper into the mud, your hand print enlarges. Your hand can create an infinite number of track sizes, the deeper it goes into the mud.

Mountain lion and grizzly bear researchers jointly recognized the problem of variable track sizes and tried to develop means for overcoming it. During their lion research, Fjelline and Mansfield (1989) developed a method for measuring tracks, we call the "Minimum Outline Method."

Remember the first contact area of your hand with the surface. If your hand went no deeper into that surface, your hand print would have only one size—the *Minimum Outline*. If your hand sank deeper into the surface, it would create a number of variable outlines as the mud moved around the curved surface of your hand and fingers. All footprints have a minimum outline, but only prints that sink into a surface have variable outlines. Therefore, minimum outlines are the only consistent sizes in tracking.

To measure the minimum outline, study the bottom of a print to determine where the rounded pad turns upward. The break point would be the minimum outline edge. Use this edge to measure tracks.

While the variable outline of a footprint may only be several millimeters wider that the minimum outline, those few millimeters have a large visual effect. The human eye sees area and area increases with the square of a linear measurement. In short, a few millimeters of width adds a lot of area to a footprint.

Minimum outline size does not change for different surfaces (assuming you have a clear track) and therefore provides cross-surface comparison, for example from snow to sand. While an animal may leave many sizes of footprints depending on surface, slope, and speed, there is only one minimum outline for every print.

Assigning the break point is a subjective judgment and no two people will always mark it at exactly the same point. However, experimentation has shown that an individual tracker can reduce personal variation in measurements and that groups of trackers trained in minimum outline methods will become more consistent in their measurement of tracks. Quality measurements are the tracker's goal and using minimum outline methods greatly reduces overexaggeration and variability of track size.

Whenever someone tells you they have measured an especially large track, determine if they understand the effect of sinking into a surface. Be very cautious of any measurements where the measurer does not specify that an effort has been made to control for the foot sinking into the surface.

To report the track size for an individual animal, it is best to measure several different tracks and average them. A good report would also include measure of variation (e.g., standard deviation). To do a good job describing track size for a species, minimum outline measurements of several individuals should be averaged and variation measurements reported for both individuals and the species.

For your personal research and learning effort, develop a minimum outline set of measurements for species that you can easily access. Remember to measure different ages, and sexes. Even doing this for common pets and dogs, would be worthwhile. I am not aware of any such data sets for household pets. Be the first on your block and send a copy to TRAcks. Also, once you have several measurements of different age animals, you can develop growth curves for footprint size.

A parting thought, be careful of any data set that lists only one measurement for a species. If it is an average, how many tracks and animals were averaged? What were their ages? What were their sexes? What was the variation in the data set? A range of measurements would be better, but the same questions still apply. Trackers must do quality work nowadays! You can help by developing good data sets and quality data sets, take time to develop.

Reference: Fjelline, D. P., and T. M. Mansfield. 1989. Method to standardize the procedure for measuring mountain lion tracks. In Smith, R. H., ed. Proceedings of the third mountain lion workshop. 1988, Dec 6–8. Prescott, AZ. Arizona Game and Fish Department.

Reprinted from TRAcks, 2(1):3, the journal of the Trackers Research Association, www.tracknature.com, 406-848-9458, P.O. Box 989, Gardiner, MT 59030.

Marking Tracks in a Trail: An Exercise in Seeing Patterns

When measuring, it is helpful to first identify the front feet from the hind feet. In the red fox, for example, the front foot is larger than the rear foot. Study the details in the accompanying photograph that cause one foot to appear bigger than the other. For instance, the toes of the smaller hind foot are pulled in tight, while the front foot toes are spread out. Depending on the animal you're tracking, the comparative sizes will vary. For instance, bobcats and coyotes have larger front than hind tracks because they carry a greater proportion of their weight in the front. In contrast, bears and porcupines carry a greater proportion of their weight in the rear and thus have larger hind feet than front feet. Usually animals in the same families have similar weight distributions, so if you can narrow your possible species down to a single family, such as Canidae, you have a good place to start.

EXERCISE

To figure out which track belongs to which foot on the animal, place Popsicle sticks or twigs in front of the toe of each track in the pattern. If you're using twigs, break them into long pieces for front tracks and short pieces for hind tracks, so that you can see from a standing distance which tracks are front and which are hind. If you're using Popsicle sticks, you can mark the tips with different colors, such as red for

Red fox track on left—larger front foot. Red fox track on right—smaller rear foot. JONAH EVANS

Side trot of domestic dog: dark Popsicle sticks in front tracks; light colored sticks in hind feet.

front and blue for hind. You will be amazed at the obvious patterns revealed. The next step is determining what gait the animal is using. Field guides differ with regard to the names of gaits, so it's best to read up on gaits in your field guide of tracks.

Measuring Trails

When you've found all four tracks of your animal—left front, right front, left hind, right hind—you're ready to take some measurements. The three measurements most useful when referencing field guides are the trail width, stride, and group length.

Trail Width. To measure trail width, find the leading track in one pair and then find the next leading track in the next pair. This measure-

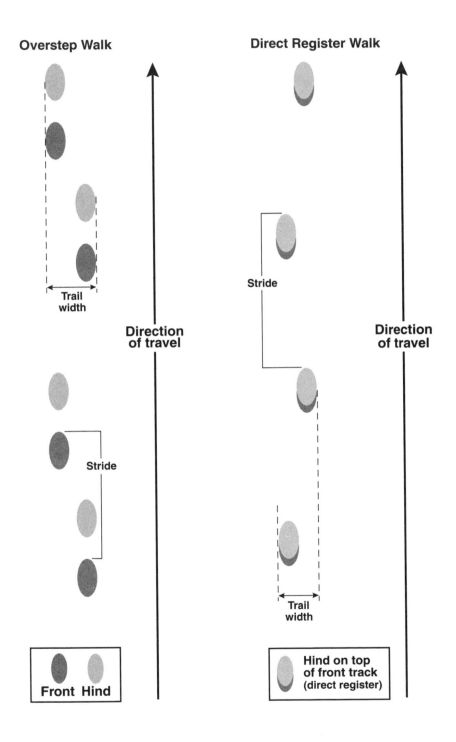

Overstep Walk

Direct Register Walk

Trail width

Direction of travel

Stride

Stride

Direction of travel

Trail width

Front Hind

Hind on top of front track (direct register)

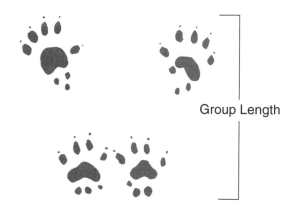

Group Length

ment is taken from the outside edges of the two leading tracks, meas-ured straight across rather than at an angle. It helps to use a tape meas-ure or a stick to mark a line from one leading track to the other for reference when measuring the width.

Stride. Start your measurement from the tip of the toe on the front foot, and end it on the tip of the toe of the next front foot in the line of tracks. This is the measurement used for all walks and trots, except for direct register. For direct-registering trots and walks, measure from the tip of the rear—which is the track that lands on top of the front in the sequence—to the tip of the next rear in the line of tracks.

Again, there are discrepancies among field guides with regard to measuring stride and width, so check your guide.

Group Length. This is a useful measurement for lopes, hops, bounds, and gallops. Find a group of tracks that consists of all four feet, and measure from the heel of whichever foot falls the farthest back to the toe of the leading foot in front.

With enough practice taking accurate measurements, you will no longer need a tape measure. The details that differentiate similar tracks will be obvious to you without this aid. I've found that using a tape measure can actually become a hindrance when trackers rely too heavily on the size of tracks rather than trusting other visual impres-sions, such as negative space, shape, and form. There is more informa-tion in the morphology of a track than in its dimensions.

4

Seeing and Identifying

It is hard to overvalue the power of the skillful tracker. To him the trail of each animal is not a mere series of similar footprints; it is an accurate account of the creature's ways, habits, changing whims, and emotions during the portion of life of which the record is in view. These are indeed autobio-graphical chapters and differ from some other autobiogra-phies in this—they cannot tell a lie. We may get wrong information from them, but it is our own fault if we do; we misread the unimpeachable document.

—Ernest Thompson Seton
Animal Tracks and Hunter Signs

J.Y.

SEARCH IMAGES AND RELATIVE AWARENESS

There is a story I like to tell that illustrates a phenomenon that occurs when people are learning a new search image. They tend to see that new item everywhere they go—even in familiar places, such as their own yards or their secret spots. The story involves the "appearance" of Red-tailed Hawks in my hometown, where I was teaching science at a private high school and teaching nature and tracking after school. Although I would never claim to know anyplace completely, it is safe to say that I knew this place pretty well. I was aware of the favorite nesting, roosting, soaring, and perch-hunting areas of the local Red-tailed Hawks. Each day on my way to and from work, I noted the birds in their favorite places and came to expect to see them there. I was rarely disappointed, and when I was, it was cause for further investi-gation—at least a good look around for a moment or two. Sometimes I would find them a bit farther down the road in a less frequented area, or I might not see them at all that day. But they would usually be back in their usual spots within a day or two.

One morning, a student appeared at my desk and said, "Mr. Young, did you notice all the Red-tailed Hawks that have moved into the area?" He went on to tell me, location by location, about all the hawks he had seen—at the same spots where I had been seeing them every day (we took the same route to school). What was new? He had just learned about Red-tailed Hawks in the after-school program I was leading. For him, there were "new" Red-tailed Hawks in the area. For me, the other instructors, and more than a few bird-watchers and naturalists, there was nothing new at all. The hawks had been there all along. But this student's perception was that Red-tailed Hawks had suddenly moved in where before they had been absent. This story is noteworthy because it happened several times that year with several different people.

From the student's point of view, there was only the "truth" of his perceptions. But what is this truth, anyway? Where do we get it? How does it change? What is our experience of this change? The student experienced a change in the external world—where there was no change at all! The change really occurred in his perceptions due to new search image data. I try not to burst people's bubbles during these rites of passages of awareness. My goal is to keep people excited and motivated, so I just ask some leading questions to get them to go back and look again or to do a bit more research.

This story illustrates the concept of relative awareness. It is about search image "storage and retrieval," but it is also about people's perceptions from two points of view: (1) if we lack search images, we may not recognize the existence of something in the environment around us; (2) if we have misguided images or inaccurate information, we will project a misguided or inaccurate perception.

Helpful in this context is the idea of "truth." The truth is that hawks existed in the area. The truth is that if several people with training in Red-tailed Hawk and tree identification went to this location at the same time, wrote down what we saw, and then compared notes, we would discover that we had seen the same trees, the same hawks, the same behaviors, the same hills, the same sun position and clouds, the same roads and other obvious land features. As individuals, however, we would have noted different small details, recognized and remembered different aspects of the landscape and nuances of behavior. This is the nature of our perceptions, and it is always changing and, hopefully, getting more refined and more accurate each day. This is the essence of primary learning on the tracking and awareness journey.

This process is at the heart of both the Kamana Naturalist and Shikari Tracker Training Programs. Ironically, when I move to a new area, some of the search images follow me and help me see the truth around me, whereas others are actually a liability of sorts. Why? When something looks a lot like something else—when you are used to seeing something in an entirely different and faraway context—misidentification is possible.

PERCEPTUAL FILTERS

The subconscious and trained aspects of tracking involve a dependence on what I call search image recognition "file cards." This is a good thing when it comes to quickly identifying loved ones, our houses, pets, stop signs, logos, and speed limit signs. In fact, we take the search image recognition process for granted in familiar environments and situations. In tracking, however, there are many situations when the search image characteristics are very small or subtle (such as telling the difference between the tracks of a male and a female). This subtlety is frequently altered by changing substrates, pressures, and other incredibly diverse variables that can distort a track. Therefore, the potential to project previous experiences (for better or worse) onto a new search image experience is great. We have a lot of things to project, especially when we are new to something.

Here is an example. A young man discovered some "dog tracks" by the creek near my house. He described their size and shape, but when I interviewed him about his observations, assumptions, and conclusions, we both discovered that many of his conclusions about the "dog tracks" came from his assumptions about the area; those assumptions became filters or projections that altered his experience of the situation and skewed his sense of the "truth" (remember the Red-tailed Hawk story).

Here are his assumptions: (1) there are many dogs in the neighborhood (based on his experience from his own neighborhood, which resembles mine); (2) the animal must be a member of the canine family, and because there are no wolves here, coyotes don't get that big, and there are no local wild dogs with feet that big, it must be a domestic dog; (3) there is no other explanation for these tracks.

Although he made some good observations, his description told me that the animal's gait was one that dogs don't use in places like this. Let's see how his assumptions helped create filters that covered the truth:

1. There are, in fact, *no* dogs in the neighborhood. There is only one large ranch surrounding the creek, and the dogs that live there have never—in the four years that I have tracked this creek—been seen there, nor have their tracks. The only other possibility is an old Labrador retriever who would be far outside his range.

2. Although it is true that there are no wild members of the dog family in the area with feet that big, this correct fact can actually skew the truth. A correct fact gives us confidence and can therefore overshadow the basic assumption—that the tracks were made by a canine—is false. Applying a true fact inappropriately renders it useless. Our perceptions, however, allow this to happen seamlessly. This is a good example of how our filters operate.

3. There can be no other explanation for this track—unless we're dealing with search images yet unlearned. This young man didn't know that there were mountain lions on the creek. It just didn't fit with his experience.

When I tracked the young man back to the places he had been, I discovered that his "dog tracks" were actually very clear mountain lion tracks, located where mountain lions are seen about once every other month, on average. Our motion-detecting TrailMaster cameras have captured five still images and one twenty-second video of at least two individuals from that same creek corridor in the last two years.

For those of you feeling smug right now, saying to yourself, "I would never confuse mountain lion and dog tracks," be careful. It happens more than you realize, even to experienced trackers. A false sense of security seems to emerge from an intermediate amount of experience, aided by the need to be right.

When and where do our filters get in the way of seeing what is really there? This is a question that must be asked routinely if you are committed to tracking in a real, honest way. Don't be afraid to challenge your assumptions, recognize your mistakes, and let go of the need to be right.

BRAIN PATTERNING

The intention of this chapter is to hardwire your brain so that you can perceive tracks and sign. First-time trackers sometimes see the most bizarre things. Whereas I can clearly see the toes, heel pad, and claws, they may see something entirely different. It's almost as if they are suffering from some kind of visual impairment. And in a sense, they are. They have an inability to recognize track patterns.

Consider an anthropological study that was done when the Native Americans were taught to read English. At first, they were unable to recognize the patterns of our language. All twenty-six letters of the alphabet looked the same—random symbols unassociated with anything in their brains. It wasn't that they couldn't *see* them; they just couldn't *perceive* them. They had to be shown flash cards repeatedly until they could see each letter, recognize it, and understand its contextual meanings.

The process of learning to read is similar to the way tracking is learned. Tracking is a whole collection of brain patterns created by using your eyes and senses to perceive compressions in the ground. You start with clear print identification—the ABCs—and build on those brain patterns for every other aspect of tracking until you're able to read stories.

Now imagine a person who has spent her whole life in a house, leaving only to drive to another building or to walk on a sidewalk. Her closest encounter with nature is her lawn. Imagine twenty years of brain patterning only on what humankind has created. Neurological studies have shown that people with only this type of input have a very limited view of the world. They lack the exposure to dynamic sensory input and can't see what's wrong with their world because they've never stepped outside of it. This blindness explains why people are capable of destroying the earth in the first place, and why it's vital that humans pattern their brains on nature.

If such a person is given the opportunity to interact with nature— bathing her senses in a manner that accesses part of her original blueprint—she will become sensitive to and aware of things she previously could not perceive. She will realize that nature has value and that society doesn't notice what nature is experiencing—what the plants, animals, trees, and waters are experiencing.

In 1970 Colin Blakemore and G. F. Cooper studied the effects of selective rearing on vision and the biology of the eye in house cats. Kittens were raised with limited exposure to light and in large tubes of either horizontal or vertical lines—allowed to view only one of these patterns for five hours a day. Later tests showed that the kittens had developed apparent "blindness" to the line patterns to which they had not been exposed. Thus, kittens habituated on vertical lines did not respond to, or "see," rods held horizontally; the opposite was true of kittens raised in tubes with horizontal lines. The challenge is to see what is truly before us, to see the actual track and remain uninfluenced by our filters and projections, to see without wanting to see something in particular.

OWL VISION

In *Jungle Lore,* Jim Corbett writes: "A human being has a field of vision of a hundred and eighty degrees, and . . . it is necessary to train the eyes to cover the entire field of vision. Movements straight in front are easy to detect and easy to deal with, but movements at the edge of the field of vision are vague and indistinct, and it is these vague and indistinctive movements that can be most dangerous and are most to be feared."

In his book *Sacred Hoops,* Phil Jackson talks about some of the innovative techniques he used when he led the Chicago Bulls to several NBA championships. One of the skills he describes is peripheral vision training. He recognizes, as do many successful coaches, that developing this aspect of seeing actually stimulates the brain and body to function more effectively. This moves an athlete's performance more effectively toward the much-desired state described as "the zone."

For most of my career as a teacher and mentor, I have been fortunate to work with people who are interested in tracking or naturalist skills and committed to spending the time and resources necessary to take the learning journey. In my early years as a tracking mentor, however, I worked in the public schools, at after-school programs, and in several inner-city programs. This could be challenging, because the youths we worked with didn't always know why they were even in the program. I had to completely throw out my expectations for lessons and meet the students on their terms. In the last few years, I have reached out to the "not-so-interested" public again through two different venues: the Riekes Center for Human Enhancement in Menlo Park, California, where nature studies is part of a larger teaching mission involving music, creative arts, and athletic fitness; and the Bass/ Nature Camp in Nashville, Tennessee, an innovative program started by world-class bassist Victor Wooten.

The challenge in these programs is finding commonalities between nature and music or nature and athletics. At the Riekes Center, we have to ask what nature skills and tracking have to offer an athlete or a videographer or a hip-hop musician. Such challenges make for interesting teaching and storytelling dynamics at both the Bass/Nature Camp and the Riekes Center. One of the bridges has been the concept of peripheral or "owl" vision training. At the Bass/Nature Camp the other instructors and I discussed this phenomenon and agreed that it was a great skill to teach. Many musicians agree that using peripheral vision during a performance or practice helps their playing. This is also an aid to improvisation—an important skill in the music genres represented at the camp. Great emphasis is placed on this skill, and students report positive results early in their training.

The reason we use the term owl vision instead of peripheral vision is related to our commitment to the storytelling aspects of our brains. We are well aware of the importance of developing good visualization skills in tracking and nature awareness training—if for no other reason than it makes for great teaching and storytelling skills later. This ensures that the trackers we train are also interesting and engaging teachers, helping the art and science of tracking to be passed down through competent leadership.

EXERCISE

Imagine yourself as an owl. Most owl species have large eyes for the purpose of gathering light in dim conditions. Owing to the oversized eyeball, the eye socket bones are interrupted, and the eye protrudes beyond the bone. For this reason, an owl cannot move its eyes very much and instead must turn its entire head to survey a new direction. During this exercise, we emulate the owl for four reasons:

1. The stillness of the eye in the socket. Keep the eyes looking directly forward at all times while practicing this exercise. (When not practicing, use the full range of motion of the eye.)
2. The stillness of the owl itself. The bird sits very still and stares without moving for long periods. This is what you should do in this exercise—sit very still and watch in one direction (blinking when necessary). It is good, like an owl, to pick a perch in the shadows, outside the main flow, partially obscured from view, but where you have a good view of the landscape around you.
3. The owl's quiet and patient nature. Emulate the owl; feel the wind lift your feathers (so to speak), and drop down into the quiet, relaxed pose of the owl.
4. The owl's gliding movement. While walking, be aware of how still your head stays as you move. Get to the place in your

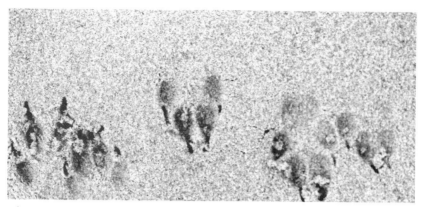

The coyote on left was moving toward the top of photo; the coyote on right, toward the bottom.

walking where you feel like you are gliding from the waist up—as if you were on a cart rolling on rails or on a skateboard being pulled along a smooth surface.

The basic exercise of using owl eyes is as follows, but there are endless variations in applying these principles. I encourage you to improvise.

1. Find a comfortable position (at first seated, then standing, and later on while fox walking). Hold your head still and look toward the horizon (if you cannot see it because of an intervening wall or thicket, pretend that you are looking at it). After leveling your gaze with the horizon, raise it a degree or two above this line.

2. Keep your eyes very still, and find a point to fix your gaze on. Later, abandon the point as you become better at this exercise.

3. Relax and stare straight ahead while activating the edges of your peripheral vision. Spread your arms out to the sides and wiggle your fingers to find the edges, but continue to hold the straight-ahead stare. Note the movement of leaves, birds, clouds, insects, or other objects in the edges of your vision without moving your head or eyes toward them.

4. Record the results in a short paragraph, describing the feelings and challenges you experienced during this exercise.

Practice this exercise for at least twenty minutes a day in the field. Every so often during the day, challenge yourself to go into owl vision while eating or working on something. Try using a skill that requires manual dexterity while practicing owl vision.

VARYING VISION

I can't tell you how many times I've looked at a track from one angle and concluded which direction the animal was traveling, only to view the track from a different angle and discover that I was wrong. This also happens when identifying tracks, because the direction of travel tells you where the toes are in relation to the heel pad. Without this basic bit of information, the track can belong to any number of species. The simple solution is to vary your vision—move around the track and look at it from different angles. But this is easier said than done, because once the mind attaches itself to an answer, such as the direction of travel, it's hard to let go of that conclusion. The following exercise is designed to help you remember to see not only tracks but also all things from different points of view.

EXERCISE

Find a local tracking spot where you can locate an animal trail in fairly difficult, but not impossible, substrate. If there's an animal trail you've wanted to follow but haven't had the time or it seemed too difficult, this would be perfect. Bring Popsicle sticks with you to use for track markers. Your challenge is to find 25 to 50 tracks and mark them with sticks. Do not skip tracks; if you have difficulty finding the next track, vary your vision. Look at the track from directly above and then slowly lower yourself until your face is hovering just above it. From there, tilt your head so that you're looking at the entire trail from the point of view of an ant. Try getting up and walking a few feet away, returning, and switching sides so that you're looking at the track from a different angle. There are many different ways to vary your vision, and I encourage you to try all of them. When you're really stumped, this tool can be indispensable for helping you to see things in a different light.

Speaking of light, did you know that it's much easier to see tracks in the early-morning hours or in the dwindling twilight? When the sun is directly overhead, tracks lack subtle details. Observe the same tracks at different times of day and see for yourself the subtle and often dramatic changes that light has on their appearance.

MORPHOLOGY

Specifically this exercise involves the morphology of animal's legs and feet. Studying the legs and feet of animal species you are interested in, can lead to enlightening discoveries of how that animal's tracks are made. Study the images of the deer hoof and track; compare the morphology of the foot with how the track registers. There are details in an actual foot that may not always register obviously in the track. If you have a mental image of the foot, you're more likely to find the subtler details in the track that help to positively identify the animal that made it.

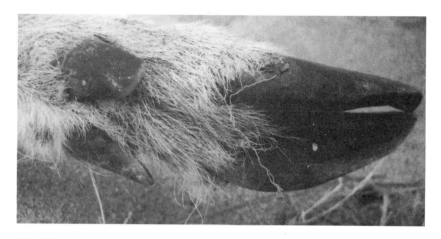

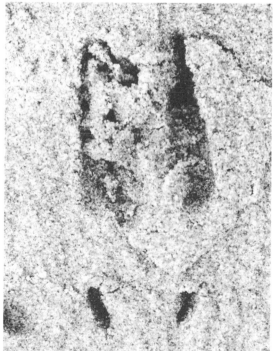

Study the top picture of the deer hoof and notice the high placement of the "dewclaws" on the leg. This explains why dewclaws only register in deep substrates such as those in loose, wet sand as shown at left.

Track Morphology
Wood rat tracks

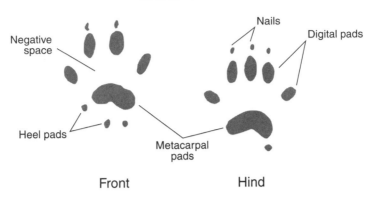

Negative space

Heel pads

Nails

Digital pads

Metacarpal pads

Front   Hind

EXERCISE

Draw the feet of any twenty-five mammals and five birds of your choosing. For this, you will likely need numerous resources, such as Paul Rezendes's *Tracking and the Art of Seeing* and Leonard Lee Rue's *Sportsman's Guide to Game Animals.* You may have to go to a museum or a university collection to finish this project. You can either draw while visiting the collection or photograph the feet and draw them at home.

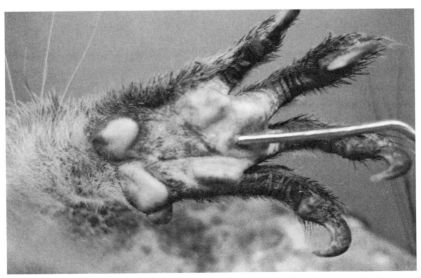

The front foot of the gray squirrel (and family Sciuridae in general) shows long nails on four toes, central metacarpal pads have fused and appear as three prominent bumps in track. Two heel pads at posterior edge plus a vestigial thumb often don't register. RANCHO DEL OSO NATURE AND HISTORY CENTER

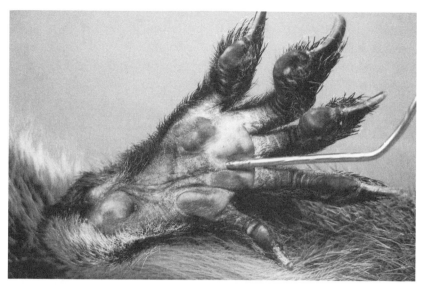

The hind foot of the gray squirrel (and family Sciuridae in general) have five toes with nails. Central metacarpal pads are fused, showing four distinct bumps in track. The heel pad is furred and typically doesn't register.
RANCHO DEL OSO NATURE AND HISTORY CENTER

Squirrels in the family Sciuridae have similar morphology of their feet and legs; thus, they have similar tracks. Studying one member of this family will teach you much about the others. Compare these tracks of the California ground squirrel to the morphology of the gray squirrel feet pictured. Bottom track is the front left foot; top track is the hind left foot.

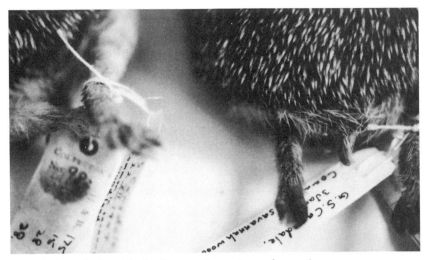

Morphology deals with the form and structure of organisms. MUSEUM OF
COMPARATIVE ZOOLOGY, HARVARD UNIVERSITY

EXERCISE

Rent several animal videos, and record the titles, production companies, and any other reference information in your notes. Watch the
videos and record whether the mammals that cross the screen are
plantigrade, digitigrade, unguligrade, or odd-unguligrade, defined as
follows:

Plantigrade. Walking with the full length of the foot on the ground
during each stride: toes and sole. Humans and bears are examples.

Digitigrade. Walking with most of the length of the digits, but not
the soles, in contact with the ground. Dogs and cats are examples.

Unguligrade. Walking on tiptoes, often on hooves. Deer and moose
are examples.

Odd-unguligrade. Walking on just one toe. Horses are an example.

By the end of the videos, you should have a list of species and how
they move. You might notice that certain species move in more than
one way.

SHALLOW AND DEEP SUBSTRATES

This is a simple exercise in track identification—your own tracks. Grab
your favorite pair of shoes (this is important), and bring a journal and
a pencil to record your observations.

First, find a clear patch of ground that will make a nice, clear track.
A bit of sand or mud will do nicely. It doesn't need to be very large, just
big enough to fit two footprints next to each other. Snow will also

Bobcat tracks in dry mud. *How can you tell that these tracks were made after the mud had dried and not while it was wet?*

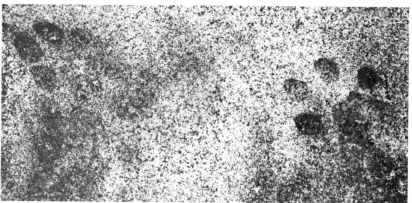

Bobcat tracks in damp, firm sand. *Notice that the minimum outline of these tracks is more obvious than in the other examples.*

Bobcat tracks in shallow mud. *Notice how mud affects the outline of the track, causing toes and heel pads to look larger than they actually are.*

work, although it's not as good as clear soil. Even if you live in the middle of the city, you should be able to find something suitable right around your home.

Once you have found a good place, pick a foot and make a single track with your shoe. Don't run or do anything tricky yet. We'll get to that later.

Then sketch the print made with your shoe. Pay attention to what you see, not what you *think* you see. Take a long look at the print, noting its size, shape, tread, patterns of wear, and the like, and then turn away from the track and sketch (the objective is to sketch from memory, not to copy). If you need to look at the track again, put your pencil down. Don't look and draw at the same time. Complete a full-page sketch.

One you have done this with your shoe, repeat the process with a bare foot. While sketching this time, pay attention not only to the size and shape of your whole foot but also to the size and shape of each toe relative to the others, the arch, and other features of your foot. Again, use the whole page and sketch what you see.

Don't take too long doing this. This exercise should take only half an hour.

STORYTELLING

Here is an exercise we picked up in a workshop with Mark Elbroch. You'll need a notebook, a pencil, and a track—either one in the field or an unidentified plaster track. The track can be made of anything—lizard, bird, or mammal. The only requirement is that you definitely *cannot* identify what made it. The less confident you feel about the origin of the track, the better.

When you've chosen a track, go ahead and draw it. Include measurements, and make sure that the drawing is accurate enough that when using references at home you will be able to identify the track.

Once the drawing is complete, you are ready for the next step. Tell the story of an average 24-hour day for this particular animal. Where does it rest? What time of day does it move about? Is it nocturnal or diurnal? What size is the animal? What does it eat? What are its fears? Does it have any predators? How fast does it move? Can it climb trees? Can it dig burrows or probe for insects? Does it hunt by stealth?

You may wonder how you can answer these questions without knowing what kind of animal made the track. But I would argue that you have all the answers you need right in front of you. The morphology of the foot is a direct result of living in a specific manner, of exploiting a specific biological niche: the foot is the direct link between earth and animal. Long claws are for digging and climbing. Webbing is for swimming. Feathered feet retain heat. Ask yourself good questions and be a detective.

The last part of this exercise is using a resource to identify the mystery track and then reading up on the animal to see how accurate your deductions were. Most people are amazed at how much they can tell from a track. They may not have known that it was a porcupine track, but they guessed the size of the animal, that it was slow, an herbivore, a tree climber, a digger, and wide-bodied.

VISUAL CHARACTERISTICS

Certain core concepts in drawing and art are used to teach students to see well and fully, and they are also wonderful tools to teach students of tracking to see more in the field. In this exercise, developed by Mark Elbroch from concepts taught by Charles Worsham, you will practice looking for four visual characteristics in a track while completing a series of five drawings—the fifth combining all four visual characteristics. For this, you'll need to head out into the field and locate one clear track; bring along a pencil and a notebook, and expect this exercise to take at least an hour. Below are instructions for the drawings. Do each one in order.

Drawing 1: Shapes. Draw the primary shapes—circles, triangles, squares, and so forth—that you see forming the track and the surrounding patch of ground.

Drawing 2: Textures. Draw all the textures—rough, smooth, and so forth—that you see in the patch of ground in and around the track.

Drawing 3: Edges. Draw all the edges you see—not only those that form the track.

Drawing 4: Light. Draw the various levels of light and shade that fall across and around the track.

Drawing 5: Combined. In this last sketch, draw the track and its surroundings in their entirety, combining all the elements.

These five drawings provide wonderful insight into how and what you see. Which drawings are fullest, and which have the greatest holes? Any blank space on a page indicates something you missed. Most people have strengths and weaknesses in what they see in a track, and these sketches will point these out. Certain people see edges well, but struggle with texture; others struggle with shapes.

Another interesting exercise is to have several people make these drawings from the same trail or of the same track. Then compare each person's drawings to see the diversity of how and what people perceive.

This is also a good tool to determine which details within and around the track you may be missing. Practice this exercise every so often to see your improvement.

SQUARE FOOT EXERCISE

Take three pens or pencils of different colors, head out into a nearby woods or field, and sit down. Choose a square foot of earth in front of you and draw it in a single color—a visual inventory of everything you see there. Then put down your pen or pencil and study the square foot again for five to seven minutes. When your time is up, choose a second color and add anything you missed in your initial drawing. When you're done, spend another five to seven minutes studying the same piece of earth, and use the third color to add anything you missed in the first two drawings.

This is an exercise in breaking through levels of seeing. With practice, you'll see more and more with the initial look, but there are always deeper levels to strive toward.

5

Interpreting Tracks and Patterns

Man has lost his power of tracking by scent but has developed greater intellectual refinement. He can read a more complex story in footprints than mere identification and direction of travel.

—Olaus J. Murie
Animal Tracks

J.Y.

LEARNING FROM THE DOG

If you shaved a wild, healthy coyote or a red fox or a wolf, what would you notice about its body? First, you would see its ribs sticking out—quite noticeably. In fact, you might say to yourself, "That animal looks awfully skinny. Somebody ought to feed it." But the fact is that wild, healthy canines are supposed to have their ribs showing through their skin. When we see them in the wild, with their thick fur, we don't realize how trim they are.

In contrast, consider domestic dogs, which are overweight compared with their relatives in the wild. Maybe it's because we think that if a dog is skinny looking, it must be starving and unhealthy. And that would mean that we're not taking good care of this animal, which is part of our family. So, we tend to overfeed our dogs.

The tracks and trails of wild members of the dog family, free to wander according to their ancestral ways, differ from those of their domestic cousins. When a wild canine trots along a level surface in a natural rhythm, the back foot falls directly into the front foot track—called direct register. If the rear track completely hides and overwrites the front track (at least to most eyes), it's called perfect register. Foxes, coyotes, and even wolves are capable of perfect register. I observed that healthy, prime adult animals seem to achieve perfect register more often than adolescent, injured, or older members of the pack; when wild dogs get tired, they also fall out of perfect register. Perfect register seems to be reserved for expressions of true wild and natural dogness, and it is clearly a sign of health.

In contrast, domestic dogs from the average American neighborhood are simply incapable of perfect register; they can barely manage direct register (exceptions are cattle dogs or farm dogs in general, which tend to be leaner and better exercised). If you know what to look for, there are all kinds of indicators that family dogs are unhealthy, overweight, and underexercised.

So I started thinking, what if I raised a dog, fed it a diet similar to that of wild coyotes, and gave it lots of exercise? What would I get? Would I get perfect register from a domestic dog?

Scout was a dog that I picked up at a music festival just a few days after I had these thoughts. I was playing the upright bass with some other bluegrass and folk musicians I had just met. And as we were resting between songs, a young girl walked up and asked, "Hey, do you want a puppy? He's half Labrador and half Irish setter." She had obviously asked a lot of people the same question and was looking a bit tired and disappointed. The day was drawing to a close, and people would be leaving soon.

"Sure," I said. Good breeds in the mix, I thought, and good price—only $20. So that was how I found Scout.

I raised Scout as I had planned, to test my theory. He was underfed by most people's standards, even though his wild cousins were still eating less than him. And I exercised him a lot—sometimes 10 or 12 miles at a stretch. Scout grew up fast and legged all the way out, and he had perfect register when in a trot. Scout was an amazing dog, and I am filled with pride thinking about him, especially the way he carried himself with so much dignity. Today, he is buried in an unmarked grave in the Pine Barrens at the first place I camped with Tom Brown, along Cedar Creek.

Scout taught me a lot. His nose was better than my eyes. He always found the subtle trails—especially the fresh ones. But most important, Scout taught me to read trails. Tom had always told me that dogs could do this for us. What I learned from Scout applied across the board to all members of the dog family, and the physics of track and trail interpretation applies to all moving things.

Our routine was a strenuous one. Keep it mind that I raised Scout for this purpose—he was trained since six weeks old for long-distance running. He ran in the rainy spring, in the hot, dusty summer, through the windy fall, and even in the frigid winter. Scout thrived on it, but you wouldn't want to take an overweight, five-year-old Labrador and run him on a dirt road for 10 miles. You could easily bring on a heart attack or do serious damage to the dog's hips or other joints. Be moderate and thoughtful in how you work with dogs; above all, be kind and loving to them, and they will repay you a thousand times.

Scout and I would get in the jeep and drive to a sand road in the Pine Barrens. All sand roads are not alike; some are better suited than others for a study of this sort. "Sugar" sand is deep and soft, like the beach, and is not the best kind of substrate. Hardpan roads with a perfect layer of fine sand are the best, and these became our regular routes. On the way to these roads, I would put Scout outside the jeep and drive along at speeds between 10 and 25 miles per hour. At first, he would always run as fast as he could in long, zigzagging patterns from the forest on one side of the road to the other. He would sniff wildly at the ground, and his head would yank to one side if he suddenly caught a fresh scent. Then he would quickly lose interest and be off again at a dead run. This kind of crazy galloping lasted only a few minutes. Then he would stop and leave a scat; sometimes he would do this twice in close succession, with some good running in between. After a bit more galloping, he would drop—kind of suddenly—into a trot. I adjusted my speed of travel based on his interest in running.

Learning from the dog. DAVID FORTHHOFFER

After about ten minutes, he would have gotten rid of whatever excess energy he had. Then he would settle in to his natural rhythm.

Settling in for Scout consisted of dropping into a rhythmic, harmonic, and seemingly comfortable trot. It was almost hypnotic to watch, and we would move along that way for miles and miles. He never got tired, but I could drive for only so many hours before I started to feel guilty, even though there was no visible sign that he was done. Scout's gait was clearly energy efficient.

In the beginning of this study period working with Scout, I would stop the truck, get out my notebook, and study the trail. Scout would often have perfect register, which meant that my experiment was a success. I drew many tracks of many trails in my journal and took a lot of measurements. His gait was so harmonic and rhythmic and symmetrical on a level road that his tracks fell into a pattern of perfect measurements that repeated again and again—his tracks in a trot were about 24 inches apart. He was about two years old at the time and had not been neutered. I noticed that other male dogs that sometimes accompanied us did not have the stamina or the body design that Scout had, and I think some of it was attributable to the hormones still available to Scout but not to his emasculated friends.

Once I had established the baseline patterns of Scout's trot signature, I began to study his "events." Scout would be trotting along in perfect harmonic rhythm when all of a sudden his head would be yanked down by something invisible; his head would turn to the right or left, and then he would kind of "bump" over this little imperfection in an otherwise perfect series and continue. When he settled down a few steps later, I would stop the truck, get out, and study and sketch the tracks and trail he had just made. Scout would rest in the front seat while I did this.

There was always a reason for his events, and after many study sessions with Scout, I learned where to look. So, when I was tracking a coyote and found a skip in the rhythm, I would recognize it (this is a form of cluster tracking). There is always a reason for the skip in the baseline rhythm—a scent mark, a cross-trail, a change in vista.

I used the same process to learn other gaits. For instance, I would speed up a bit and hold at a new steady pace. Scout would respond by picking up his pace. With a slight increase in speed, Scout would move into a side trot, providing a whole new baseline to study and journal. Any events out of that trot were cause for me to stop, study, measure, sketch, and journal.

Sometimes I would put the jeep into low gear, especially when Scout would start walking and sniffing, which he did from time to time. I think it was often in response to core areas of foxes or coyotes or near campsites where dogs were camping with their families. Scout would go into a slow, almost thoughtful kind of mode: walking, sniffing, stopping, urinating, sniffing, walking. Then, all of a sudden, he would just start trotting again, and I would stop the jeep to study and journal.

This same systematic process went on for lopes, gallops, all kinds of trots, and walks. Any time Scout felt the urge to actually turn off the road completely, to follow a fresh trail, I knew that it would be an interesting one. Sometimes I would leave Scout in the jeep and go it alone, trailing the dog's find. One time I found a fresh set of gray fox tracks that I followed for about 20 yards, track set by track set. The trail led off the road and up to a little level place at the top of a hill. The fox was following a subtle but visible run—probably its own, judging from the size and condition of the wear patterns. At the point where the run struck the top of the little ridge, there was another run perpendicular to the original one. The ridgetop run was parallel to the dirt road a few yards away and below. When this particular fox got to the top of the run, instead of crossing the ridgetop and continuing the same trajectory, it hung a left without missing a beat in its gait pattern. The fox maintained a trot the whole way, and it was a perfect register for the most part. It traveled along the ridgetop run for about 5 yards before reaching the overhanging branches of a large pitch pine, which provided welcome shade and cover on this hot day. When I looked back toward the jeep, I could see Scout filtered through a screen of branches. If I were as camouflaged and as small as a gray fox, I would be all but invisible to Scout, or to anyone else. This was a great lesson.

I also found a day bed in this spot, and right in the middle of the little worn-in area under a pine branch was a Mourning Dove carcass. The dove was lying on its back, breast into the air, entirely intact. Not a feather was out of place, except for the breast, which was clear of both feathers and skin. There were a few blood drops glistening on the downy feathers surrounding the skinned circle of red meat showing through. The blood was still wet, as was the glistening breast muscle. The meaning was clear: the fox was very close by, and this was a fresh kill. Now, I wish that I had backtracked and looked for the kill site. I did foretrack the fox for a few yards, just to see where it had gone to hide.

Today, every time I see a head turn, a sniff, a pause-to-scent mark, a sudden stop to look or listen, or any other event in an otherwise consistent, harmonic, and rhythmic set of tracks, I am grateful to Scout. I don't think you can learn these skills without some good experience and the ability to verify results by watching the tracks being made and then stopping to study them while the animal's movements are still fresh in your mind.

BASELINE

J.Y./T.M.

To learn gaits—especially baseline, when an animal is comfortable—study the gaits of canines, whether fox, coyote, wolf, or domestic dog. Study all gaits, but pay close attention to when the canine is in a trotting pattern. Learn to distinguish this from a stalking pattern, a gallop, and a lope. Look for subtleties of behavior that reveal themselves in the tracks and show a disturbance in pattern: a quickened or slowed pace. Become so familiar with the canine's baseline gait that your recognition of it is subconscious; you can spot it out of the corner of your eye. If you concentrate on this, you will soon be able to recognize the baseline of other species, even insects. You'll be able to watch a beetle moving and know that it feels safe and comfortable—it's in baseline. You will reach the point where you're able to recognize baseline in everything. Once while tracking wolves in Idaho, I heard a radiotelemetry airplane flying overhead very slowly, the engine making a kind of subidle sound; it was out of baseline, moving slower than normal to gather information. Likewise, while searching the sand roads in Idaho for wolf scat, I had my pickup truck idling in first gear, and I could hear it was struggling to keep that pace; it was out of baseline. You'll be able to tell when a bird is flying comfortably and when it's going just fast enough to keep afloat but losing integrity of flight.

This is really a physics problem: an animal is designed to move comfortably at a certain speed; anything above or below that is possible, but only for short distances. Training yourself to see these subtleties is the key to the interpretation of gaits, but you have to start with baseline so that you can detect a disturbance.

Animal baselines vary from one species to another, however. For example, the baseline gait for a coyote is a trot, whereas a bear's is a walk. You may also notice variances within species; for example, one bobcat may have a slightly different baseline gait than another bobcat. This may be due to injury, habitat, or simply personal preference. If you have the opportunity to track the same species of animal in two different regions or habitats, compare your notes on baseline gaits to see whether the influences of weather, predators, or landscape features affect baseline. The important thing about understanding an animal baseline pattern is knowing when it's out of basiline. Investigating a breach in baseline is often the first clue in a riveting mystery.

Personal Baseline

Baseline is a rare state of mind in our Western experience, except when we're on vacation, getting ready for bed, or enjoying a leisurely Sunday morning. These are often the only times that baseline is allowed to creep into our busy minds and lives.

Imagine that you're on vacation. You wake in the morning, it's a beautiful day, and there's nowhere you have to be. You play with the idea of taking a walk but decide to sit on the deck for a while and just look around, feel the wind, hear the sounds. Soon enough you get up to take your walk, but you don't have any particular destination. You start walking along and come to a fruit stand, where you stop and buy some fruit to take the edge off your hunger. Now you're ready to stroll, walking at a slow, gentle pace; you're enjoying the view, the feelings, and the scents. This is the best way for you to understand a baseline gait in an animal. It is completely in the moment, enjoying perfect balance within its body. We might perceive this as being lazy. But taking your time, without exerting yourself, is baseline.

The early missionaries are said to have perceived the natives as being lazy. During the heat of the day, the natives would sit in the shade laughing and telling stories. They were observed spending much of their time just sitting around; however, at other times, such as while hunting, they were all business, focused, and working hard. The observation was made that they were capable of working hard but rarely did. Studies with wild wolves show the same pattern of behavior; they are generally either resting or hunting, and they spend most of their time resting. This is true of all animals; they don't exert themselves unless there is a need to do so. Thus, they have a relatively stress-free lifestyle and are typically in a state of baseline.

Children are good at achieving baseline. In childhood, a high quality relationship usually develops between a child and his or her immediate locale. A child might have a favorite tree to sit in or under while Grandma works in her garden, or the child may nap there. Frequently children talk out loud to themselves or to the objects around them. They develop an almost dreamlike relationship with their surroundings by having conversations with trees, birds, and insects. They are conditioning themselves to have a high-quality connection to the details of a place. They are beginning to understand, in a rich way, how the birds, animals, trees, and insects interact around them, leading to an understanding of the relationship among all things. This is an important time. As children learn to sit still, they learn that nature is their friend, their provider, and their safe haven. Perhaps most important, they learn to recognize baseline. They can sit in the baseline of place and know this in their bodies. They begin to see with the same eyes and feel the same internal desires as the animals and birds around them, which makes them better trackers as adults because they understand the decisions of animals and birds.

The goals of energy conservation and avoidance of danger are what guide baseline. For example, native people who survive by gathering and hunting don't have energy to waste. Knowing that danger is coming long before it arrives is the safest way to avoid it, so native people develop strategies of awareness that help them recognize the approach of danger. They learn to see changes in the clouds or the wind that predict the coming of a storm. They are trained to know that a certain bird sound means that a leopard is hiding in the tree ahead. Because of their quietness, they are able to take one step at a time and be fully present as they move, making it easier to avoid a rattlesnake strike or accidentally stepping on a puff adder.

Such things are conditioned from childhood and are very much survival tools. If you don't understand these things, you don't understand the nature of a holistic tracker. Without this kind of background, people cannot and will not grow as trackers.

Modern society does not recognize baseline as having value. For example, in the classroom, it's frowned on if a child falls into the instinctive pattern of resting, relaxing, and dreaming. In the afternoon, after a full day at school, a child may want to rest and lie down but is made to do chores instead. Children are taught to feel bad about themselves for being lazy. Baseline nowadays is confined to people sitting on the couch watching television, when they're finally allowed to rest. On vacation, we may begin to understand the internal clock that drives baseline, just in time to go back to work again, where it is quickly forgotten.

In modern life, we move in what would be considered an anxiety gait in nature. We're taught to push ourselves, race the clock, and always be in a hurry. We miss the subtle cues; moving at too quick a pace, we miss obtaining the information we need from our senses to make the cues meaningful. Much of our sensory input is just noise, not only because it is man-made and meaningless in the natural concept but also because we're moving too quickly for it to register in our brains. This patterned response to sensory input makes it hard for us to relate to baseline. We're putting a lot of emphasis on the development of baseline, and you'll have to go through many walls to get there, but the combination of sensory awareness, self-reliance, meaningful ecological knowledge, conditioned quality knowledge, and baseline is necessary to be a holistic tracker.

Journaling Your Baseline Patterns

Throughout the day, observe yourself when are you comfortable, relaxed, and content and when are you fearful, anxious, or agitated—in other words, when you are in baseline and when you are not. If you were a wild animal, baseline would be a harmonic gait, relaxed feeding, bedding down to rest. A breech in baseline would be erratic or unusual behavior—a fox in a gallop rather than its usual trot; a winter wren scolding with a loud, rapid chip; juncos fleeing the forest floor to nearby shrubs for cover.

Living in a modern setting, baseline is a quite different experience for us humans. A stimulus such as a car door slamming would send a bobcat tearing off into the woods, but we tolerate it without even flinching. Much of the external agitation in our environment is ignored, but there are many influences that cause unrest in our minds and bodies if we pay attention. Sensing these disturbances will take some retraining. However, becoming sensitive to your own baseline behavior will create empathy for the animals you track, helping you understand and predict animal behavior.

EXERCISE

Journal all the times that you are in baseline for an entire week, as well as all the times that you are not. This might be done as a reflection at the end of each day or, better yet, as notes taken throughout the day. Write a summary of your personal baseline.

NATURE PROGRAM INTERPRETATION

I cannot overemphasize the importance of watching animals as often as possible. Even a glimpse of a wild animal behaving in its natural way provides an invaluable visual reference and teaches you countless lessons in natural history, anatomy, and energy efficiency.

EXERCISE

For this exercise, select a fifteen-minute segment of video footage from a nature program that you have never seen before and that includes narration—but *do not listen to the audio commentary.* Record the name and production information of the video or program as a reference.

1. Watch the fifteen-minute segment *without* the sound, and record all the animal behaviors you see—submissive behaviors, dominance, other communications, feeding, caching, and so forth.
2. Watch the segment again *without* the sound, and record what you missed the first time.
3. Watch a third time with the sound on. What do the narrators describe that you missed? What did you catch that wasn't mentioned?

The more experience you gain watching and interacting with a given species, the more fine-tuned and accurate your interpretations will become.

APPLIED ANIMAL FORMS THROUGH EMULATION

Tracking is both an art and a science. The art side draws on the creative resources of the mind. Many noted trackers and tracking authors have noted similar experiences after years of intensive tracking time: a point is reached during the trailing of an animal when one feels that one "becomes" the animal in some intangible way. This reminds me of the experiences I have had when telling a good story or playing music. The experiences of drama, music, and storytelling are quite similar. It is highly likely that this experience even draws on similar parts of the brain, but that research remains to be done. Such artistic experiences can be quite compelling, powerful, and engaging. This, however, does not make them real in the tangible sense. It is important to sort these things out carefully and handle this exercise in a mature and humble manner.

For now, let us assume that storytelling, acting, and music are important to the development of the skills and methods of tracking. This assumption can be justified by noting that the many traditional societies around the world that produce great trackers also value storytelling, music, and drama. It seems logical that if these arts were unimportant to peoples who depend on practical survival skills and lead pragmatic and efficient lifestyles, they would simply disappear. However, the reverse is true. Humans the world over seem to have a need for these experiences, starting at a young age.

If we can assume that all human civilizations were once based on hunting and gathering and that this pattern of life led tracking to emerge in the first place, then it stands to reason that the ancient art of storytelling, drama, and music have some role in the learning of tracking. If we also assume that trackers' experience of "becoming" the animal is also related to the storytelling aspects of the mind (watch *The Great Dance* video or DVD available from www.senseafrica.com), then it is reasonable to assume that practicing these cultural routines could develop these skills to a higher degree. The goal is to open up those parts of your brain that can help you project your mind into the mind of the animal you are trailing and speculate about the animal's next moves. This can save a lot of time when trailing and greatly enrich your tracking experiences. Your ability to do this depends on your knowledge of the animal you are trailing, your knowledge of the landscape, and your tracking experience.

ANIMAL FORMS EXERCISE

Choose an animal that you often see the tracks of or that you see at your sit spot. This animal should be fairly familiar to you, and it should be large enough to travel at least a mile or two on its rounds—perhaps a raccoon, deer, fox, bobcat, or coyote. Choose an animal that moves through your area but may not be there when you get there.

Study this animal's habits for a few days: read about the animal, watch it in the wild if you have the opportunity, write in your journal about the animal, imitate its motions around the house, watch a show about it if you can. Track the animal throughout its range, finding dens or beds, feeding sign, dropping and scent markings, runs, and ultimately tracks—especially fresh ones. When you have absorbed this animal for a few days and feel like you could act it out in a play, head off to your sit spot emulating your chosen animal.

First, begin by practicing a good and full sense meditation. Put your street mind to rest by attuning yourself to the sounds, scents, sights, and feelings of the place. Listen to the wind; try to determine the shapes and feelings of the wind forms as they move by. Tune into the quietest sounds around you. Read the bird language with your feelings, not through analysis. Just be there and revel in the beauty and mystery of the nature around you.

Tracking with Your Body

Walker Korby

The pair of whitetail does crossed the stream in front of me just upwind and did not notice me sitting motionless behind a fallen tree. As I stood to follow them, I found myself hunched over and high-stepping on the balls of my feet with one hand in front of me and one behind. This was the most comfortable posture for traveling through the dense undergrowth. As I walked, I tried to match my footsteps to those of the two deer ahead of me, and I soon found myself walking in that unhurried yet cautious and concise gait that deer fall into when comfortably browsing. Occasionally they would stop, raise their heads, and look at me intently, and I did the same. I matched the nervous flick of their tails with a quick wave of my hand behind me. When they put their heads back down to continue feeding, so did I. Then I stopped and looked up at them, and they followed suit. I flicked my "tail" and then continued "feeding," and so did they. With the wind starting to shift, I let them move ahead of me, and I sat down to ponder the true meaning of "shape-shifting."

A year later, my interest in tracking picked up and my natural curiosity led me to the study and understanding of gaits. I was having trouble making sense of the circles and squares and RFs and LFs used by various books to describe an animal's galloping patterns. Blessed with a long stretch of soft summer grass and the guidance of Jon Young, I set out on all fours to unravel the secret of the galloping horse tracks I had found in one book. By placing my relative "feet" where the book had placed the hoof tracks, I soon learned that in order to make that pattern I had to be moving rather quickly. Within hours I had mastered the rotary gallop and had begun to figure out the other gaits described in the book.

Soon tracking began to take on new meaning for me; I was able to fill tracks with images of the animals themselves moving across the earth. Instead of my brain frying over the mental acrobatics it took to picture four highly articulated legs moving simultaneously, the muscles in my body began to twitch with recognition. Not only could I easily picture the animals moving across the landscape; I could also sense it in my bones.

The realization that tracking was a whole body experience and not limited to the brain intrigued me. You would rarely find me outside just standing up. I'd bound like a weasel, gallop like a horse, trot like a wolf, walk like a bear, and crawl like a turtle. I even considered spending a summer on all fours like a cougar but feared what it would do to my body. My favorite "dirt time" is on beaches, where endless stretches of soft substrate allow me to record my passion for imitating animal movements.

In our quest for understanding animals, we often forget that we possess the same skeletal components as our four-legged brethren. We read in books about indigenous cultures and learn that they danced the dance of their animals and told their stories. Yet we modern trackers often forget to dance the dance of the animals we track, missing out on a key component in our relationship with them.

Just as actors take on the qualities of the characters they play, you can incorporate the qualities of the animals you track into your own being. You will then be better able to track those animals. When you start walking like a deer, you start thinking like a deer. And if you practice enough, you might "become" the deer, rendering tracks obsolete.

Using your own body as a tool for understanding animal movement will help you make sense of the complex art of interpreting gaits. As a student of tracking, you must get down and dirty. You may get funny looks from people as you gallop along the beach after their dog, but it's worth it.

Practicing animal forms. D. F.

Move slowly at first, taking in all the sounds and sights. Then begin to move pretending that you are the animal. Picture your hands as paws or hooves. Feel that animal moving in all your moves. Act it out as if you were telling a great story to your best and most trusted friends. Let the story be told by your actions alone. Move in a foraging pattern, if appropriate, or perhaps in a hunting pattern if you have chosen a predator. Whatever the animal, put on its mind and head toward your spot following a route you are *called* to follow. Don't think your way there; simply release yourself into the animal you're emulating and let your feelings tell you where to go.

Afterward, write a reflection. Explain the process you followed to prepare, such as the research you did, the observations you made, the tracking you did, and the ways you rehearsed the emulation at home. Next, describe the day you chose to first use this emulation technique to go to your sit spot—the sights, sounds, sensations, bird activities, and other feelings you had. Then discuss your emulation journey and what you saw and learned on the way. Try this a few times over a month, keeping a journal each time.

GAIT INTERPRETATION

Gait interpretation can be defined as comprehension of body mechanics via track patterns. For instance, if a trained tracker sees a series of footfalls on a dusty road, he or she can determine the mechanics of the animal's gait at that time. Such detailed information can be useful in determining the mind-set of an individual animal; for example, a deer in full gallop across a meadow indicates that it was disturbed from its daily maintenance patterns of feeding and resting.

Building on your understanding of baseline, we are now going to divide the different speeds of animals into categories and further refine our interpretation. The three speeds are fast, baseline, and slow, and each of these speeds can be subdivided into three categories, such as slow-minus, slow, and slow-plus. Thus, you have nine possible interpretations of a gait. This might seem confusing at first, but it is an attempt to simplify the complexities of gaits and help you move straight into interpreting animal behaviors rather than becoming stuck in technical gait analysis and never understanding what any of these gaits mean.

Let's consider an example: the bobcat. We would divide the bobcat's gaits (as defined in *Mammal Tracks and Sign*) in a shallow substrate (along a dusty trail) in the following way:

Slow-minus	Slow stalk
Slow	Stalk
Slow-plus	Understep walk
Baseline-minus	Direct-register walk
Baseline	Overstep walk
Baseline-plus	Trot
Fast-minus	Lope
Fast	Gallop
Fast-plus	Stretch gallop

Understand that there is no one gait attached to baseline, slow, or fast; it depends on the species and the substrate. For example, the baseline gait for a kangaroo rat is a bipedal hop, which is entirely different from the bobcat's baseline gait, an overstep walk. And if the bobcat were moving in deep snow, its baseline gait would be a direct register walk.

The Canine

Let's look at the canine family again, because most people are familiar with how dogs move even if they haven't consciously watched the animal's mechanics in motion. All species of canines—dogs, wolves, coyotes, and foxes—can direct register. This means that their hind feet land in the tracks of their front feet, obliterating evidence of the hind tracks. The tracks form a straight line, with a little deviation to the left and right of center. A canine in a direct register is easy to recognize because it's a nice rhythmic pattern. Canines can direct register in a walk but do so more often when trotting. If you were to measure the stride of a gray fox in a trot, it might be 10 inches. If you continued to measure the strides of a trotting gray fox on a level surface, there would be little variation in length: 10 inches along the entire trail. In music, it would sound like *dat-dat-dat-dat-dat-dat*—the rhythm of a fox, coyote, or wolf trotting. The stride length differs among species, but they all have the same rhythm when using their baseline speed, which for canines is a direct register trot. This trot is congruent with the physics of a canine's body, allowing it to move and cover distance without wasting energy.

When a coyote is trotting along and catches a scent on the wind, it slows down to gather information. Typically, it shifts its gait into an overstep walk. In this gait, the distance between the front tracks shortens, and the fronts fall behind the rears. The coyote is in an information-gathering mode: slowing down and sniffing. An overstep walk is, for the coyote, a baseline-minus speed.

By the same token, if a coyote is in a hurry, its stride stretches and the rear feet get out ahead of the front feet. These gaits, which can vary, are called overstep trots and are the baseline-plus speed for canines. The canine may have a destination in mind or may be avoiding danger. For example, a coyote may hear you coming long before you see her, so she will transition from baseline to baseline-plus to put more distance between the two of you. Since there's no immediate danger, there's no reason for her to go tearing off into the woods, possibly putting herself at greater risk.

Loping and galloping are the fast speeds for canines. They can indicate that the animal is either being chased by or chasing after something. Loping for a coyote would be the equivalent of a human running, and a gallop would be like sprinting. What would cause you

This raccoon transitioned into a shorter stepped walking pattern to walk down an embankment.

to run? Imagine that a dog is chasing you and you think you can make it to your front door just in time to escape inside. As you reach the front yard, the dog is at your heels, and you must transition into a sprint as a last-ditch effort to reach the door. Coyotes utilize these speeds in a similar fashion. They don't waste energy galloping just to cover distance; typically, there's an apparent cause for the use of speed. These gaits are like signposts signaling a major change in behavior from baseline into something worth investigating. In wolves, or foxes, lopes can be observed as a means to cover distance—like jogging—as from a den to a hunting area that is more productive.

Transitional Gaits

Don't make the common mistake of focusing too much on transitional gaits. You may come upon a set of coyote tracks where the coyote is in baseline and then suddenly, 20 feet later, it's in fast-minus. You could spend several hours trying to re-create this, trying to figure out how it went from a direct register trot to a lope. But in the end, the conclusion is simply that the transition just represented acceleration, and that's all you really need to know. The mechanics of a transitional gait, though revealing a little about the physics of the animal, teaches you nothing about the animal's behavior except that it increased its speed.

CLUSTER TRACKING

Sometimes there are just too many things going on to make sense of in the field. Take the example of a cluster of coyote tracks. Trying to interpret every movement these coyotes made would take hours. This is when looking at the big picture comes into play. If you look toward the bottom of the accompanying photograph, you will see a plastic food bag that the coyotes are investigating. This tells the story of these tracks. You don't need to know that the coyote took two steps to the left, stopped, and then turned right in order to interpret these tracks.

It is important to know when to step back and look at things with the bigger picture in mind. You must learn when to group information in larger patterns so the details don't overwhelm you. Tom Brown calls this cluster tracking.

Cluster tracking is helpful when describing a longer time's worth of bird or animal behaviors. For instance, a Song Sparrow is scratch feeding on the ground continuously for ten minutes; its mate is singing nearby. A California Towhee is also scratch feeding. A pair of Lesser

Multiple coyote cluster. J. E.

Goldfinches is feeding on rosemary flowers just beyond that. A squirrel is foraging in the leaf litter 20 yards to the left. It is easy to cluster all these individual behaviors together in a single observation: the birds and animals in a 20-yard diameter are in their baseline pattern for this time of day.

Tracking often allows us to make similar clusters of activities by one or more individuals. In the accompanying photo of a cluster of coyote tracks, there's a confused mass of different individuals visiting one place. This information alone forms an interesting question: why are all of these coyotes attracted to the same place? This may seem simplistic, but it's an easy question to overlook if one gets too caught up in the details. We could get down on our hands and knees and study each individual track, take measurements, decipher how many individuals there are, the age of their tracks and what gait each is using. Sounds pretty exhausting doesn's it? While this might be a useful exercise when you have the time, in the majority of cluster tracking situations you don't need to analyze each individual track. In these instances, you will gain the most insight into the animal's behavior by stepping back and looking at the big picture. Look again at the photo of the coyote cluster; notice in the bottom of the photo towards the middle there is a crinkled plastic bag at the center of the coyote activity. All of the tracks lead to and from this piece of refuse, suggesting that at one time, probably before the coyotes discovered it, this bag had some king of food remains in it. And we didn't even have to get down on our knees.

DRAWING GAITS FROM VIDEOS

In a workshop with Mark Elbroch, he assigned us this exercise between sessions. It was a huge eye-opener to learn how to interpret animal gaits, and we highly recommend it, especially if you have trouble with abstract thought processes. In the beginning, interpreting gaits was like figuring out abstract word problems in math class. We couldn't visualize the animal in the tracks; having never consciously watched an animal move, we didn't trust our impressions. Interpreting animal gaits is difficult for most people. And even if you're an expert, this exercise is bound to teach you something profound about the way animals *actually* move compared with how you *thought* they moved.

EXERCISE

You'll need a wildlife video or DVD, preferably one focusing on an animal you're curious about. You'll also need a notepad, a pencil, the remote control, and plenty of mental focus. Because you're going to be concentrating and drawing, do this exercise when you'll have some peace and quiet.

Watch the video and look for a single animal moving in a gait that interests or perplexes you, for instance, a walk, trot, lope, or gallop. The clip should show the animal moving across a landscape with its legs and feet visible. The clip should last five seconds or longer, because you'll be creating twenty drawings from it. On your paper, draw lines about 3 inches apart lengthwise all the way down the page. These lines represent the ground, which is important for determining which foot or feet are touching down. Pause the video at the beginning of the clip. Starting in the top left corner of the page, quickly sketch the animal's position and write the number 1 above it. While studying the screen, pay close attention to the animal's legs and which feet are touching

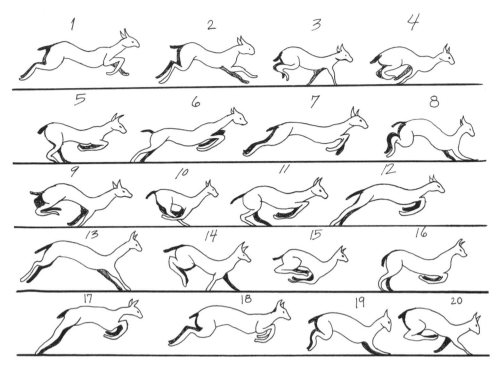

Gazelle in a gallop.

down making tracks. Simple circles to represent the animal's body and sticks for the legs are sufficient. When you're done with the first drawing, play the video for just a few frames until the animal is in a noticeably different posture. Pause the video and draw the animal again, labeling this drawing number 2. Continue in this way until you've drawn the animal twenty times and feel that you have a basic understanding of the gait the animal is using.

Simply watching the video in slow motion will go a long way toward teaching you about gaits. I also recommend watching how your pets move. Take your dog to the beach and observe closely as it moves across the sand. Envision what its tracks will look like in the sand, and then check to see whether you were right. Remember, though, that domestic animals move differently from wild animals, even if they're in the same family. If you really want to test the accuracy of your gait drawings from the video, create a flipbook of the individual drawings and watch your animal in action.

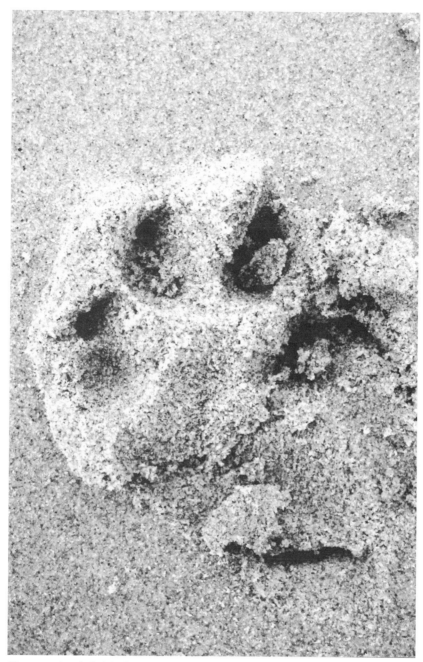

Dog turning left. Notice the buildup of sand at the edge of the left toes.

TRACK DYNAMICS

Reading and interpreting track dynamics can be fairly confusing at first. The subject can be better understood if the many confounding variables are separated for easier analysis. Another name for track dynamics used by Tom Brown is pressure releases. If you are interested in learning more, check out his helpful book on the subject, *The Science and Art of Tracking*.

Separating the Variables

What is a track? For our purposes, a track refers to those marks made by the passage of animals, birds, or humans; footprints are the basic track. Therefore, a single, basic track is caused when weight is applied to a foot as it comes to rest on the ground for a moment and is then removed. More specifically, a track is a dent, compression, stain, scratch, or other mark caused when a foot, paw, or hand is pressed into a surface substrate and subsequently removed, leaving a record representing the physical characteristics of the body part.

In the physical study of objects in motion, there are usually several components acting at once. For example, there are three directional components (three dimensions) or vectors acting on three different trajectories at once—horizontal, vertical, and diagonal. There are twisting vectors as well. There are also vibrations in objects caused by such things as muscle tension. When considering the motion of living things on a surface substrate such as the ground, there are other variables, including the slope of the ground, the nature of the substrate, and the physical condition of the animal itself. For instance, the animal's weight, density, speed, motion dynamics, and muscle tension all affect the track dynamics.

This is a complex subject with many variables, all of which impact the way a track compression looks, as well as the ground in and around the track itself—thus the term *track dynamics*. Essentially, a track is a record of all the physics of the moving object (foot), the animal, and the characteristics of the ground.

SIMPLE COMPRESSIONS
FROM A SIMPLE, SMOOTH OBJECT (1)

In the beginning, it's a good idea to deal with the variables separately and practice reading the dynamics with simple problems.

First, find some damp, leveled, and carefully tamped sand with a smooth surface. Take a 1-inch by 2-inch board that is a few feet long (something like a cane) with a smooth, sanded surface (so the sand doesn't stick). For this exercise, simply press the stick straight down into the ground about 1 inch deep. Don't tilt or twist the stick. Just press it straight down and then carefully pull it straight up and out.

Remember how hard you press down, because you'll be varying the pressure in the next exercise. If you wish, you can use a scale to approximate how many pounds of pressure you are exerting to make a 1-inch-deep track.

Now study the track and journal it. Notice that even though you didn't twist or tilt the stick, there are dynamics in and around the track that seem to indicate that you did. Draw the track (it should be a simple rectangular hole in the ground). Study the floor of the track (the bottom of the hole), and note the angle of the floor. Is it level? Is it tilted? Note the walls of the track. Are they straight up and down? Are they tilted?

Draw these features from a top view, both in the track and around it. Draw the cracks, dents, bumps, and other little geologic features that form from the making of the track. Next, look down into the track and journal it from a side view, as if you cut a cross section lengthwise down the middle. Then repeat that side view as if you cut a cross section crosswise down the middle.

VARYING THE WEIGHT (2)

Repeat exercise 1, but this time, increase the force with which you press the stick down into the ground, making the track about 1.5 inches deep. Again, repeat the top-view and two side-view cross-sectional sketches of the track.

Repeat the process two more times—once making the track about 2 inches deep, and once pressing very lightly, making a track that is only ⅛ to ½ inch deep. Do all the same studies and journals as before. Now compare these drawings and describe how they are similar and different.

VARYING THE ANGLE (3)

Do the same series of pressures in exercise 2, but this time, press the stick into the ground at a slight angle, being sure to use the same angle with each change in pressure and depth. How do the cracks, mounds, walls, and floor of the tracks and the dynamics surrounding them vary with this angle as compared with the results in exercise 2? Be specific.

VARYING THE DYNAMICS WITH A TWISTING MOTION (4)

For this exercise, repeat the same three depths as in exercise 2, but this time push the stick straight down into the ground and then give a quarter turn (90 degrees) to the right before lifting it out. Again, make comparisons with the previous exercises.

VARYING THE DYNAMICS WITH TWISTS AND ANGLES (5)

This time, make tracks using the same angle as exercise 3, the same twist as in exercise 4, and the same three pressures and depths as in exercise 2. Again, make comparisons.

STUDYING REAL MOTION DYNAMICS WITH A HARD SHOE (6)

For this exercise, wear hard shoes with smooth soles. Set yourself up a walkway leading to a sand trap; then walk up to the damp sand, step into it, turn 90 degrees to the right as you walk 5 and step out of the damp sand. The first time, step lightly into the sand and turn, trying not to go deep into the sand. Then repeat the process, stepping a bit harder and pressing down a bit more. Journal both results.

Repeat the exercise a third time wearing a backpack holding 20 to 80 pounds or carrying something heavy in your arms in front of you. Journal these results and compare them with the earlier ones.

The variables are endless. Hooves have one effect on sand, whereas soft cat feet have another and the hairy paws of a red fox yet another. There will be similarities among all of them if they are moving at the same speed, on the same substrate, and in the same time range (dampness varies with time of day, which can affect the substrate). The gait an animal is using, what its head is doing, its health conditions, and other subtle physical factors affect the track in obvious and subtle ways as well.

INTERPRETING ANIMAL BEHAVIOR

For this exercise, we've included three photos of different animal behavior. Your assignment is to study the photographs and make some educated guesses about what the animals are and what each is doing. There are enough clues to help you answer both questions. We've provided the answers in the back of the book, but take the time to do your own research and formulate your own theories.

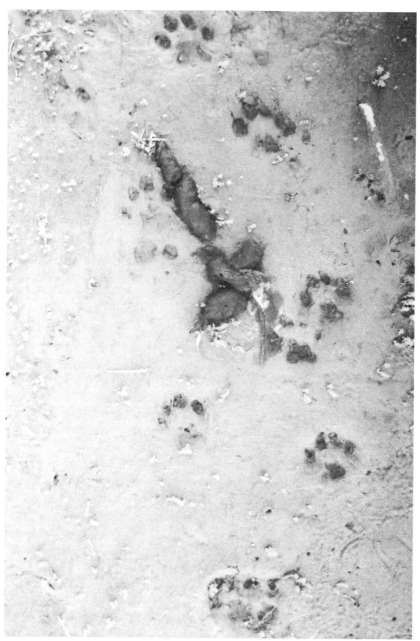

Hypothesis 1—Interpreting Animal Behavior.

Hypothesis 2. J. E.

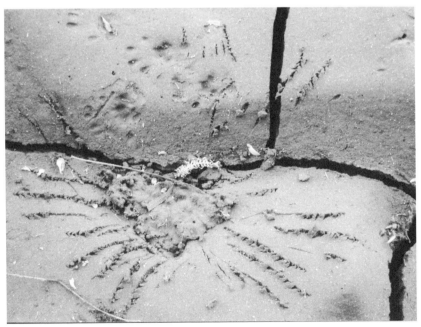

Hypothesis 3. J. E.

6

Awareness

I once knew an educated lady, banded by Phi Beta Kappa, who told me that she had never heard or seen the geese that twice a year proclaim the revolving seasons to her well-insulated roof. Is education possibly a process of trading awareness for things of lesser worth? The goose who trades his is soon a pile of feathers.

—Aldo Leopold

T.M.

BLACK BEAR IN JERSEY

I was sitting on one of the few damp pieces of earth that New Jersey had to offer that summer. A soft stump whose torso had long since decayed cushioned my back. This was a place I had returned to every day for a month to observe the many birds that bathed in the tiny creek that curved around my feet and then straightened into Catfish Pond. A low canopy of witch hazel trees spread out over my head, providing welcome relief from the focused rays of the sun. Blueberry thickets drooped with richly colored fruit and cradled me on all four sides. In many ways, I felt protected and comfortable here, even though I couldn't see more than 20 feet in any direction. With this lack of visual information, my other senses were brought to full attention. Rustlings and footsteps in the leaf litter on the opposite side of the blueberry thicket instantly piqued my curiosity. When a sound was particularly intriguing and I needed to know the source, I would climb the narrow but sturdy trunk of the closest witch hazel tree and sit on its shoulder. From this vantage point I could see 360 degrees around me and was just high enough to be invisible to people and deer—the most common cause of the rustling. At the base of this tree laid an enormous bear scat that had been deposited two weeks after I had started visiting this place. Since

99

that time, it had decayed considerably and wore a fuzzy cap of mold caused by its solid blueberry content. It was a constant reminder of the possibility of encountering the bear that left it—a situation that I was hoping for yet wary of.

As was my routine, upon arrival I slowly tuned in to all my senses. I softened my vision so that my eyes weren't focused on any one thing and could take in the entire clearing where I sat. This allowed my other senses to awaken. The warm wind felt pleasing on my skin. A crisp, cool smell from the creek filled the air and mixed with the earthy smell of decaying leaves and ripening blueberries. My ears picked up a quiet, distant rustling east of where I was sinking deeper into the spongy stump. My eyes closed slightly.

I had already become complacent and assumed that the source of the rustling was the doe that came to feed on blueberries nearly every afternoon. A small flock of titmice hardly made a peep as they bathed in the creek near my feet. Meanwhile, the rustling sound on the opposite side of the brush was becoming increasingly louder. The titmice flitted away down the creek toward the pond, and my interest in the rustling was renewed. I pulled myself up to investigate and was soon quietly perched in my trusted little tree like a pelican on a fence post. From this vantage point, I could see that one of the blueberry bushes was more excited than its neighbors, wagging and swaying in a chaotic rhythm. Between branches, the bottom lip of a doe became visible as she reached for blueberries. I became engrossed with the twisting and curling of the deer's neck as she tried to reach hidden fruit with the edge of her teeth. A couple of Black-and-white Warblers dipped their feathers in the creek below me, and the sun radiated heat from above. I scanned the doe's body for signs of sweating and noticed her ears placidly flicking at flies. Then, without warning, those ears shot upright and she snorted with an intensity that nearly knocked me off my branch. I scanned the area for the cause of her terror and was perplexed when nothing jumped out at me. Within seconds, the doe had vanished. I had never witnessed a deer in the area respond with such urgency. Hunting wasn't permitted, so human encounters generally warranted only a casual disappearance into thick cover—often just a few feet from the trail. This reaction hadn't been caused by a human disturbance, and I waited anxiously for the offender.

It was minutes before my senses picked up any sort of sign that something was approaching. My ears were the first to sense a disturbance, a hollow smacking noise just out of sight and in front of me. The outline of an oak tree was momentarily disrupted by a furry black form obscuring its large gray trunk. Only with this obvious visual clue was I able to decipher what the deer had known long before I had sensed anything: a bear was approaching. A brown and black nose poked out from behind the tree trunk and sniffed deeply at the air, like a vacuum sucking dirt out of carpet fibers. She was on her hind legs, using the oak as support, and I noted that she could easily reach the highest branch of the flimsy tree I was in. She lowered herself back down, out of sight. I monitored her movements by observing the shaking brush. I had previously seen entire blueberry bushes knocked over by bears so that they could reach the highest fruit. It occurred to me then that I was trembling with a mixture of excitement and fear.

In a small clearing just below me on the opposite side of the brush line, the mother bear reappeared with two young cubs tripping at her heels. The bears had three sets of eyes—two very curious, and one hypervigilant. I waited anxiously for them to discover me eavesdropping on their afternoon forage. The cubs sniffed at the ground, poked their noses into bushes, and climbed over a log while their mom rose up again on hind legs and pushed her nose into the database of scents surfing on the waves of air. Strangely, part of me hoped that my scent would reach her nostrils; another part prayed that it wouldn't. She seemed suspicious of my presence, constantly smelling in each direction, yet she never saw me—or if she did, there was no reaction. I was easy to see, just above eye level with very little cover a mere 20 feet away. But she probably didn't expect to find a human there. It was clear to me then how much bears rely on their noses to experience the world, even though they can see as well as humans. She moved on a little, so that just her rear end was poking out of the brush and into the clearing where the cubs were still exploring. With the mother's head temporarily hidden, I tentatively stood up on my branch to get a better view of the cubs. They were just like two little kids lost in their own world of play. They bumped into each other like wind-up toys and bounced off in opposite directions. One of them sat up on its hind legs and sniffed the air just as its mother had, but it was easily distracted. Then the imaginary cords that connected them to mom were suddenly pulled, snapping the cubs back to her side and into the brush. A few minutes after they had all passed out of sight, I heard the startled yelp of an unwary hiker on a nearby trail in the direction the bears had gone. I laughed a little to myself, as I imagined the shocked look on the hiker's face as the bears crossed his path meaning him no harm. I was thank-

ful that my experience with the bears had been one of quiet ovserva-
tion and I credited all of my senses for providing me with the gift of
watching the mother and her cubs undisturbed by my presence.

SENSE MEDITATION

Preparation

Before beginning the sensory awareness exercise, find a pleasant
location and a comfortable position, then relax. In the beginning, you
should start off in a sitting position, but this particular exercise can also
be done while lying down, walking, running, driving, or just about
anytime. Your goal is to be able to enter this clear awareness by simply
focusing your mind on this intent. We suggest that you do this exercise
every time you visit your sit spot and before each tracking expedition.
The benefits of tapping into your senses are twofold: your mind is qui-
eted, and your senses are piqued, exposing the nuances of nature and
wildlife to your awareness. The exercise works through your senses in
order of dominance.

SIGHT

For most people, sight is their dominant sense. Imagine that you are an
owl, with eyes so big and powerful that they've actually outgrown
their sockets and are frozen in place. Look straight ahead and imagine
that your eyes are stuck in place; to look at something outside your
range of vision, you have to move your entire head.

Now look straight ahead in the direction your body is facing.
Choose a spot in front of you and train your eyes on it without moving. That spot is your focal point; if your eyes wander off, simply bring
them back to that spot.

Notice that, while you're staring at your focal point, you can also
see the ground below it, the sky or ceiling above, and the walls or landscape on either side of it. Using your peripheral vision, you can see all
this at the same time without moving your head. Practice using your
peripheral vision so that you can see all five things at once: your focal
point, the ground, the sky, extreme left, and extreme right.

HEARING

While maintaining your focal point and expanded vision, notice the
sounds around you. Imagine that you are a deer with a set of incredible
auditory receptors that swivel to catch the slightest sound. Twitch your

ears and prick them up to the slightest sound. Like the deer, you are able to hear the faintest sound from a far-off distance and are warned long before any danger approaches.

Listen simultaneously to every sound that surrounds you. Perhaps you can hear the wind in the trees or the hum of traffic on a distant road. Maybe you hadn't noticed that there's a chorus of crickets just outside your window. Can you hear the buzzing of the refrigerator or the hum of a light? Notice that even when there is no sound, you can still hear the sound of silence—a low-pitched vibration as background noise. There is sound coming from 360 degrees around you at all times. Using your ears like radar, sweep the area, seeking sounds in all four directions as well as above and below you.

COMBINED SIGHT AND HEARING

Now return your awareness to your vision, to your focal point. Make sure that your whole peripheral vision is turned on, and simultaneously listen to all the sounds around you. Now your eyes and ears are fully engaged.

TOUCH

Raccoons earn their living by the sense of touch. Have you ever watched a raccoon as it investigates for food? Its little hands touch the ground, feel around rocks, or dig through compost in search of tasty morsels. All the while, the raccoon's head is up and staring off in the distance, it's not looking at what its hands are doing. Raccoons, it seems, can see with their hands. They are the masters of touch.

Allow your body to become like the raccoon's hands. Feel the sensations around you with your whole body. How does it feel where you are sitting? Is the ground cold? Is there a rock sticking in your back? How do your feet feel inside your shoes? Can you feel moisture in the air or the sun warming your face? Is the wind blowing your hair? Tune in to these sensations.

The skin is the largest organ of the human body and the primary receptor for the sense of touch. It's capable of receiving the subtlest sensations from sunlight to gravity.

COMBINED SIGHT, HEARING, AND TOUCH

While you are aware of your focal point, the ground, the sky, the birds singing to your right and left, and the sound of wind in the trees, also be aware of your hands resting on your knees and the weight of your body wherever you happen to be sitting.

SMELL AND TASTE

Sniff the air the way a dog does—short inhalations to see whether you can pick up an intriguing scent. When you catch a whiff of something, explore it with the focus of a dog's nose, intent on extracting the meaning from the mystery of the smell. Is there a stagnant smell? Perhaps there's a source of water you hadn't noticed. Is there a pungent odor? Maybe it's garbage day in the neighborhood. What is that sweet fragrance? Perhaps it's a flower that's just beginning to bloom. The dog's nose is capable of sniffing out the fresh track of another dog, a squirrel, or a rabbit. The human nose struggles with such subtleties but is capable of smelling clues that can lead to a greater understanding of wildlife.

Smell and taste are closely linked. As you use your sense of smell, notice all the tastes you can sense with your tongue. Is that a hint of morning coffee there behind your molars? Can you taste the pine tree off to your right?

COMBINED SIGHT, HEARING, TOUCH, SMELL, AND TASTE

Train your eyes on that focal point again while taking in all the sights around you. Your eyes are softly focused, like in a daydream, but don't let your mind wander off without your other senses. Instead, perk up those ears and listen for the obvious sounds—voices, engines, and roadways; now listen harder for subtle hums, ticks, and breezes. While you are softly seeing and intently listening, activate your skin and the sense of touch. Let the sensations wash over you like a wave. Focus on what feels good: the warmth of your sweater, the direction of the wind against your cheek, the pain in your knees and the tightening in your neck. When you're feeling like a sensory machine, poke your nose into the air to search for scents; open your mouth slightly to activate those taste buds. Draw in some deep breaths through the nose and mouth, and then return to a normal breathing rhythm. At this point, all five senses are engaged.

Combining all five senses is more challenging than it may seem and takes some practice. Luckily, it can be practiced anywhere and is easy to remember. You may want to choose two senses to focus on and then build to all five. Because of the important role your senses play in becoming a competent tracker, the rest of the chapter is devoted to exercises that can help you access the enormous amount of sensory input that all five senses have to offer.

SENSE OF SMELL

Have you ever seen a coyote, a fox, or even a wolf as it approaches something it doesn't recognize? The animal lowers its head to the ground and swings it from side to side slowly, seemingly obtaining the information it needs. Deer do the same thing.

OLFACTORY OVATION

We are going to work our noses in a similar fashion to dogs and deer. In the beginning, this exercise may not work for you, but please stay with it for a full two weeks. If, at the end of that time, you've seen few or no results, wait two weeks and then repeat it for another two weeks. This may give your brain a chance to realize that you are serious about developing this untapped resource and let your brain cells catch up with you. I am convinced that, with enough stimulation and regular practice, this will work for almost anyone anywhere.

Has it ever occurred to you that the wind may be moving in different directions at different heights? Did you ever stop to think that your body works like a rock in a river, creating eddies of air? Some eddies are trapped, some swirl in the opposite direction as the main flow, and some move up your body like a chimney. If you could only see what the wind is really doing. Occasionally, this is possible with smoke or fog, but seldom do we really get to understand these flows.

The first step is to calibrate your sense of wind direction and your nose and olfactory sense system. You'll need a pocket notebook, something to write with, and perhaps a compass.

Part 1. Wind Direction

Go into the field, in the yard, in the woods, or, as a last resort, in the street or driveway. Try to find a patch of natural earth that is growing or at least has leaf or bark litter decaying. Once you find this place, stand there and figure out which way is north. Face north, figure out which way the wind is blowing at face level. Look up to the trees catching the wind. Which way is the wind blowing at treetop height? (*Hint:* The birds can help you if you study their soaring and flying behaviors.) Now squat down to the ground level and place your hand near the ground. Which way is the wind blowing at this level? Note these three levels of wind direction, marking "F" for face wind, "T" for treetop wind, and "G" for ground wind.

Part 2. Olfactory Calibration

Relax, take a deep breath, and stand facing west. Breathe normally, in through your nose, and note the smells around you. Some descriptions will have to be somewhat subjective, as smells are hard to pin down. It is more important to be aware of the smells than to identify them accurately.

Then, turn to the north and repeat the exercise, noting any differences from what you smelled while facing west. They may be subtle, and you may want to turn west and start over. That's okay. Just have fun.

Next, turn to the east and then to the south, noting all the smells and all the differences.

You can repeat this cycle two or three times. It's interesting how the sense of smell gets better the more you use it.

Part 3. The Dog Sniff Exercise

Watch a dog sniff the air. It takes about ten shallow breaths in and out in rapid succession, followed by a long exhale. Then it repeats this again and again while facing in other directions, with a slow tilt to one side or the other as it figures out which way the scent is coming from (or where it is most noticeable). This exercise is the same as that in part 2, except that you sniff like a dog rather than breathe like a human.

Facing west, sniff through your nose for half a second and then pause for half a second. Repeat this about ten times. Do this whole cycle of ten sniffing, halting inhales for a total of four to five rounds. I have timed this at about twelve seconds. Note how the results differ from those of the last exercise.

After a forceful exhale to cleanse the airways, face north and repeat. Do the same facing east and south.

Note the overall differences between the dog sniff style of olfactory sensing and the normal breathing through the nose method. Which works better? What are the differences?

Variation

Try parts 2 and 3 again, but first wet the insides of your nostrils. As your nostrils dry out, rewet them. How does this change the results overall?

Part 4. Adding the Ground Component

Repeat parts 2 and 3, but this time do it while kneeling and bending so that your nose is close to the ground. Note your results.

Part 5. The Sniffing Walk

After you have finished calibrating your sense of smell, go for a very slow walk. Stop every ten steps, or every time you get a new rush of scent that seems different. Do this for about ten minutes. While walking and stopping, try turning to the four directions and see what happens. Alternate between regular breathing and dog-style sniffing. Also vary your height—standing, bending or squatting, or placing your face near ground level.

Walk to a different place each time you do this exercise. Note how stream corridors differ from high and dry hills, lawns, forests, and parking lots. Try walking in different parts of the forest. The world will come alive with new information.

When you have completed two weeks of this, write about your overall impressions. What have you learned about the animals around you? Did you notice that you can smell trails now?

"Scentual" Poet

T.M.

A few years ago I took a snow-tracking workshop with Paul Rezendes in Massachusetts. We started out with the tracks of a coyote—a direct register trot down the middle of a snow-covered dirt road. I can still see those tracks in my mind's eye: a near perfect line of left rear on top of left front alternating with right rear on top of right front. We didn't linger on the coyote tracks for long because we were seeking the more elusive red fox. The class took a dramatic turn when the snow became sparse and the focus shifted from what we could see to what Paul could smell. Red fox urine has a distinct, pungent, almost skunklike smell. Paul bent down to sniff a post at the intersection of the road and a trail. He was like a hunting dog after that first whiff, which sent him off smelling every bush and twig, while the rest of us unsophisticated sniffers followed behind. I didn't believe that we were hot on the trail of anything until we reached the snow, where the trail of a red fox magically appeared. It wasn't really magic, of course. It's simply a matter of training your nose to recognize scents. We tend to underutilize our sense of smell, but with a little training, you too can track like a bloodhound.

EXERCISE

Ask a friend to gather six smell-rich items—items from the kitchen, the garden, or a nearby woods should bring in a nice assortment—and put each of them in a separate container. Then blindfold yourself or shut your eyes, and have your friend gently waft one of the items under your nose.

The challenge is to use words to describe what you are smelling without naming the item. Ask your friend to remind you to be descriptive and to use adjectives. When you've exhausted your vocabulary and your nose, move on to the next item. After all have been sniffed, remove the blindfold and see what you have smelled—perhaps for the first time.

SENSE OF TASTE

How can your sense of taste improve your tracking abilities? Even though we are primarily visual creatures, tuning in to our other senses is the key to a more holistic approach to tracking. Our senses of taste and smell are intricately connected, so developing one inadvertently develops the other. We spend a large portion of each day preparing and eating food, so focusing on the sense of taste is not only practical, it's also enjoyable.

TASTE TEST

You may have played this game as a child and been pleasantly or unpleasantly surprised. Have a trusted friend pick out different foods for you to taste, perhaps chopping it up or otherwise disguising the shape, so that it's truly a mystery. While blindfolded, chew each bit of food slowly, thoughtfully, and tastefully; allow the flavors to permeate your tongue, and describe the experience.

Variation: Do a taste test with different brands of the same food or drink. This is especially fun to try with a product that you love and a close imitation, just to see whether you can tell the difference between the two.

EATING IN THE DARK

This is an exercise that I was introduced to at Coyote Tracks, the Tracker School's summer camps for kids. Although this exercise perks up your taste buds, it also trains your senses of touch, smell, and hearing. We recommend that you practice it often, and since it can be done anytime you eat, there will be plenty of opportunities.

The next time you sit down for a meal or a snack, eat blindfolded or simply close your eyes. Take it slow and, if it's not too messy, eat with your hands to get the benefit of feeling the textures with your hands as well as your mouth. This will likely evoke a sense of thanksgiving for the food you eat, so with gratitude in your heart and a mix of flavors in your mouth, involve your other senses for a full sensory experience—excluding sight. Pay attention to the sounds in the room: the hum of the refrigerator, family members talking in the next room, a lawn mower in the distance, birds chirping outside the window. Pick up that carrot and experience it with your sense of touch, first with your fingers and then with your teeth and tongue. Notice how it feels as it travels to your stomach and how the taste in your mouth changes with the absence of food. Now reach for a sandwich and just before it reaches your lips, pull its scent deeply into your nose. Try to pick out each individual smell: mustard, lettuce, turkey, cheese, bread. This exercise is versatile; each meal provides a new and dynamic sensory experience.

Variation: Concentrate on the sensations and flavors in your mouth, and then write about your experience as if you were your tongue; include the textures you felt, the temperature of the mouth you live in, and, of course, the flavors. Be creative and have fun.

SENSE OF TOUCH

Years ago I worked as a teacher's aide in a second-grade classroom. It was Easter time, and the walls were dotted with decorations. One of those cutouts taught me a valuable lesson: it was a bunny holding a pink tissue-paper egg that folded out accordion style to create a honeycomb shape. Whichever child arrived at the table first had the grand privilege of sitting next to this egg. As I read to them each afternoon, a little hand would brush back and forth across the soft, crisply folded paper, sometimes for thirty minutes. Whichever child it was that day appeared to be more content than the others, and it struck me that they had all been enchanted, simply by the feel of a thing.

ENCHANTED TOUCH

For this exercise, all you need is your walking shoes and your sense of touch. It doesn't need to be a long walk, perhaps just to your sit spot or around your yard. Recall something from your childhood that you loved the feeling of—your blanket, a stuffed animal, or a cool stone. As you stroll along, evoke that memory of being enchanted with touch and reach out to the things in nature that entice you: smooth leaves, fuzzy fruit, an insect crawling up your arm. Spend extra time with the things that really delight or satisfy you.

This is a great exercise to do at the beach; shells, seaweed, and sand offer a variety of textures and feelings. If you want more of a challenge, go out on a rainy day and just pay attention to the sensations of wet and cold, without attaching any negative connotations to these experiences. Go home and get warm when your senses are satiated and your clothing saturated.

MEET A TREE

I've learned that getting to know a tree can take a lifetime. Their change is slow with emerging fruit, flowers, and leaves, living and dying. Sometimes it's dramatic with branches lost in storms, a family of raccoons moving in, or damage from lightning. Trees have been through it all, but it takes time and patience on your part as an observer to draw these stories out. This is an exercise for your sense of touch, but it's also an exercise in sensitivity toward your surroundings, providing you with an opportunity to meet a tree in a new and dynamic way.

You need a friend, a blindfold, and a forest or park with plenty of shrubs or trees. After you have been blindfolded, have your friend disorient you and then lead you in a roundabout way to a single tree about 100 to 200 yards away. With your senses, discover the uniqueness of that tree. Rub your cheek on the bark, wrap your arms around it, and ask good questions. Are there animal signs on the tree? Are there plants, moss, lichen? How old is it? Give it a good whiff with your nose. Explore that tree until you feel like you know it, and when you're done, have your friend lead you away using a different route until you are back where you began. Remove your blindfold and search for your tree, this time with the help of your eyes. Can you find your tree? Were there things you saw with your eyes that you missed with your hands? Were there things you felt that you never would have seen?

Get to know the trees in your backyard this way. Simply close your eyes and use your other senses to experience the richness of these trees. You're bound to discover things about them that wouldn't be apparent with your eyes alone.

SENSE OF HEARING

J.Y.

As trackers on a journey, we must develop a keen ability to self-analyze, to look at ourselves and be critical of our techniques in the field. Begin-

Triggers

Matt Wild

Triggers are things that remind you to practice sense meditation or the other sensory awareness exercises outlined in this chapter. The best triggers are things that you already do or see many times a day. If you condition your brain and senses to consciously see and hear the trigger every time it happens, this can help you remember to tune in to your senses.

I have a few triggers that I like to use, depending on my day. My favorite ones are a ringing phone, walking through a doorway, hearing or seeing a bird, and stoking a fire in the woodstove. When I'm here at the Wilderness Awareness School office, I use the sound of the phone and walking through a doorway. Do you have any idea how many times the phone rings each day? This trigger helps me remember to pay attention to my surroundings while not distracting me from my task. When I'm at home or in the woods, I use birds and fire. You can choose anything at all, as long as you know that it will actually trigger you. You don't need half a dozen triggers—start with just one.

Whenever I share this idea with people, I ask them to let me know what their triggers are. Here are a few examples: hearing your name, seeing brake lights in front of your car, flipping a light switch, seeing a screen saver on a computer, hearing the sound of a city bus, seeing an airplane. Anything will do as long as it happens to you more than ten to fifteen times a day.

ning trackers are prone to look down at the ground and become self-absorbed, thinking the whole time about what they're going to see or what they're going to prove to others. They miss all the sounds around them, so we emphasize the need to listen when in the field.

Tom Brown did a lot of that kind of work with me. Whenever we were out in the field, he would constantly pause and give me the "shush" sign. Then he would look to one side or the other, as if gazing into the distance at a sound he had heard. Constant repetition taught me how to listen while I was tracking.

LISTENING QUESTIONNAIRE

After a day of tracking, challenge yourself to answer these questions:

1. Did you hear the wind?
2. Was the wind strong? Was it fierce? Was it gentle? Was it just a ripple?
3. Did you hear the sounds of traffic or human activity in the distance?
4. Did you hear the sounds of water falling, flowing through the creeks?
5. Did you pause to appreciate the feeling you got from hearing these sounds in nature?
6. What insect sounds do you remember hearing?
7. What birds could you identify by the sounds they made?
8. What bird alarm sequences do you remember hearing?
9. What other sounds came to you?
10. What were the sounds of your own footfalls?
11. Did you hear the sounds of animals moving off in the distance?

These questions should be answered after every hike while you're working on your sense of hearing.

HUNTING THE WATCH

This is an exercise suggested in David Scott-Donelan's book *Tactical Tracking Operations*. Have a friend hide a ticking watch somewhere and then track it down. It's dual practice in moving quietly and listening hard.

SEARCHING FOR SOUNDS

A simple listening exercise is to choose a sound on the landscape and track it down until you find it. It can be a birdcall, a squeaking tree, or any mysterious sound you wonder about as you move through the forested landscape.

SENSE OF SIGHT

It's amazing how obvious changes in familiar landscapes can go unnoticed by even the most careful observers. Perhaps we become so accustomed to looking for subtleties that we miss what's right in front of us. As trackers, we often get stuck in a rut of staring at the ground, which narrows our focus even further. This exercise is designed to help you broaden your visual capacity to see disturbances in the forest at every level—from the trees to the trail.

UNNATURAL OBJECTS

Have a friend set out a trail of ten to twenty unnatural objects, consisting of things you wouldn't typically find in the forest: dishes, T-shirts, pens, toys, and so forth. Everyday objects you have at home or in your backpack will suffice—nothing fancy. Have your friend hide the items along a trail in the woods or at a park so that just a fragment of each one is visible. These objects should be placed at varying levels in the forest: on the ground, in bushes, behind rocks, in trees. Once the trail is complete, go to the starting point and walk the trail alone, looking for the hidden objects without leaving the trail. Keep a mental note or write down the objects you see and where they are located. When you are finished and reunited with your friend, review your list together to discover what you found and what you missed.

To add difficulty, include more objects placed more inconspicuously. After you've practiced with unnatural objects, collect natural objects and put them in unnatural places: a rock in a tree, a stick in the mud, a pinecone in a hole. Be creative.

7

Ecology and Mapping

Intricacy is that which is given from the beginning, the birth right, and in intricacy is the hardiness of complexity that ensures against the failure of all life.
—Annie Dillard
Pilgrim at Tinker Creek

It seems to me that one can think of mapmaking as a fundamental human activity, if not the fundamental human activity . . . learning consists of looking at something new and beginning to see paths into it. You construct a map or a series of maps, each one an approximation and probably wrong in many details, but each one helping you to go further into the territory.
—Tony Callet
"Homo Cartographicus"

Tracks and animal signs can be divided into two major categories: primary and secondary. Primary sign is defined as track and sign left directly by the animal in question. For instance, when tracking wolves, primary sign would be wolf tracks, scat, trails, and other signs made by wolves. Secondary sign is defined as track and sign made by other mammal or avian species associated with the primary subject. For instance, when tracking wolves, secondary species would include elk, mule deer, beaver, and coyote. By default, secondary sign tracking provides an ecological context for the study of a species or group of species. When trained trackers find a set of wolf compressions along a ridgetop devoid of ungulates, they immediately scope out adjacent trails, browse patterns, landform relationships, habitat variations, hydrology, and vegetation patterns. With ecological interpretation, trackers avoid the trap of narrow-minded tracking.

In this chapter we introduce you to a mapping and journaling process that can profoundly increase your knowledge of ecology at your sit spot and other places that you regularly track. With time and practice, any natural place that you visit will unfold to reveal the layers of mammal, bird, reptile, and amphibian activities as they relate to water, soil, plants, trees, weather, sun, moon, and people. You will be able to create field inventories and corresponding maps of your area to record your observations and questions from the field. This is a slow process, but over time, you will witness significant results. I had been practicing this system of journaling for three years when an experience with a gray fox taught me that recording my observations and questions could lead to a depth of understanding that spanned years, and it eventually taught me to trust my impressions of animals and their relationship to the landscape.

GRAY FOX DEN

T.M.

I moved to San Gregorio, California, in the fall and had been living there for a month when I saw my first gray fox walking nimbly across the driveway. I was taken by its beauty and how exquisite and dainty the creature looked—closer in size to a cat than to a coyote or even a red fox. Having heard that the gray fox was elusive and rarely seen, I felt rather privileged to be standing there soaking up the essence of this quiet yet knowing fox.

That glimpse was all I needed. It drove my curiosity, and for the next two years my interest and studies shifted to the gray fox. What did it eat? Could it really climb trees? Where did it sleep? How did it survive? How did it avoid bobcats? Would I see one again? The questions were endless, but the answers were finite. It was nearly impossible to find any literature specifically on the gray fox, so I ended up studying the red fox to glean information about red fox habits that might cross over to gray. I quickly exhausted my literature resources and switched my focus to the field, where a remarkable amount of learning would eventually take place.

Every day that I visited my sit spot, I recorded my observations and questions in a field journal with a corresponding map I had drawn of the area. About the gray fox I had many questions and didn't know whether I would ever find the answers. I slowly chipped away at this mystery, and it seemed that as I did, the foxes revealed their activities to me with more frequency. It's possible that I was simply more aware of them, so it just seemed that they were becoming more visible. But I believe that animals can sense your intent, and since mine was a harmless curiosity, I didn't offend the fox. It required months of careful observation for me to distinguish the fox's tracks from those of the bobcat that frequented the same meadow, and it took even longer for me to realize that there were two foxes. After an entire year, I had figured out that one was male and the other female, and I could even differentiate them. My attention, however, wasn't focused on how long it was taking me to learn; I was immersing myself in a quest that was timeless.

Eight months later, I noticed a shift in the female fox's behavior. She was using a trail that led from the compost pile in my garden to the far edge of the field, where my sit spot was located, and into a thicket of ceanothus. I noticed, too, that the fox scats on the trail were often filled with leftovers that had ended up in the compost. As might be expected, I started to see the fox with more regularity in the garden beds, as well as on the trail I used daily to visit my sit spot, which the fox was now using more often than I was. These observations were all leading up to a discovery that hadn't even occurred to me until a peculiar sound whispered from the brush pile at the edge of the ceanothus thicket—an unmistakable sound like puppies whimpering. It took me a moment to realize the implications, but gradually the recent changes in the female fox's behavior made sense. If there were fox kits in the brush pile, it would explain why the fox was using this trail with more frequency and why she was taking greater risks to eat from the compost pile in plain view of the house. The following is an excerpt from my field journal at that time.

May 9, 2003
Today I visited the location where I had heard the gray fox kits whimpering. No sounds were emitted this time, so I continued down the wheel rut trail searching for fox scat. I wonder if the parents are the same foxes that sneak down to our garden for compost? I've seen leftovers of squash and rice in their scats on this trail. No sooner had I thought this and there she was—the female fox perched on a brush pile 10 feet from me. She paused for a minute, our eyes transfixed on each other. I relaxed my shoulders, gazed at her softly, wished her luck with her babies, and asked only for a harmless glimpse of them. She seemed to relax too, blinking occasionally with a

placid expression. I admired her coat where the sunlight was highlighting patches of groomed fur, and she slipped back into the brush pile. When she was gone I rejoiced: "Her kits must still be nearby!"

I looked and listened for the kits frequently. I even set up a motion detector camera where the whimpering sounds had come from, and while I captured many images of the mother fox, but I never saw the kits that season. The story doesn't end there, however, and the second half is an excellent example of how journaling your observations and questions can eventually lead to unexpected discoveries.

A year later, the fox answered my request in an astonishing way. At the time, my home-office window provided an exceptional view of the local wildlife. On an overcast spring day, I caught a glimpse of the female fox before she slid her narrow frame into the gutter pipe that runs under the driveway from one end (right below my office window) to the other. Although foxes were frequent visitors to the yard, I had never seen one go into that gutter. My curiosity was piqued. I described to coworker Mark Elbroch what I had seen. The following day, a contractor hired to inspect the roof brought his black Lab with him, and the dog couldn't keep her nose away from the metal grate in the driveway where water drains into the gutter. Although the grate had slats in it, affording a view into the gutter, we couldn't make out what the dog was so excited about. Mark reported later that evening that he had seen tiny twisted scats in the dirt at the bottom of the drain, which looked like weasel feces. Because weasels are rare to nonexistent in the area, the most likely explanation was that they were the scats of gray fox kits. I went out to the drain, and a foot beneath the grate I saw twisted scats the size of Tootsie Rolls. I knew then that the kits were in there, and it was just a matter of catching a glimpse of them when they were under the grate in plain view.

The following day, Mark and I stepped outside and I peered over the edge of the drain, where there was movement. "They're in there," I screeched, not intending to be so loud. I inadvertently spooked all but one kit back into the culvert. Mark carefully lifted the cover off the remaining fox pup and gingerly lifted it out of the drain into the bright sunlight. She didn't look to be more than a week old and was slow to wake up. We would later learn that she was the runt of the pack. He quickly handed the pup to me. She relaxed in the warmth of my arms but barked threateningly at Mark, who was trying to take a close-up with his camera. When I handed the pup over to Mark, the fox barked at me and relaxed into Mark's arms. Its eyes had only recently opened, its squint revealing bluish, gummy eyes behind the lids. The other foxes had escaped quickly into the safety of the culvert, but I had definitely seen three of them before the other two managed to get away. We didn't want to disturb them too much, so I placed the fox back in the dirt where we had found it and closed the grate.

For the next week, it was fairly common to find a pile of five kits in the sunny corner of the drain when the afternoon light hit it just right. The kits were about two weeks old before they ventured to the end of the culvert where I had first seen the mother enter. They took timid, shaky steps into the light. It became clear that this was a risky time for the kits; they weren't very coordinated and were definitely incapable of planning their escape with the speed necessary to get back into the culvert. They also needed training in what to be afraid of and how to sense danger before it was upon them. Their first week out of the den, most of the youngsters would allow us to hold and pet them. Gradually, the mother stayed in proximity when we were observing her young, and when she barked with a certain pitch and intensity, they knew to run. Eventually they put it together that she was barking at us humans and would run into the den at our approach. In the meantime, we took every opportunity to observe, film, and photograph the activities of these marvelous creatures.

Below are selected excerpts from my journal. The first entry is a week after we found the kits, which is when they started to venture out of the pipe where we could observe them. Of note is that we discovered the gray fox pups on May 10, 2004, almost exactly a year after my journal entry on May 9, 2003, when I asked the female fox for a glimpse of her young ones.

May 18, 2004
I returned home late just as one of the fox kits ran across the driveway. All the kits were out and playing at the end of the culvert. They've formed a latrine just outside the entrance, which is accumulating the twisted scat that increases in size every week as the foxes age. After one of them added to the pile, it dragged its rear end across the ground in the dirt. I whistled to them and they responded by coming over to investigate; I wiggled a branch with dangling leaves over their heads that they gladly swatted at and chewed on.

May 19, 2004
There's an interesting new behavior developing among the youngsters. As they pass one another, they lift up a back leg to the other one's face. Perhaps this is to be able to recognize each other by scent or it's a display of dominance. Sometimes they simply lift their leg over the back of another. I don't know whether this is clumsiness or another piece of the ritual. While the largest one of the litter slept, the smaller ones lifted their legs over its back and the runt mounted the larger sleeping one briefly. One fox ventured freely from the den at a 30-foot distance. I petted him while the others hid. I've noticed that they either dug out a dish in the dirt or their bodies formed the spot, but this is where they sleep when outside the den.

May 20, 2004, 1:00 pm
The kits were gnawing on a wood rat that the adults left for them during the night, and as I took pictures the mother came up behind me. When I looked back she ran off. I went back in the office to give her some space and noticed the father fox on one of the decks. He held a wood rat gingerly in his mouth, which I assume he came to deliver. Both parents seemed anxious and nervous to approach too close to the den site. They generally leave kills for the kits around the back of the office, 20 feet from the den entrance, which creates a situation where the most daring kits get to the meal first. I wonder whether this is intentional so as not to give away the den entrance to predators or scavengers. I hope that we haven't disturbed them too much and realize we are testing the theory of whether she will move them because of our scent on them or simply being disturbed. The kits didn't emerge for the rest of the day or sleep under the grate in the afternoon because the sun never showed. I hope that the cold weather is what's keeping them inside.

May 21, 2004
The fox mother barked at us today while we crossed the driveway. The kits responded immediately to this warning; without looking for the danger, they darted back into the culvert. On most occasions, when the mother isn't present they hardly respond to us at all. They are learning.

Gray fox group.

May 23, 2004, 12:00 pm

I peered out the window today to check up on the kits and one of them was scratching and rubbing its nose incessantly. I went out to have a closer look and wondered whether it had tried to eat a banana slug. The slime from a banana slug is difficult to remove even with water, and that was the only thing I could think of that would be causing this fox to act possessed. The fox was easy to catch and I held him carefully on my lap, pulling the slime off his face. He didn't make a sound, just squirmed a little, and I was able to clean him off. I wonder how much he ate to get so slimed.

May 23, 2004, 5:00 pm

Mom arrived with a young rabbit kill and waved it over the grate for her kits to smell. She left it by the grate and walked over to the entrance of the culvert and waited while the kits slowly emerged one by one to suckle. The pecking order started up and the runt was pushed away. They fed for about ten minutes and then mom's ears turned like radar toward something in the garden. Another fox emerged on one of the garden decks, which didn't seem to be the father, judging by

An individual fox.

the mother's response. The kits retreated to their underground cavern. Mom was very alert as she moved toward the rabbit kill and picked it up in her mouth. I wonder whether the other fox had followed her here because she had food. The kits scrambled out again and took little interest in the rabbit; the mother set it in the woodpile, which is near the house, but there is good cover. When the mother moved away, one kit moved in on the rabbit and once it got a taste for it growled and barked if the others came within a few feet. The others played nearby, occasionally testing the boundaries of the feeding fox, but none were successful in wrestling the rabbit away. The mother stayed on watch for a time, looking in the direction of the intrusive fox, and then she retreated into the woods.

May 25, 2004
I noticed a scat outside the den today, which contained yellow chunks of slug flesh; I doubt that fox will make the mistake of eating a banana slug in the future. The parents sat in the driveway today pulling ticks off one another and guarding the entrance of the den. The adults are more of a presence now, perhaps because the kits are venturing further and for longer

stints. Also the adults are bringing more kills. I wonder if this stage in the development of the young is similar to human teenagers: the young are hungry and wild.

May 26, 2004
Mark found the remains of a fawn at the entrance of the den: the head, neck, and front legs were still intact but the hindquarters were missing. It is surprising to think of a small gray fox tackling a fawn. Teeth marks were apparent on the neck, but no puncture wounds, which led us to believe that it was suffocated. Later in the day the young dragged the remains of the fawn into the culvert and a fresh rabbit kill appeared at the entrance. According to Mark's camera trap pictures from the previous night, the fawn was brought at 3:30 am, followed by a gopher and a wood rat, all in one night!

May 31, 2004
Mom was in the yard with kits again. Another fox approached, which she barked at. Usually when the father is around she doesn't bark, so I assume it's an intruder. The fawn legs were

Remains of a fawn killed by a gray fox parent.

strewn across the driveway and the kits went to sleep under the protection of the drain. The mother barked at me as I stood in the doorway of the house and then she retreated into the forest.

June 20, 2004
I've been out of town so wasn't able to observe the den for all this time. However, when I returned on June 20 the kits were frequenting the den site again. They take long forays with the adults but return to the den site, sometimes as a group of five, but more often just a few of them are around at one time. It's been roughly two months since they were born and it seems early for them to be venturing out for such long stints. According to my research they don't start venturing out until three months of age.

Eventually the juvenile foxes left the security of the gutter and the surrounding area. Their forays away from the house increased in distance almost daily, until it was rare to see them except on the fringes of the property. It was staggering how quickly they grew up and how

Taken in August 2006, this shows the runt from the 2004 litter. She's the only one that remained in close proximity to the house. She utilized the same culvert she was born in to raise her own litter two years later—only one of which is known to have survived.

much of their development I'd missed. But I couldn't have asked for a better location for the den, which provided me with an intimate view of their activities, often while I worked at my desk. I'm still amazed by the connection I developed with the mother fox as we learned each other's rhythms and the trust that grew between us, to the point where she sought safety for her family right under my feet.

SIT SPOT MASTER MAP

The master map is one that you will create of your sit area with your anchor point (sit spot) located in the middle (see chapter 2). This map will be a reference for all the other maps you'll draw in this exercise. We recommend that you first make a fast sketch of your sit area in pencil and revise it several times before settling on a final rendering. The final revision will be your master map, which you will redraw each time you create a new field inventory.

Keep this map simple and uncluttered with detail (see the sample map). The master map should contain the following:
1. Anchor point (sit spot marked with an "X").
2. Circle of 200 paces in diameter (100 paces from the anchor point to the edge of the circle in any direction).
3. Four cardinal directions marked.
4. Major land features to help locate directions and the edge of the area.

Walk out 100 paces from your anchor point, and prepare to outline the area by walking a circle with the anchor point as the center. Using normal walking paces, the area should be approximately 200 paces across in diameter. By walking 100 paces from your anchor point in any direction, you will land on the edge of your circle and the edge of your study area. Don't worry if you can't quite get it at first. Just keep working on it, and you will figure it out. A helpful hint is to imagine yourself soaring above your spot and looking down on it. Use your mind's eye right from the start.

Use a compass (or the sun at noon, which will be very close to due south, or the north star at night) to help you locate the four directions as seen from your anchor point. Stand at your anchor point, hold a compass in your hand, and look to where the needle is pointing, which is magnetic north. You must adjust the compass so that the north indicator on its numbered wheel is pointing toward true north. This is called declination, and every area has its own declination adjustment.

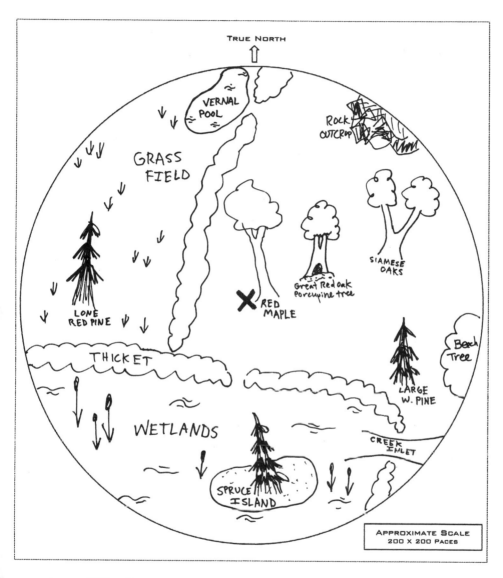

NAME: Tiffany Morgan   **DATE(S):** April 10, 2002

TITLE: Sit Spot Master Map

SOURCE: Rayne's Neck, Maine

The reason for this is that magnetic north is actually south of the true North Pole. You can obtain the correct declination from an environmental consultant, a library, the Internet, or a local topographic map.

On a piece of field journal paper, mark an "X" in the center of the page to denote your anchor point. Now, using the entire page, draw a circle. This circle represents the area you paced out. Include the four directions on your circle (north at the top). Pick a tree, rock, or distant landmark from your sit spot that represents each direction, and draw a symbol on the map that represents that landscape feature. Also include on this map any other major land features that will help you orient yourself and recognize the boundaries of your area.

ADDITIONAL ECOLOGY MAPS

In addition to your master map, you will create maps that are an in-depth study of the lay of the land. You can use those maps for future exercises in ecology. Animals are greatly affected by land features, and this knowledge is vital to your ability to predict an animal's behavior. Without such information, you will be dependent solely on tracks that you can see.

To begin, go to your spot with the intent of looking for obvious geographic features as well as those that are more subtle. Take a walk from your anchor point to the perimeter of your area and circle around. Do this for each of the following maps, and you will be amazed at how much more you see each time around the circle.

VEGETATION MAP

Note the landmark trees—the big ones that you can see in all directions from your anchor point—and the dominant species of low-lying vegetation, such as ferns, berry thickets, and vines. Note where the grasses and mosses are. If it's winter, look at the organic matter or forest litter. Oak leaves tend to stick around for a long time, whereas maple leaves have probably already disintegrated. Note where pine needles are lying thick on the ground.

TOPOGRAPHY MAP

Hills, Hollows, and Hummocks. Look for little hills and hollows. Look for a place where an old tree was uprooted and left an indentation. Notice where an old mine may have been filled in. The cause of hollows is not really a concern; you just need to locate them. Also look for little bumps known as hummocks, which are often caused when a

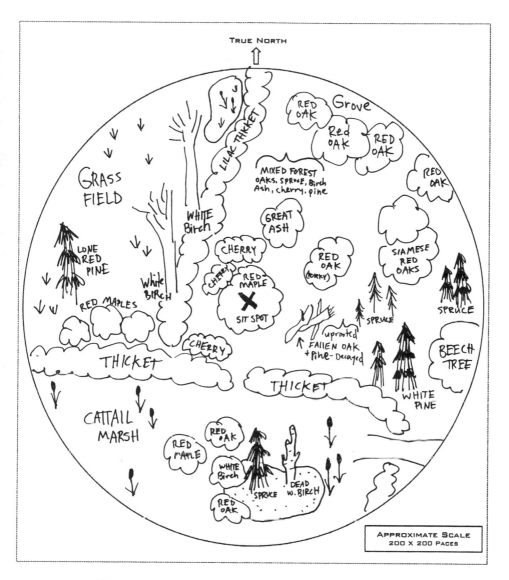

NAME: Tiffany Morgan   **DATE(S):** April 15, 2002

TITLE: Sit Spot Vegetation Map

SOURCE: Rayne's Neck, Maine

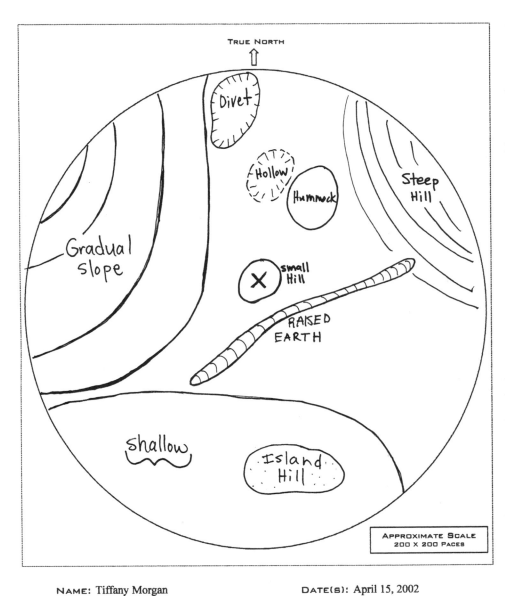

TRUE NORTH

Divet

Hollow

Hummock

Steep Hill

Gradual Slope

X small Hill

RAISED EARTH

Shallow

Island Hill

APPROXIMATE SCALE
200 X 200 PACES

NAME: Tiffany Morgan

DATE(S): April 15, 2002

TITLE: Sit Spot Topography Map

SOURCE: Rayne's Neck, Maine

large tree falls over. The root ball rots and disintegrates into the ground, leaving a little bump on the land, usually right next to a little hollow.

Erosion. Look for elongated dips in the ground that were formed by erosion. Look for gouges in the land such as ravines or gulches. In the summertime, these features may be hidden, covered with raspberry bushes, grasses, or wild herbs.

HYDROLOGY MAP

Waterways. Pay attention to which way the creek flows, for it may be dry in the summer or hidden from view. Follow the streams as they move through the landscape, always checking the little tributaries and following them until you find where they begin. As springtime advances, springs become more difficult to see, and they may be unidentifiable in summer.

Vernal Pools. During late winter or early spring, you may find vernal pools—ponds used by some amphibians and fishes for only certain months of the year. By the time late summer comes, the pools dry up and disappear. The only signs that they were ever there are discolored leaves at the bottom of the former pool and some live vegetation that favors wetland sites.

SOIL AND GEOLOGY MAP

Soil. Look for places where sand is available. Later, the grasses will grow in and cover these places. Also find out where there is heavy clay, mud, and loam.

Rock Formations. Make note of major rock formations in your study area. If there are none, note that too. Look for erratic boulders left over from glaciers, things that look like they don't belong. Large boulders with scratch marks or gouges may be erratics.

TRAILS MAP

Using your master map for reference, begin sketching where you believe trails to be. At first, this may include only obvious human and deer trails, but you can keep adding to this map as you learn where the trails actually are. Leave out the ant trails; start with rabbit-sized creatures and larger. On the sample map, notice that the key in the upper-left hand corner contains three categories: human and other mammals (the wide, obvious trails used by multiple species, including humans), large mammals (e.g., deer, coyotes), and medium and small mammals (e.g., raccoons, weasels, foxes). If there is only one animal species using

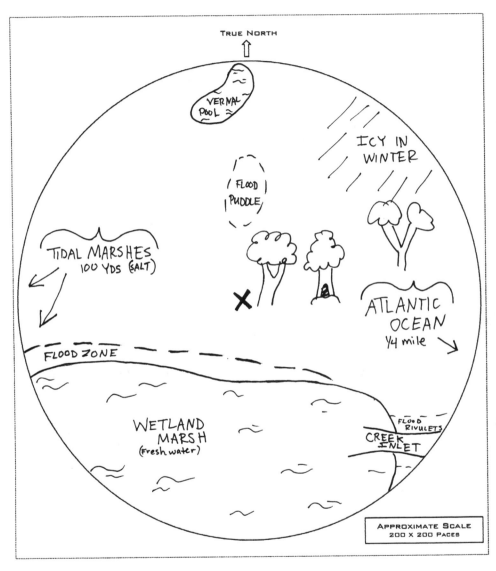

TRUE NORTH

VERNAL POOL

ICY IN WINTER

FLOOD PUDDLE

TIDAL MARSHES
100 YDS (SALT)

ATLANTIC OCEAN
¼ mile

FLOOD ZONE

WETLAND MARSH
(fresh water)

FLOOD RIVULETS

CREEK INLET

APPROXIMATE SCALE
200 X 200 PACES

NAME: Tiffany Morgan   DATE(S): April 15, 2002

TITLE: Sit Spot Hydrology Map

SOURCE: Rayne's Neck, Maine

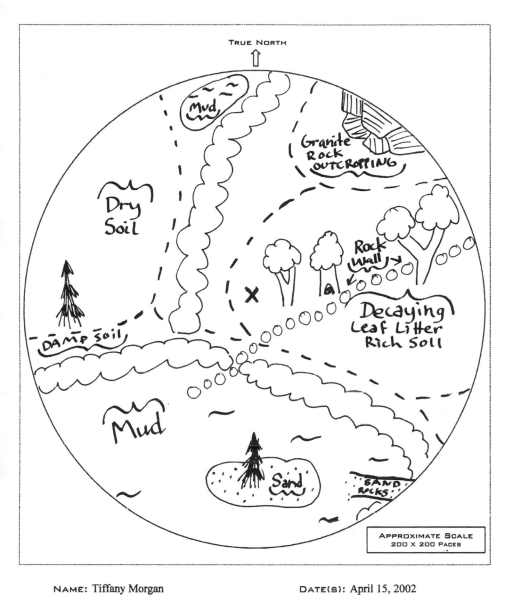

TRUE NORTH

Mud

Granite Rock OUTCROPPING

Dry Soil

Rock Wall →

DAMP Soil

Decaying Leaf Litter Rich Soil

Mud

Sand

SAND ROCKS

APPROXIMATE SCALE
200 X 200 PACES

NAME: Tiffany Morgan   DATE(S): April 15, 2002

TITLE: Sit Spot Soil/Rocks Map

SOURCE: Rayne's Neck, Maine

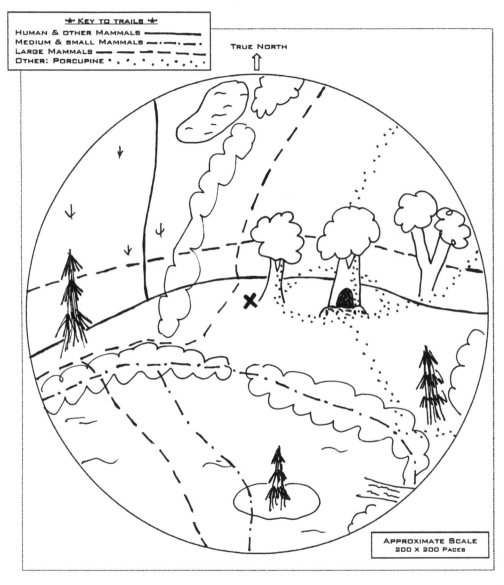

NAME: Tiffany Morgan   DATE(S): April 15, 2002

TITLE: Sit Spot Trails Map

SOURCE: Rayne's Neck, Maine

How Well Do You Know Your Study Area?

I'm always surprised by what people still have to learn about familiar trails in a familiar patch of woods. When venturing from the trail to do a little investigating, they are often startled to find a creek just over that little rise, a huge boulder or cliff, an eroded gully, a ravine, or an old farm field they never knew existed. Until you've done some exploring, there's no telling what landscape features you'll encounter, and the exploration itself can be great fun.

a trail, it is likely a run (runs described in chapter 9). Include these in the category marked other. Our example shows porcupine in this category.

If you're not sure which specific animal is using a trail, use your observation skills to judge the size of the animal using it. If it's a trail through a thicket with lots of low-hanging branches, it's probably used by small to medium animals. If it's a trail in an open clearing with no overhang and a well-worn pattern, you're looking at a large mammal trail. These are generalizations, but they give you a starting point. In the beginning, just noticing where the trails are—even if you don't know exactly who made them—is an excellent start.

To find trails, look for visible lines on the landscape. These may consist of slightly discolored leaves or vegetation on the ground or a tunnel through a thicket where the leaf litter or soil is flattened. Depending on the vegetation, trails can take many different forms, so don't get locked into a single idea of what one looks like. Journal anything that you suspect is a trail. If you find out later that it was just your imagination, you can remove it. This is an ongoing process.

One way to recognize a trail is to imagine yourself as the animal using it and get down to its level to see if there is a tunnel in the thicket or through the grass. If you have a live sighting of an animal, take a mental note of the trail and investigate. Journal your observations as soon as it's convenient to do so. If the animal is escaping, it may not use one of its regular trails, so look around for a regularly used trail nearby. Typical locations for trails are at the edges of fields, along creeks, near water sources, in places hidden from view, and around large objects such as steep hills, large rocks, and fences.

Do a thorough search of your area, and don't be afraid to get dirty; this exercise will likely take a little investigation into some tight places. When you have located some of the major trails, draw them on your map.

FIELD INVENTORY

Each day that you visit your sit spot, journal and map your observations from that day. This may sound like a lot of work, but with your master map and a little ingenuity, it should take only ten to twenty minutes. It's important in the beginning to re-draw your master map so you can make changes to it as your knowledge of your place expands and grows. We've provided examples to help you understand the process and get you started.

By now, you should have six different maps: master, vegetation, topography, hydrology, soil-geology, and trails. For this exercise, you need to copy your master map onto another sheet of paper. If you find that your master map has too much detail and is difficult to reproduce, don't fret; this is a learning process, and you can refine your master map until you have it just right. When you record your observations on this map, you may find it helpful to have your additional ecology maps handy for reference, but you don't need to copy them.

Your master map copy is used for a one-week period of journaling; after the week is up, you'll need to draw another copy of your master map. In the field inventory sample, the inventories are numbered on the map and correspond with the numbered text. For example, if you look for the number 2 circled on the field inventory map and then at the corresponding number 2 in the field inventory text, you'll read that this is the location of wild turkeys performing a mating dance. What it doesn't mention is that it may take months of questions and observations about wild turkeys (or whatever animal you're interested in) before you know enough about their habits to find them in the wild. You may not get the answers right away, so it's important to write down your observations and questions and continue to visit your sit spot. Eventually you'll make the discoveries that lead to your answers.

The sample field inventory is one day in the week of April 13–20, 2002. If you were to read through the entire week (which is not included), you would notice that the inventories contain observations about water, soil, plants, birds, mammals, people, trees, sun, moon, and stars. We've included a prompt at the bottom of the field inventory journal page to remind you to include these elements. This portion of the

TRUE NORTH

APPROXIMATE SCALE
200 X 200 PACES

NAME: Tiffany Morgan   DATE(S): April 13-20, 2002

TITLE: Sit Spot Inventory

SOURCE: Rayne's Neck, Maine

	DATE: April 13, 2002 **TIME: 6:00am**
1.	Our neighbor, Wes, had told us that the turkeys were doing their mating dance by the white fence between 6-6:30am. I got out there around 6:15am, but there were no turkeys by the fence. I picked up my pace and startled the turkeys that were down by the creek inlet into the wetland marsh. There were two females and one large male that I could see. I let them be and went to my sit spot.
2.	On my way home from my sit spot, I saw the turkey mating dance by the lone red pine! The male fanned his tail feathers and spread out his wings while shuffling and strutting for the females.
3.	I picked off a piece of birch fungus for a coal extender and approached the great red oak that houses the porcupine. I scanned the tree hoping the porky would show itself, just as I neared the stonewall; old porky emerged from his den. He began the ascent up the tree's trunk and walked out on nearly every large branch only to back up and try another. Eventually he settled on one that hangs out over my sit spot. While I relaxed at my sit spot, old porky scratched his belly with the claws of his front feet.
4.	Pine and spruce chewed by porcupine.
5.	A redwing blackbird; the first of the season or at least that I've heard. I spotted him from a fallen log that I walked out on over the marsh. He had a black body with yellow wing bar showing and was singing the most incredible tune, complete with drum and base.

ECOLOGY AND LINKING: Water-Soil-Plants-Birds-Mammals-People-Trees-Sun-Moon-Stars

WEATHER NOTES: Cold one day warm the next—warm weather attracts many bird songs.

NAME: Tiffany Morgan   WEEK DATES: April 13-20, 2002

TITLE: Sit Area Field Inventory

SOURCE: Rayne's Neck, ME

inventory is called "Ecology/Linking" because it encourages you to pay attention to all aspects of nature and how they relate to one another.

LINKING

J.Y.

Linking is a process and an exercise that involve paying attention to how one thing affects and is affected by another. For example, the presence of a fast-flowing, oxygen-rich river with a rocky bottom and clear, clean water can be linked to trout and salmon. The presence of spawning salmon is linked to the sudden appearance of birds called "dippers" that feed on the salmon eggs. Black bears also start to come downriver to feed on the salmon, even as Bald Eagles congregate in the trees. The eagles' appearance, in turn, affects the ravens, whose vocalizations change in agitated response to their presence. The salmon run can be linked to the rains that raise the river's level, the rains to the clouds, the clouds to evaporation, and evaporation to the temperature of the sea. The salmon's gathering can be linked to the seasonal position of the sun in the sky and how it relates to the dark cycle of the moon.

All these links are tough to keep track of, but if you are asking good questions on a daily basis and using the observation and exploration activities in this book combined with good research, you will begin to build a map of all these linked phenomena in your local environment and bioregion. It is important for you to read about the local environment, to figure out what the important food resources are, such as grass, mast, voles, insects, berries, fish runs, and the hatching of millions of bird eggs and the raising of thousands of baby birds. What about fawns? Worms? Caterpillars? Moths? How do all these relate to one another and to the plant systems, the weather, the seasons, and even the full moon?

When you are studying links in the environment, one of the most important influences is human activity. This is the single most powerful influence out there, next to sun, soil, and water. Human structures create habitat; lawns interrupt habitat and make edges. Lawns are mini-larders of grass and herbs for plant eaters such as deer, bears, and rabbits; you will find their trails leading to these places. Highways create strange little eddies devoid of human activity (the noise and speeding cars cut people off from little pockets along interstates near parks and open wild places). Here in these hidden eddies are bear beds, coyote dens, and raven nests. The lack of human influence created by the intensity of human influence causes this safety zone for these shy creatures' homes.

The salmon linking story related earlier can also be told backward. For more than a year, I have been going to the same tracking spot along the Skykomish River in western Washington. I have been using this as my sandy study area, but it is also my wetland and my forest, because the area combines a mile-long sandbar, a large forest, and a river. The only things missing here are grasslands and meadows, which are several miles away. Lately, I have been going to this area almost every day.

On the sandbar there are a few coyotes, a female and two males that I have been able to identify; there may be others. I'm beginning to know their habits and behaviors as they hunt for snowshoe hares in the shrubs and among tufts of grasses. Their stories are everywhere in the sand of the river bottom, making it a great place to learn about their world.

One day when I got to the sandbar I noticed that the coyotes had been playing, using gaits I had not seen them use before. They were dancing, it seemed, and so were the hares. "That's strange," I said to myself. "Why are the hares out in the open? And why are these coyotes playing?" With my natural curiosity and sense of mystery, I simply had to know. So, I told people around me what I had seen and asked them to think about it with me.

Soon, I realized that the coyotes were playing because there was extra food around. That was also why the hares weren't afraid to be out in the open where the coyotes were playing (probably at different times on the same night). This was unusual—a break in the pattern that I was used to seeing at this place. This was an event. So, using the concept of linking, I first linked the coyotes' play to extra food; this was linked to the rabbits' sense of safety, because the coyotes weren't interested in them. Additional links were the sounds the ravens were making—again, different from what their normal calls; eagles calling to one another; and an osprey flying by—the reason for the eagles agitation and maybe the ravens. I then linked this to the bear tracks I had found along the mud bank, and all of it spelled one thing: salmon run.

Sure enough, at the river's edge there were numerous large chum salmon in an eddy pool, as well as a few picked carcasses along the way. Bones and skin were hanging from the salmonberries below good eagle perches. The smell of fish remains was in the air. I had been away from this place for only a few days, but in that short time there had been a lot of changes. Coyote scats contained salmon bones and skin and sand, where the coyotes ingested the sand below the carcasses to get the precious oils.

In the coming days, the dippers started to gather, and I knew that there were salmon eggs at the bottom of the river. The adult salmon were dead or dying, but trout were gathering to find the eggs too. There were also otter tracks around, and raccoons. This is linking.

LACKS AND LARDERS

Understanding animal and bird behavior requires a thorough awareness and knowledge of the local landscape and all its physiographic features and ecological conditions, along with how these features offer advantages and disadvantages to inhabitants at different times of the day or year and during different weather conditions. I call this an understanding of lacks and larders.

A larder is a supply of food or a place where food is stored. With regard to a specific animal or bird, the definition can be expanded to include its favorite food items. For instance, a bear's potential larders at a certain time of year, in a particular ecological zone, and at a certain time of day can be very specific.

A few years ago, I helped lead a workshop in California that took us to many parts of the state that I had never seen before. In one northern location we explored the habitat of the black bear. Apples from the many orchards bordering the forested areas constituted one important larder, especially at night. Another larder was fish in the river, but when we visited no fish runs were apparent. These two larders largely determined where the bears traveled regularly and where their tracks and scats were found, leading to many interesting discoveries.

Likewise, when the fish are running in the Skykomish River, I know where to look for bear tracks. When the apples are ripe, I know which fences to search for breaks and other openings where the bears have gone through. When the new, tender grasses are growing in the spring, I know to look there for bear sign. In other words, the presence of food larders in the landscape greatly increases the likelihood of an animal's presence in those locations.

Another example: In winter in the Santa Cruz Mountains of California, the rains settle in for several months. During this time, the grasses green up and grow fast to provide an enormous larder for voles. This, in turn, creates a fantastic larder for a wide variety of predatory mammals, reptiles, and birds. One larder becomes another.

Decide which species you are interested in tracking and understanding. Consult books or other resources and get to know their diets, including seasonal variations. Start to predict where these animals and birds might find their favorite food larders, and then go there and see whether you are right.

In contrast to a larder, a lack is the absence of something. The lack of something physical—warmth, good views, breezes, wetness, shade, cover, and sunlight, to name a few—causes animals and birds to seek what they need. This is not unlike us. When it is raining, we seek some kind of overhead protection. When it is hot and sunny, we look for shade. Animals do the same thing.

Back in the 1990s, along the Skykomish River, I found the tracks of a bobcat that followed a peculiar pattern in the sand. The trail waved back and forth as if the cat were following some kind of invisible and wiggly shape. The next day, while I was tracking, I happened to look up and noticed that the shape of the treetops in the distance was the same shape as the bobcat's trail. When I projected the path of the moon from the night before, I realized that the moon had cast a shadow onto the sandbar in this exact location. This lack of cover and lack of shade at night determined the bobcat's path of travel.

When you add the effects of larders and lacks, you can be almost 100 percent accurate in predicting animal and bird behavior in an area you know well. When you have developed these big-picture aspects of tracking, you can begin to test your knowledge of local animals.

Compile a list of physical and physiographic landscape features that are important in your bioregion. For example, such a list for a western Washington rain forest would be vastly different from one for the plains of South Dakota or the deserts of Arizona. There are many things to consider. Here is a short list of things to think about: presence of human infrastructure such as highways, fences, roads, houses, and yards; wetlands, ponds, streams, and other water features; tidal zones; windy areas; topography, including slope and aspect; size of level areas in the presence of slopes; rocky outcroppings among plants or plants in rocky zones; cliffs and other steep or impassable areas; clearings in thick areas or thick areas in clearings; hedgerows in open spaces or open lanes in thick areas; paved or compacted zones among leaf litter or leaf litter zones in otherwise compacted areas; sun in shade or shade in sun; rain cover in wet zones or wet areas in dry zones or seasons; dark where it is otherwise light or light where it is otherwise dark; high where it is normally low or low where it is normally high; shallow water where it is normally deep or deep water where it is normally shallow; fast water where it is normally slow; and so on. When compiling a list for your area, consider different times of day, times of year, and weather patterns.

EXERCISE

Using a topographic map or aerial photographs for your tracking area, pick one mammal or bird and generate a list of larders and lacks for the current season. Repeat this exercise several times a year for each species you study in depth. Make some predictions that you can verify later in the field. Predict where you will find feeding sign and relate that to larders and lacks. Predict where you will most likely find beds, lays, or dens and where trails and runs will be a result of recent activities.

Record your predictions on a hand-drawn map showing where you expect to find each sign, track, and trail. Then go afield and see how well you did. This will take some practice, but in time you'll be surprised by how much you can determine in advance when going into a new tracking area. This saves a lot of time when searching for species such as mountain lions or wolves in wilderness settings.

Ask yourself: What did I assume going into this exercise? How were my assumptions correct or incorrect? What will I do differently next time?

8

Trailing

*When we track, we pick up a string. At the far end of that
string a being is moving, existing still connected to the track
that we gaze upon. The animal's movement is still contained
in that track, along with the smallest of external and internal
details. As we follow these tracks, we begin to become the
very animal we track.*

—Tom Brown, Jr.
The Science and Art of Tracking

TRAILING THE WILD BUCK

T.M.

A sleek raven hovered a few feet over our heads as the three of us ran
on a thin trail that paralleled the ridge we were climbing. Its feathers
were glistening, and it called out *caw, caw, caw,* seemingly to encourage
us. I instantly thought of native stories of the raven as a trickster, and
then my mind snagged on a lucid memory of ravens assisting native
hunters in finding game. Was this raven involving itself in our pursuit?
Whether it had planned to or not, the raven was helping us find the
buck we had been trailing for nearly five hours.

A group of twelve had started out just as the sun lifted over the
hilltops in Cuyama, a desert directly east of Santa Barbara, California.
It was early spring, and a drizzle of rain throughout the night had
drawn us out of our tents early that morning. Our hope was to find
fresh deer tracks to follow for the entire day. The rain had dissipated
with the night sky, taking with it the tracks of any animal activity during the night. This eliminated much of the guesswork of trying to age
tracks. We knew that any tracks we found would have been created on
that bright morning.

We broke up into two groups of six and my group found the fresh
trail of a large buck right away. The soft sand was damp from the rain

Fresh deer tracks in damp sand.

and held the tracks nicely. This made for easy trailing as we meandered across the flat desert pan just as the buck had done moments before. At the foot of a ridgeline we came to a cluster of oak trees, where the deer apparently liked to cluster as well. We lost our deer's tracks repeatedly in the maze of other bucks, does, and yearlings. The challenge then became to create a mental picture of what our buck's track looked like.

At first glance, all I noticed was the size, which was bigger than the majority of other tracks. But when our buck mingled with another large buck, I became lost and had to return to the last known track. My second look revealed the depth of our buck's track and the texture within the track; it was moist and crisp, and none of the surrounding soil had fallen back into the track. Each time I lost the trail, I was drawn back to a clear track and to the details that made it our buck's. I also looked at how our buck was moving and what his purpose appeared to be. He wasn't lingering in the area like the other deer, which were perhaps foraging and staying in a group for safety. He moved through decidedly, and we followed him to the edge of a cluster of tracks where he left the other deer behind and moved swiftly up to the top of a ridge. Out of breath, we crested the ridge. I looked out over the valley where we had started and could see why the deer had chosen that particular spot to rendezvous. It was well covered and had many escape routes. A black bear or cougar, both of which inhabit the area, wouldn't be able to see deer activity from the ridge where I now stood.

Our buck curled up and took a nap on one of the finger ridges that spread out like veins from the main ridge. A dusty patch indicated the outline of the buck's rounded torso, and two depressions showed where the front legs had folded neatly under the buck's chest. It was encouraging to find this lay, because it meant that we had a better chance of catching up with this sleepy creature. After another hour of tracking, it became clear that our deer habitually traversed up and down these ridges, and finding a deer lay at the top of each ridge also became predictable.

The next valley between ridges created a funnel for leaves to collect in and was bordered by thick brush. The only visible tracks were slightly disrupted leaves; the ones that had been stepped on were moist, while the surrounding leaves had dried out in the sun. The buck slipped easily through the brush, and the tracks disappeared in the shade. We worked as a team to find where the tracks reappeared on the opposite side of the brush. Three people went through the brush to

Deer trail.

comb for tracks on the other side, and three of us stayed on the last visible track to try to determine the direction of travel, which would help us figure out the likely exit point on the opposite side. Eventually, two different trails were found on the opposite side, and there was much speculation and debate about which one was our buck. Half the group followed a trail down into the valley, and the other half followed a trail up the next ridge. I went with the latter group, because climbing the ridges seemed to be our buck's pattern.

At the top of that ridge was the predictable lay of our buck, which gave me the confidence I needed to stay on the trail. The ridge flattened out, and the soil became hard packed, making it difficult for the tracks to penetrate. In my group were Neal White and Roger Moore, both of whom are focused and dedicated trackers. I had confidence that we had a good chance of seeing our buck. We took turns looking for the next track, but even this became challenging in the afternoon heat. Our buck seemed to be walking in circles, remaining stubbornly on the hard-packed soil.

After an hour of arduous searching, the tracks became clear again. The buck stayed high on the face of the ridge, slowly dipping in and out of erosion gullies. We were thankful for the soft soil and easy trailing this provided. We bumped up onto a finger ridge where our buck had laid down for another nap, and we decided to take a little siesta ourselves. In the valley below we could hear the other half of our group. We called out to them as they approached, and they climbed up to meet us on the ridge. They had lost their trail in the valley, where increasing deer activity had made it difficult to distinguish the buck's tracks. After we reported that we were sitting in another deer lay that seemed to be linked to all the others we had found, they decided to rejoin us.

From his lay, the buck climbed slowly up the finger ridge toward the peak, where he would likely rest again. But halfway up he surprised us all and made a sudden, unexpected change in direction. He dove 15 feet down the face of the ridge toward the valley floor and continued down in a full gallop. Up to this point, we had only seen him walk and occasionally trot for short distances. We all took off running in pursuit. My thoughts were also racing, trying to grasp how incredibly close we were to this elusive creature that was now apparently aware of our pursuit. Because of the buck's speed and energy, his hooves were digging in deep, creating crisp little "V" shapes even where the substrate was hard packed. This allowed us to maintain maximum speed, because we could clearly see the tracks without bending over to be certain. In places where the tracks became less visible, we fanned out, and the first person to find them would be on point, following the visible tracks while the others looked for a change in direction in case the point person lost the trail.

The buck clipped along with purpose, veering off his straight path only to dart around bushes. He reached the base of the hills and leaped onto a trail that cut narrowly out of the hillside and angled steeply toward a plateau. We fell in line behind Neal and jogged uphill at a discouraging pace. As if sensing our plight, the raven drifted in and hovered just over our heads, pointing its beak down and cawing loudly, seemingly to encourage us. I quickened my pace slightly, and the edge of the plateau moved closer. At the top, Neal was nowhere in sight; the only other member of our group that I could see behind me was Nicole, my sister. The buck's trail seemed to go in both directions and reminded me of a snowshoe hare I had tracked in New Hampshire that was trying to evade a fox. The hare's trail wound in wide circles and then tight ones, all the while zigzagging, which was quite effective at throwing me off course. Our buck was utilizing a similar strategy on a bigger scale. However, in this case, we had the benefit of multiple sets of eyes, so I followed the trail north and Nicole went south. Somehow, we both ended up on the east edge of the plateau fifteen minutes later. I turned my head to call out to her just as something caught my eye. In unison we both exclaimed, "There's our buck," as its graceful, tawny body slipped through the air and cleared an entire ridge. Nicole and I stared for a moment in disbelief and then ran to the edge of the plateau. From there we could see the buck skipping down to the valley floor with the raven still in pursuit, flying in tight circles over the buck's head. The two of them raced to another ridge across the valley, and as the buck climbed the steep face, the raven cawed wildly, as if begging us to continue the chase and provide a few scraps for it to eat. The raven continued in this way until it was just a speck against the sky. But we had already gotten what we were after—a clear view of the buck, an affirmation that we were on the right track.

TRAILING THROUGH THE SEASONS

Having lived mostly in snowless territory, I can tell you that nearly every habitat has some opportunity for trailing during certain times of year. The simple exercise below will help you find habitats in your area that host trailing opportunities. Even if you do live in a place with snow, it doesn't last all year. With a little research, you can be trailing animals year-round.

EXERCISE

Obtain a good map of your area—a topographic map or one that shows parks and recreational areas. Look at the map with the intention of finding areas that have trackable substrate. You will likely find places that you never thought of as tracking hot spots. Then investigate these places in person and choose a few that are seasonally trackable. For example, one spot may be perfect in the spring because of the mud created by heavy rain or melting snow. Then in the summer, when everything has dried out, your tracking hot spot might change to a dusty road that shows perfect, detailed tracks. With time and research, you should have four tracking and trailing locations—one for each season.

Suggestions

There's a plethora of places you may have overlooked, simply because you hadn't considered them. For example, there's usually enough mud or dust below underpasses or bridges to hold a string of tracks long enough to trail. Creeks, streams, and rivers also host trackable substrate either on their banks or on sandbars. These spots might be seasonal, depending on the height of the water, so check them at different times of year. Beaches, sloughs, marshes, and estuaries are wonderful tracking spots. If you're investigating an area that's tidal, make sure to check it at the different tides; these places can be great for learning the age of tracks made below the high-tide mark. If there's a desert area close enough for a day or a weekend trip, make the effort. Desert areas can be as revealing as snow; I've had good luck with sand dunes, dry creek beds, and desert valleys. Ask the locals where the good substrates are. Even if they don't track, they'll know which places have mud or sand. Go off-trail with a map and a compass and do some exploring; you're bound to turn up with something unique to your area.

TRAILING IN WINTER WITH A GUIDE

T.M.

I arrived in New Hampshire in late summer, long before the first snow. Having tracked only in Southern California, I had no idea at the time that snow would be the key to unlocking the mystery of life there.

Whenever I move to a new place, the first thing I do is find a sit spot. I've learned from experience that visiting the same place in nature is one of the best teachers. I found a little patch of woods just outside of town that bordered the local sand lot. A creek paralleled the main trail into the heart of the woods. At the first opportunity, I jumped off the trail and cruised down the embankment to a curve in the creek that wasn't visible from the trail. Waterways are often teeming with wildlife, so I parked myself there under a striped maple tree.

Not long after I had sat down, I saw in my peripheral vision a dark tan form slinking under ferns and over rocks. Within moments it had climbed right up on a rock in front of me. I could clearly see that it was a longtail weasel, and she wasn't alone. A listless chipmunk dangled from her clenched jaws. I sat motionless, trying not to disturb this small but formidable creature. The weasel carefully rested the chipmunk on the rock, raised her body up to a standing position, and gingerly sniffed the air while I held my breath. Somehow I remained invisible, perhaps not to her nose, but she didn't see me. Eager to get that tasty morsel into her stomach, she picked it up by the nape of its neck and dashed out of sight, the chipmunk swinging like a pendulum.

This was a splendid beginning, and I took it as an indication that this would make a fine sit spot. Unfortunately, after sitting there for four months, this clearly was not the case. Sure, I'd seen a few squirrels and roaming flocks of chickadees, titmice, and woodpeckers, but the area was a virtual wildlife dead zone. Where were the animals?

One glorious evening in December it snowed, and my question was answered. A soft, white blanket covered every flat surface outside my window. This wasn't like driving from the warm valley of San Diego to the snowy mountains. I was related to this snow; it had started pumping through my veins in the fall, when the weather turned cold and my blood thickened. Now it was here like a long-lost friend that I couldn't wait to see. The next morning I wasted no time getting to my sit spot. Where were the animal trails? What had I been missing, and what would I find?

I shouldn't have been surprised, but I was. There wasn't a single track within 100 yards of my sit spot. There must be tracks somewhere, I concluded, and set out to find them. At the top of the hill behind my sit area I crossed a red fox trail, and thus began my first all-day trailing experience. For the first time, I felt as though I was following the animal itself and not just the tracks it left behind. There was enough information for me to see the animal moving in my mind's eye. It hopped up onto a fallen tree and nimbly walked the length of it. When it jumped off at the opposite end, the one fox became two. The second one had been trotting in a perfect direct register on top of the other one's tracks. If you had put your ear to my head at that moment, you would have heard new pathways being created in my brain. I couldn't believe what the animals were teaching me just because I cared to look. The red foxes led me to the south side of the hill, where they circled around each other in a playful manner and then reunited in a cluster of tracks that was difficult to decipher. I wondered whether this cluster could be an indication that the two foxes had mated. I wasn't sure whether it was mating season for red foxes, and that question led to a dozen others that could be easily answered with the assistance of a field guide to mammals.

Even though I could finally see the animals' trails, I felt like I was missing a large piece of the story. I could look up the information on red foxes when I got home, but I had prematurely ended my questioning process by not carrying the guide with me. I drew the cluster of tracks in great detail and continued to follow the foxes into the heart of an animal junction containing the tracks of every animal known in that forest. So *this* was where the animals were. For the next three months, every time I returned to this place I chose a different animal to trail and research with my mammal guide, until I had traveled all their trails at least once.

Field guides to the mammals in your area are indispensable. The more you know about the natural history of an animal you're tracking, the more depth your trailing experience will have. Bring the guide with you so that you can research questions of natural history that are bound to arise. A mammal guide can tell you how to identify the animal and provide information on its range, similar species, habitat, habits, and raising of young. If it's too cumbersome to carry a guide, take excellent notes and research your questions when you get home. With the combination of trailing and research, you will quickly gain intimate knowledge of the animals in your area.

THE LOG DRAG

J.Y.

For people who have not had much experience in trailing, the log-drag game is a great way to get started. Trailing can be challenging for beginners and can be discouraging for many. It helps to have some techniques to practice that give good feedback. The log-drag game can do this, and it can be adapted to a variety of settings, situations, and skill levels.

I originally learned the log-drag game while working with the Boy Scouts. The log is a piece of firewood with a dozen or so nails driven halfway into it. The spiked log is then tied to a short, sturdy rope. The idea is to work with the same log and the same trainees for a series of exercises in the field. Over time, as the participants get better at following the trail left by dragging the log, nails are pulled out until finally there are none left in the log. Eventually, you can use a lighter log and then no log at all when the participants have enough field trailing experience.

Alternatively, you can use a dragging stick about 1 inch in diameter and 5 feet long. With this method, you can vary the pressure on the shaft of the dragging stick as you walk; for example, in softer substrates, where footprints are more easily seen, you can lighten the pressure on the stick or even pick up the stick altogether. When I use this method, I hold the stick under my left arm, near the armpit, and apply pressure with both arms—my right arm on the stick's base, palm oriented upward, and my left hand a few inches toward the long end of the stick on the ground, with my left palm facing downward. I vary the pressure with the hand facing down and switch sides when my arms grow tired. This allows me to walk facing forward and watch my forward trail without having to worry about what the stick's end is doing behind me.

This game is best practiced in hardpan soil situations, such as sun-baked pastures or meadows, or in forests when the ground is frozen or hard and dry. Don't do it where sensitive spring wildflowers are growing.

EXERCISE

Send one person out as the trail maker while the others wait behind. The trail maker marks the start of the trail with a ribbon or some other indicator and then creates a log-drag course through the forest. The trail followers should not watch or listen to the trail maker's progress. The initial trail should be about 50 yards at most and serves as a test trail. If it is too difficult, that will become obvious fairly quickly, and the trail maker may have to start over making a new trail in a new area. At the end of the trail, the trail maker leaves something to indicate that the trail followers have finished the course.

Once the trail has been made, the trail followers start at the beginning and try to follow the trail to its end. Over time, the game can be varied by making the trail longer and more subtle. Another variation is to play hide-and-seek this way or to have a treasure hunt along the way.

TEN STEPS

If you're stuck at home or don't have much time to practice your tracking skills, this is the exercise for you. Years after having been introduced to this exercise in the Shikari Tracker Training Program, I still use the lessons learned to find the next track in difficult substrates.

EXERCISE

Head out to a patch of grass large enough for you to walk about fifteen paces. Bring ten Popsicle sticks, or the equivalent. Once you arrive at your destination, pick a landmark in the distance and walk toward it for ten paces, moving in your normal walking stride. Before you take your first step, mark your first track by placing a stick in the ground at the base of your heel. This will be your first footprint in a string of tracks that you are going to leave behind and then come back and follow. Similarly, leave a stick at the heel of your tenth and final track. When you're done, circle back to the right or left to your first track.

Now, find each one of your tracks. Don't skip any tracks, and make sure that each track is actually a track. Don't go on to the next track until you're sure you've found the previous one. At each track you find, place a stick at the back of the heel. As you progress, you will create a string of visible markers indicating your trail. Keep an eye on your landmark, and check to see that the distance between sticks is indeed your natural stride. Change your angle of view often, being careful not to trample the tracks. Even tilting your head can change your perspective enough to see the tracks in a new way. Add more tracks to the trail as you gain confidence.

PICK TRACKING

Choose a place outside where you can make a track, but one that isn't too clear. Grass, forest litter, or bark chips in a garden will do. Once you have chosen a suitable site, make one track by stepping in it. Then spend twenty minutes studying the track in this manner:

1. Use the first five minutes to study the area inside the track, but don't dig through the track yet. For now, just look at its

features: breaks in sticks and pine needles; the way the soil is compacted, the way leaves are broken, creased, or crumbled; the way the track is raised around the edges. Don't sketch yet, either. For now, just observe, and when the time is up, move on to the next step.

2. Spend the second five minutes studying the area around the track, but don't look inside it. Do the same thing you did in step 1 for the substrate the track was made in.

3. For the final ten minutes, compare the area within the track with the substrate it was made in. How are they different? Use a small stick or tweezers and pick down into the track. Pull out individual pine needles and study the breaks on them. Pull out leaves and see how the creases go through the layers into the soil below. Then sketch these things: study a piece of the track closely and then set it aside and sketch it. Turn back to the object periodically to refresh your memory. Don't spend too long on any one part of the track.

When your twenty minutes of pick tracking are up, wrap up the exercise by writing a reflection paper. What did you notice toward the end of the ten minutes in step 3 that you didn't perceive at the beginning? Can you apply these observations to animal tracks? How would they be different?

TRAILING IN EASY SUBSTRATE

Where I live, there isn't much opportunity for trailing an animal in easy substrate. So when I get the chance, I drive thirty minutes west to the sand dunes at the beach. If you can't travel to a place with easy substrate, then an animal trail made visible by pushed down grasses, bare earth, or tunnels in brush will work as well. Follow the rhythms of that trail while practicing the following exercise.

EXERCISE

Find an animal trail to follow for at least three hours. While trailing, pay attention to the animal's behavior: beds, lays, elimination, feeding sign, change in gait, stalking, escaping, and so forth. How does the animal behave when it approaches a road? Does the animal climb hills, or does it choose to stay low? If it does climb, how does it move, and what route does it take? You're like a detective gathering clues, uncovering evidence of this animal's passing. Carry a notepad to jot down your observations. A good detective always does some research ahead of time to get background information on the subject. Is it mating season? Might it have young? Is it preparing for winter, gathering food? If you don't know what animal you'll be trailing, these questions can be researched later. This is an exercise in learning animal behavior. It encourages to draw on your understanding of the needs and motivations of animals to help you to predict an animal's direction of travel when you've lost the next track.

Write down all your observations. Even if they seem irrelevant or insignificant now, they may turn out to be useful as your questions about a place develop and change. If you're unsure about a finding, document that in your notes and return to it when you have more information. It's also important to write down the date, time of day, location, and weather for future reference.

DEER TRAILS

> *The esthetic value of deer cannot be measured. There are fully as many, if not more, people who just enjoy watching deer or photographing them as there are hunters. Both groups are sure that the world is a better place because of the deer.*
>
> —Leonard Lee Rue III (1968)

Any ungulate will suffice for the following exercise, but for the purpose of demonstration, I will be referring to deer. If there are deer in your area, chances are you've found yourself on one of their trails: any well-worn, obvious trail that isn't a human trail is likely a deer trail. Although other animals may be taking advantage of it, deer are likely the primary users. Deer are habitual and use the same trails repeatedly—sometimes for hundreds of years, if left undisturbed. Therefore, documenting and mapping their trails will teach you volumes about the deer in your area. You will be more successful if you do some research on deer ahead of time. Find out, for example, when they mate and have young and whether they migrate in winter and spring.

EXERCISE
Choose a 2- to 5-acre piece of land that you know has heavy deer traffic, and draw a map of the area. This may be your sit spot or a different location. On the map, include major land features such as large trees,

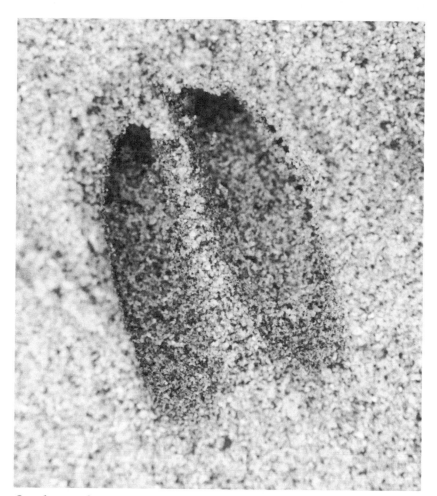

One deer track.

rocks, or hills for reference points. Be sure to mark the four directions. Travel every trail that you suspect is deer and draw it on your map using the land features as reference points. A compass will enhance your accuracy and help you get your bearings. It may take a few visits to the area before you feel confident that you've found all the trails. When you're satisfied with your master map of deer trails, redraw it on another sheet of paper. On this copy, record all the tracks and sign that you observe while traversing the trails, including scat, browsing, markings, digs, beds, and feeding sign. Be sure to indicate any actual sightings of deer on your map—the number seen, male or female, and their ages (fawn, yearling, adult).

Draw a new master map each time you visit the area and record your findings for that day, including the date, time, and weather, all of which have a significant impact on deer behavior. Visit at different times of day and, if possible, at night or at first light. In order to observe dramatic shifts in behavior, carry out this exercise for at least two seasons.

100 DEER TRACKS IN A ROW

As soon as it's springtime, when the snow has started to melt, that's when you really learn to trail deer. Tracking in snow can teach you the rhythm of deer, the choices they make, the size of their feet, and the distance between their steps. Once the snow is gone, test yourself by attempting to follow 100 deer tracks in a row. It takes a lot of practice, and two or three years from now, you may be pretty good at it. It all comes down to seeing minute differences in foot sizes, minute differences in the way they walk, and minute differences in step.

PREDICTING DIRECTION OF TRAVEL

The purpose of the following exercise is to determine the direction of travel using a single track as your guide. Human tracks are suitable for beginners, but with practice, you'll be able to apply this method to the tracks of anything from voles to coyotes and deer. It's especially useful when you lose the trail of an animal, because predicting the direction of travel can help you find that next track.

Although this exercise is best done with a partner to verify your conclusions, it doesn't require one. Start in an easy substrate such as sand or dust; then try grass or leaf litter. If you're doing this alone, find a place with plenty of human tracks: the beach, a local park, or a well-traveled dirt road.

EXERCISE

If you have a partner, turn your back while he or she draws a circle in the sand, steps in the middle of it with one foot, and then makes a dramatic change in direction. Have this person brush away all the tracks surrounding the circle, so as not to give away too much information. Turn around to view the track in the circle, and use your skills of observation and deduction to determine in which direction your partner moved out of the circle. Left or right? Backward or forward? Once you've reached a conclusion, your partner can verify your results.

If you're alone, you'll have to use preexisting tracks and then speculate or use surrounding tracks to verify your findings. Either way, make note of how the substrate reacts to changes in motion and direction. With practice, you'll be able to recognize subtle changes, such as someone simply looking over his shoulder, and how the soil responds.

Pay close attention to the action in the substrate surrounding the track and where there is depth or shallowness within the track. Look for patterns in where the sand piles up or spreads out. These patterns will also reveal themselves in animal tracks, helping you to determine direction of travel.

BUSHMAN TRAILING FORM

J.Y.

In the film *The Great Dance,* which depicts Bushmen living, tracking, and hunting, I noticed that the trackers had a particular way of walking. They tracked with their arm raised out in front of them and their eyes looking at the horizon. Louis Liebenberg, the founder of Cyber-Tracker, has spent a great deal of time with Bushmen, so I asked him about this walking form. Louis's fieldwork with the Bushmen has taught him that the best trackers hardly look at the ground at all when trailing. They are always looking about 30 meters ahead. What are the survival benefits of this practice?

1. You can see danger (predators or enemies) ahead or to the side, rather than bumping into trouble head-on.
2. With the ground in your periphery, the movement of poisonous snakes or other dangers at your feet will still catch your attention.
3. Bird language is happening all around you, and with your attention on the horizon instead of focused on the ground, you can catch important and potentially lifesaving signals.
4. It is much faster and more efficient to trail something in this manner.
5. It can be done at a run.
6. It allows a team of trackers to have silent communication while using each tracker's skills.

You may be wondering, how do I trail something without looking at the tracks? The following exercise is designed to answer that question.

EXERCISE

Find an open, relatively level area that will give you a fairly long run of tracks on the trail of a person or animal. Ideal locations might be a beach, a sand flat, a sand road through a coastal plain, a desert, a snow-field, or any other area with good tracking substrate. Review and practice the basics of owl vision and sense meditation as the foundation for this exercise.

Next, find a trail. It can be cat, dog, human, or anything that left a long run of tracks for you to follow in relatively easy conditions. As you get better at this, you can try more subtle trails.

Notice that tracks on a trail can be seen for a long distance in good substrate. Take your hand and raise it in front of your eye, as if you were sighting down your arm, over your hand, onto the distant trail about 100 feet from where you stand. Notice that you can see the entire trail connect back to the tracks at your feet. This is critical, especially in the beginning.

Now, follow the tracks with your wide-angle vision as they pass beneath your outstretched arm and hand (only glance at them from time to time; train your wide-angle vision to see them). You can "keep time" on the individual tracks as they pass beneath your hand by marking them with your fingers. Use your fingers to imitate the movement of the animal as it left the tracks. Switch back and forth between your pointer and middle fingers to match left and right sides of the body for walks and trots; for galloping patterns, move your whole hand to match a group.

Follow the animal or person, keeping your arm outstretched and sighting along your hand. This action keeps your eyes from following the tracks as they come to you (as you move to them). If you don't do this, it's hard to keep yourself from looking down at the ground.

Dan Gardoqui and I ran for miles following wolf tracks along a pack trail in this manner. When I had the tracks, Dan knew—using only his wide-angle vision—by the regular movements of my hand. When I lost the trail, my hand would drop and Dan would begin to look for the lost trail. If he picked it up, I would watch the rhythm of his hand. This is one way to communicate silently while sharing the burden of trailing an animal for long distances.

If you ever have an opportunity to trail an animal in this way with another tracker, you'll be amazed by how much ground you're able to cover while remaining on the animal's trail. It also affords a much greater chance of finding the animal at the end of the trail.

Raccoon trail on a sandy beach in Pescadero, California.

Akamba Tracker Form

"Ingwe" (M. Norman Powell)

In the shadow of Mount Kilimanjaro, hunting and gathering people survive through their astonishing skill at tracking game. These same skills impart a sense of security. Tracking has saved many lives in two ways: the prevention of starvation, and the advance detection of danger. What is especially important to note about detecting danger (from both beast and human) is that it leaves plenty of time for a calm retreat rather than a frightened escape. Through such awareness, the hunting and gathering people conserve vital energy and the rarest resource under the equatorial sun—water. Through centuries of experience, the Akamba trackers learned which routines of awareness served them best. It should come as no surprise that the wise animals of the forest live by these same routines of awareness. This is how the wisdom of the Akamba trackers can help those interested in increasing their tracking skills.

When you practice the Akamba tracker form, look at the ground only when you are standing still. When you are moving, do so slowly and steadily in a gliding motion, and keep your eyes ahead. Each time a stop occurs, drop down to a low crouch to study the ground, first looking behind you. Then, sweep your eyes overhead in an arc to the forward path again. Then sweep your eyes to the left and to the right in a horizontal arc, thus completing a basic sweep of all directions: ahead, left, right, behind, and above. This should take no less than twenty seconds. Before proceeding, use a side-heading method to study the ground farther and farther along the chosen route and identify from the squatting position where the next stop will be.

The rewards of this form are many. Birds and animals in the trees are spotted more often. Lost tracks, sign, and other subtle clues on the trail come to the forefront of awareness. Bird language is detected near and far. Alarm birds and animals such as juncos and chipmunks are spotted before they can send out concentric rings of alarm. Overall information retained from scouting and wandering explorations increases. This form also keeps surprises to a minimum.

However, people tend to have a hard time sticking to this routine. It feels too mechanical to most. Also, impatient friends will grow more so at the slow progress of an Akamba tracker.

9

Animal Runs

All good things are wild and free.

—Henry David Thoreau

A run is an accumulation of tracks by a single animal or members of the same species. Runs are easy to identify because their frequent use results in a buildup of tracks over time. (For further reading, see *Mammal Tracks and Sign.*)

Why do animals form runs and continually use the same ones? If an animal creates a run, it's for a distinct purpose. A deer may create a run in deep snow that multiple deer use repeatedly to conserve energy rather than breaking new trails. In the spring, when the snow melts, the deer return to their other trails. The purposes of runs are as varied as the animals that use them. This chapter relates to the ancestral patterns of the animals themselves, or the DNA coding that determines their behavior and thus the runs they create.

In New Zealand, there is a legend that says the Creator made the spirits of animals from the stars. He sent the stars down, and they went across the ground and laid trails for the animals to follow. Then the Creator formed the animals from clay, placed them on their trails, and breathed life into them. Since that time, the animals have followed the same trails. There's a similar legend from Africa and among the Lakota in North America. The trails came first, and the animals followed them. This is a common myth worldwide.

These legends imply that animals are following some preconditioned response that determines their runs and trails. The more deeply you understand the animals, the more likely you will begin to think like the animal which will cause you to be drawn directly to its runs and trails, recognizing them on the landscape.

Deer run in the grasses of a marsh.

IN-HOUSE RUNS

Finding animal runs became much easier for me when I realized that animals in the wild have many of the same needs as people. The consistent travel patterns of animals weren't so mysterious when I thought about them in relation to my own patterns of movement. Imagine your kitchen: the sink, the refrigerator, the table, the cupboards. Take a close look at the floor. Is it wood, linoleum, or tile? Can you see the patterns of foot traffic, the accumulation of soil? The signs may be subtle, but there are probably some worn trails because, like all animals, we are motivated by food. Your house is akin to an animal's core area, which is simply a place where it feels comfortable and safe and where it spends most of its time. Many of its needs are met there such as rest, shelter, and having reserves of food. However, just like people, animals must often leave home and travel outside of its core area in order to search for new food sources, find a mate, or defend its territory.

Voles provide an excellent example of runs because they don't travel very far. You can find their kitchen, bathroom, bedroom, and connecting runs all within a 10-yard radius. The following exercise will help you see your own patterns and what motivates your movements. When you relate this to an animal's movements, you will see that we're not so different after all, which will help you find and interpret their runs.

EXERCISE

Draw a map of your house viewed from above, including all rooms, hallways, doorways, driveway, mailbox, yard, and garage. Simple one-dimensional boxes will suffice. After your map is complete, search the house and yard for your runs. Draw the run from the front door to where you park your car and the one from the bedroom to the bathroom. Create a key so that you can identify the amount of use each trail gets: light, moderate, or heavy. When your map is complete, write down how each of your trails relates to those of an animal. For instance, if there's a heavy trail leading to the couch, this could be compared to a deer trail leading to a deer bed. Humans are complex creatures, but if you look at our basic motivations, it's clear that we're just sophisticated animals.

Animals are unique individuals, just as people are, so it's interesting to compare the trails in your home to those in your friends' homes. Use your imagination to get inside the mind of an animal to discover

Black-tailed jackrabbits form very distinct runs, showing that humans aren't the only animals who are creatures of habit.

Above: *The runs of these California ground squirrels on this hillside form a web with each branch leading to and from the various needs of these animals, including shelter, food, water, and mates.*

Left: *California ground squirrel run leading to its den.*

what motivates a fox, a rabbit, or coyote to move across the landscape. Someday you might be able to distinguish between two different foxes' trails simply by knowing their preferences.

DRAWING A RUN

The first step is to find a run and determine which species of animal is using it. There may be signs of other species, such as scat, track, or feeding sign, but there will be one predominant species. Your assignment is to determine which animal is creating the run and why. Look at the run from all angles: lie on the ground and peer down it; stand up to view it from above. In your sketchbook, draw these angles, paying attention to the width and height of the trail, which are good indications of the size of the animal that uses it. Investigate the floor of the run, identifying possible compressions or tracks; check the vegetation that makes up

Desert cottontail run used for an escape from sparse grass to dense cover.

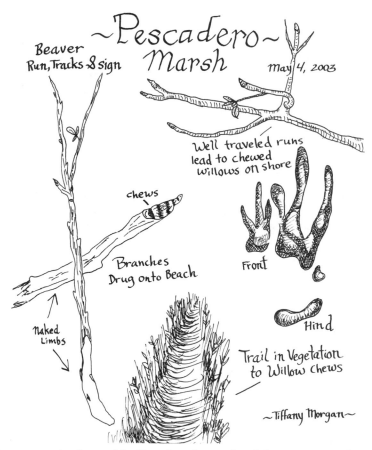

Beaver run, tracks, and feeding sign observed and drawn at Pescadero,
Marsh, California.

the walls of the run for feeding sign. Follow the run as far back and forward as possible, seeking information that will help you discover the purpose of this run for this particular animal. Does it lead to a food source? Is it hidden from view? Is the animal conserving energy by using this run? Consider these questions, put yourself in the animal's shoes, and ask, What are my runs, and why do I use them? When you have a theory about what animal is using the run and why, draw all the evidence, including the run and tracks, on a piece of journal paper.

Start a catalog of animal runs—either photos or drawings—with descriptions of their uses. These will be invaluable when you're researching specific species and require knowledge of their habits and habitats.

A VOLE'S WORLD

We often introduce people to voles when teaching people to interpret animal runs. Voles often surround us, yet we don't realize it. These animals are vital to the strength and diversity of a given environment. Many predators eat voles, and their prolific nature can lead to intense accumulations in appropriate habitats. You will focus on the meadow, long-tailed, or California vole, depending on which species is most prolific in your area. Take a moment to browse your natural history books and field guides to familiarize yourself with vole habits and habitats.

Should you live in an area where snow is deep during the winter months, the ideal time to do this exercise is in the early spring—just when snows recede and vole sign is suddenly exposed for all to see. In areas where snow never falls, or in the heat of summer, any overgrown meadow will do—the longer the grass the better.

EXERCISE

Select an area of about 10 square yards in prime meadow habitat where vole sign is clearly evident and abundant. Draw or map this entire area in detail. Comb the 10 square yards and draw in all tracks, runs, nests, burrows, scats, latrines, urine stains, feeding signs, and vole remains you encounter, as well as any tracks and signs of other animals (e.g., foxes, weasels, humans). This is a long project, so plan to devote an afternoon or a morning; take your time and produce something you'll be proud of.

If you live in the desert, voles may not be the best subjects for this exercise. Instead, draw 25 square yards of your most common rabbit's habitat. Find and map all the same signs described above for voles.

Once your map is finished to your satisfaction, take a break and read an example of this exercise by student Daniel Gray, under the guidance of Mark Elbroch.

AIR SCULPTING

Air sculpting is a term I made up, but I didn't make up the *act* of air sculpting. I have been teaching and talking about air sculpting for a long time—at least ten years. The film *The Great Dance* features trackers as storytellers, shaping things in the air as they speak, making gestures that give shape to the animals they're tracking. This is air sculpting. Your grandmother who has a habit of talking with her hands

Learning from Voles

Daniel Gray

When I was asked to participate in a drawing exercise that would be used for a tracking book, I immediately got excited. I imagined myself being brought out to a beautiful, fresh coyote track and being asked to draw it in as much detail as possible. Everyone would comment on how artistically the two front toes were made or how delicately the claws were shaded. Instead, I was brought outside to a grassy mound near the wooden structure of an old garden bed. Mark Elbroch pointed out various latrines, many small plants and trees that had been gnawed on by small mammals, a handful of nests, and tunnels. The tunnels were incredible, running crisscross, sideways, lengthways, and all ways. The ground was riddled with a giant mass of tunnels, mounds, and matted areas.

Mark walked to one end of the mound, held out his arms sideways in the air (he looked like an American Kestrel soaring over a meadow), and then walked across the entire length of the rectangular mound, which was about the size of five large cars parked next to each other. The mound was filled with dirt lines winding all over the place, large mounds of poop and numerous grass nests and holes. Mark said, "I want you to draw all this." My heart sank. This would be boring, tedious, and difficult. He wanted me to draw everything that was influenced in any way by meadow voles.

I stood there alone for a while and let the idea sink in. I was supposed to draw this large rectangular mess. I began to walk around the mound, surveying the land like a giant walking casually among the downtown streets, restaurants, and apartment buildings of a city. I did this for about an hour. Maybe it was to soak up all the information from the ground beneath me, all the tracks and stories contained in the earth. Maybe it was because I wanted to do anything but draw a map of vole mess. I can't think of a more boring animal than voles. In fact, I hate voles. As I picked up my pen and paper, I imagined the little furry creatures scuttling around in dark, musty tunnels beneath me.

continued on next page

continued from previous page

"Not bad," I said to myself as I looked at the finished map. Voles are a bit like us; they keep large stores of food, leave their garbage in big piles, and have their roads going every which way, all over the place. I found a huge pile of knobby old roots tucked away in the corner of the garden bed. I had always thought that voles were insectivores, but here they were storing roots and chomping tree bark. I read that, like other rodents, voles are herbivores, or plant eaters. I also read that voles are the most prolific animals on earth. I began to think that voles are actually pretty interesting little animals. Did you know that kestrels can spot voles while flying over a field by using an infrared scope mechanism in their eyes to pick up the lines of the animals' urine along their most used tunnels? Another thing I found out is that voles have two different kinds of tunnels: one like a rain gutter in hard ground, and one that domes up above the ground's surface. I always thought that these domes were where voles had dug underneath the soil and pushed it up. But they are actually old tunnels filled in with dirt scooped out from new tunnels. I saved the best thing I discovered for last: There were two different kinds of scats lying around that garden bed. One was small and oval; this kind belonged to the voles. The other was a more twisted, windy, long scat; this one belonged to a weasel, probably a long-tailed weasel. And like many other meat eaters, weasels love voles. Because there was a latrine—a big pile of scat where an animal goes over and over, like a bathroom—weasels might have a den there. Imagine a weasel den right next to a family of voles. It would be like having an insane, bloodthirsty murderer who prowls outside your door at night for a neighbor.

Now, everywhere I go I see vole tunnels, both gutter and domed, all along the ground. And if I don't see them, I find myself looking for them. Does this mean that I've been stepping on these little vole villages all along? I wonder what else I've been squashing beneath my feet without noticing. It seems like voles have suddenly become very active ever since I did this mapping exercise, or maybe the mapping exercise wasn't so bad after all.

is air sculpting too. It is the most rudimentary form of communication—gestures combined with a basic intent—and it uses an ancient part of the brain.

BASIC SHAPES IN THREE DIMENSIONS

This exercise is a bit like shape charades. Find an ordinary household object—something static and small enough to air sculpt with two hands. Study the object until you have it memorized, and then air sculpt the object for your partner. Carefully "describe" the object using gestures of your fingers and hands. Repeat the process until your partner either gives up or guesses correctly. When you reveal the object, be prepared for some critical feedback. Listen carefully to this feedback, measure your performance against it, and, if necessary, make adjustments in your next air sculpting rendering session. The feedback will help you calibrate your air sculpting abilities.

Hint: While studying the object, try to picture it in your mind, and sense what it feels like to run your fingers and hands over its surface. Note things such as humidity and temperature and qualities such as "woody," "greasy," "plastic," or "metallic." This is key not only to air sculpting but also to storytelling and tracking.

PROGRESSING FROM FAMILIAR AND KNOWN
TO UNKNOWN ANIMALS

To air sculpt effectively, you have to be pretty familiar with the object. In the ancestral or native version of tracking, when did the natives master the skills of air sculpting? When did they have the opportunity to study the animals they air sculpted? The ability to model an animal in three dimensions requires a familiarity that comes only from handling the animal. This is easy for hunter-gatherers, who actually catch and handle the things they eat. In *The Great Dance,* three trackers study a small antelope that they confiscated from a cheetah. They spend considerable time working its joints, brushing its coat, and otherwise being serious naturalists. They are genuinely curious about this animal, even though they have probably handled the same species many times before.

This exercise series starts with a well-known animal—a pet cat or dog. You also need a partner, but this time it won't be charades as much as live critical feedback. As you sculpt one part of the animal, your partner looks at the pet, criticizes your rendering, and tells you how it needs adjusting. When you have done one or two parts of the anatomy, switch and let your partner sculpt for you. Eventually, take turns sculpting the entire animal in a variety of different positions or postures: sitting, lying down, upright and alert, lying down on one side or the other, and standing. Be prepared to repeat the process.

For the next part of the exercise, pick an animal or bird from vivid memory and render it for your partner. This is like charades, but if your partner can't guess it, provide some hints about the fur, feathers, or scales. Then demonstrate—while envisioning these features as vividly as possible—the action of running your hand over them. You can even make the sounds or facial expressions you would make if you were really touching this animal or bird. Accept criticism from your partner to help calibrate and improve your air sculpting capability. There are three key things to remember: (1) envision these animals as if they were really present, even feeling the warmth or coolness of their bodies; (2) be open to criticism from your partner; and (3) repeat this exercise again and again until it starts to come together.

For the next part of the exercise, you will use field guides or nature videos to obtain the necessary data. But this time, you're going to add a fourth and fifth dimension to the animal or bird you're air sculpting. The fourth dimension is the surface features of the animal, such as its fur, feathers, or scales; the fifth dimension is the weight, density, and "personality" of the animal.

Using a field guide, determine the following information for each animal or bird you wish to render: size, including length and height; weight; habits; and habitat. Good photographs or illustrations of the features of the animal or bird you are studying are required. A video that shows this animal would also be helpful, especially if it portrays the fur, feathers, or scales of the study subject and shows it in motion.

Again, you'll need a partner. A measuring device, such as a yard-stick or tape measure, and a bathroom scale might come in handy.

To start, both you and your partner secretly pick a medium-sized animal or bird to be rendered (e.g., a gray squirrel to a coyote; a quail to a goose). Then each of you uses resources (field guides, videos) to study your subjects. When both of you are ready, begin the game.

One of you is the sculptor; the other is the guesser-critic, as before. Review the previous air sculpting exercises and apply what you learned here. Really pretend, earnestly, that the animal or bird is in the room. The more you use your imagination, the better for your storytelling and tracking abilities. Try to sense the body temperature of the subject; try to feel its vibrations and the twitches of tensing muscles; even smell the animal and hear its breathing or vocalizations while air sculpting. This may be a bit scary, as you are tapping into some serious power. You may even have vivid dreams or other interesting experiences as a result of this exercise.

For variety, repeat the exercise, but this time, alternate between light animals, such as a rabbit or chicken, and dense animals, such as a snapping turtle, groundhog, or river otter.

Another way to do this exercise is to picture the animal or bird standing on your open, upturned palms. For example, imagine a domestic cat standing with its forepaws on the palm of your right hand and its rear paws on the palm of your left hand. Only occasionally show your partner where its back or head would be. Lift and lower the forepaws or rear paws by raising or lowering your corresponding hands, and envision how the cat would respond to the challenge of shifting its weight, and make sure to try to catch it if it jumps off.

READING RUNS AND OTHER WEAR PATTERNS
J.Y.

Before getting to the exercise, I want to tell you a story. A friend of mine took me to visit a facility with nonreleasable wild animals, and the program director was kind enough to let me watch her bobcat for a while. After a few minutes of getting used to my presence, the bobcat chose to virtually ignore me and began to do what it apparently did quite often—pace over the wooden floorboards of its enclosure. It had worn the wood smooth and shiny where it habitually stepped.

This is the point of this exercise and this story: the bobcat had repeated the motions and turn-around maneuvers so often and so exactly that its paws fell exactly on the shiny spots. These shiny spots were arranged along the edges of the cage and on the turn-around platforms in a unique pattern. Had I seen the shiny spots in an empty cage, I might not have guessed that they were made by a bobcat. I almost certainly would not have seen the foot patterns and what the cat was doing, especially when making a U-turn. The animal kicked out its right rear leg during each turn-around on the left-hand platform, causing a shiny spot to form outside the pattern. All the other shiny spots corresponded to points below the bobcat's body while walking. Because of its placement, that kick-out spot looked out of place.

After watching the bobcat repeat this pattern about forty times, I thought I had it down. I closed my eyes and watched the cat do the same motions again and again in my mind. Then I would open my eyes and see whether I was right.

When I got home, I looked for the same patterns in an area that I knew a wild bobcat was using. And I found similarly sized worn spots in the grass and on the bare ground. After this, I begin to see these shapes again and again in a variety of habitats, and I could discern subtle compressions and wear patterns that had not quite formed runs yet.

Now it's time for a new exercise, which requires a partner, some journaling materials, and a video that shows several mammals moving in their most natural rhythms. You'll also need an area of habitat that you know contains the animal under study.

First, pick an animal. I'm going to use a raccoon for purposes of explanation, but it could be any animal that you can air sculpt effectively. It's important that you watch the raccoon walk about in its natural rhythm on the video again and again, until you can see it in your mind's eye making tracks in that rhythm. The natural rhythm of a raccoon determines its trail and run characteristics—the wear patterns that form in the forest.

Next, work with your partner to imitate this motion with your own body. Use air sculpting to shape the raccoon, and follow the raccoon with your hands as it moves across the ground again and again. Picture the characteristics of its trail and run that result from repetitive steps in the exact same places. Use all the good storytelling techniques from the previous exercises to enhance your visualizations, and use as many of your senses as possible.

Now take out your journal and draw a cross section of a raccoon run. Measure its approximate dimensions, including height and width, at both the top of the run (where its head would pass) and the bottom of the run (where its feet would pass). Describe what the run might look like on the substrate.

Answer these questions in the journaling process:

1. Would your animal walk around a low object, such as a log on the ground? Or would it step or jump over it?
2. Would the animal's run be wider at the top (head and shoulders) or at the bottom (feet)?

3. Would the paw or hoof characteristics create a "chopped" surface to the ground or a smooth, shiny surface?
4. Would the animal choose a quiet trail? Or would it happily
move through noisy substrate?
5. How would the animal relate to cover? Be specific.

Draw your predictions. Discuss your journal with your partner,
and describe to him or her what the subtle patterns would look like.
Now listen as your partner does the same. Help each other with good
questions and critiques.

For the next part of the exercise, go out into the forest or meadow—
preferably not a sandy area or a muddy riverbank. Here, you are not
looking for individual footprints or clear trails; you are looking for
the equivalent of the shiny, worn patches made by the captive bobcat.
The predictions you are making are based on the knowledge and experience you gained from the previous exercise involving what a moving
animal of a certain size, shape, weight, and other physical and personality characteristics would do to the surfaces and foliage it interacts
with on a consistent, habitual basis in its most natural rhythm on the
landscape.

Note your results, pick another animal, and try it again. This exercise challenges many parts of your mind, body, and senses. It is essential to test your hypothesis. Utilize one of the methods of trapping
tracks described in chapter 14. One simple way to find out what animal is using the run is to spread sand in its floor, pack it down (you
may even want to add water to get a nice firm consistency), and use a
stick or a board to smooth it out. Give the animals ample time to get
accustomed to a new patch of sand in their run. Before you know it, a
revealing track will appear in the run, giving away its maker.

10

Aging Tracks

Rain! whose soft architectural hands have power to cut
stones, and chisel to shapes of grandeur the very mountains.
—Henry Ward Beecher

T.M.

If you ever come upon a fresh track, there is always the possibility that the creator of the track is still lurking around. Almost without your knowing it, an ancient survival mode kicks in (depending on the animal, this could be a hunting instinct or a fight or flight response). Your movements become more exact, each step more carefully placed than the last. Or maybe you won't move at all, as your senses become magnetized to the surrounding landscape. Nuances of sound, smell, color, and texture become lucid. You feel as if something unforgettable and profound is teetering on edge, waiting to happen. Don't push this feeling away for fear of being wrong; this is the feeling that opens you up to the experience in the making.

This feeling has overtaken me many times while tracking. When I pay attention and slow down my mind and body, I often see the animal before it sees me, and I have the rare opportunity of observing a wild animal undisturbed by my presence. When I don't listen, I run the risk of stumbling onto the animal and sending it racing for cover. The following story is an example of a time when I had not only the feeling but also the visual clues (fresh tracks) to back it up.

I was collecting inventory data using CyberTracker software at the Ellicott Slough National Wildlife Refuge in Santa Cruz County under the direction of Ken Clarkson, an environmental education specialist. I had visited the location twice before but had been able to gather few data. The third time I visited was the morning after a douse of rain, which provided fresh tracks that were actually visible. Typically, the compacted earth of this place allowed only the sharp edges of deer hooves to make a mark, but this day would be different. I eagerly set out on the trail, seeking the delicate outlines of padded feet.

The first I came across was a bobcat track with a single blade of grass pressed neatly in the heel pad impression. The blade was still damp, and wet sand clung to its surface. Noon was approaching, and the day promised to be warm. The other blades of grass from the same clump, which hadn't been stepped on, were dry and springy. It wouldn't take long for a pliable piece of trampled grass to return to its light, upright state. From these observations, I concluded that the tracks were no more than thirty minutes old; more likely, they had been made only moments before my arrival. My mind traveled in the direction of the tracks to where I imagined the bobcat sitting hidden from the trail behind a thicket of coyote brush. The cat is nearby, I thought, but I'll probably never see it, even if it's just off the trail. I'd seen a bobcat hunting in an open field virtually disappear into the tall grasses, only to reappear on the other side. Unless you see one in the open, the bobcat's camouflage is quite crafty.

I was there to collect data, so I entered the fresh bobcat tracks through the CyberTracker sequence and supported my findings with a digital photograph. The next set of tracks was in mud at the edge of a puddle: a bobcat front and hind foot. The mud puddle was shaded by brush, and it was difficult to tell whether the tracks had aged. It was clear that they had been made after the rain of the previous night; there was no sign that raindrops had touched them, as the edges were still crisp. When tracks get a little bit of rain but are still visible, the edges appear rounded, even if the track has dried out. This is especially true of tracks in mud. I entered these tracks as fresh bobcat and realized that I was traveling in the same direction as the cat, which meant that I might find more of its prints for my data entry.

Around the next bend in the trail, I heard a deer feeding to the north under an oak tree hidden by coyote brush. From what I could hear, I suspected that there were two deer, so I spooked them out to determine the accurate number. One darted across a clearing, but the other remained hidden; I could hear the sound of leaves and twigs giving under its weight as it ran for thicker cover. On the south side of the trail 20 feet away, another dark form caught my eye. I thought for a moment that it was a fawn, but I quickly realized that it was too early in the season and I saw that it was actually a bobcat in a low crouch, which is a typical position for sneaking away or hunting. I was unsure

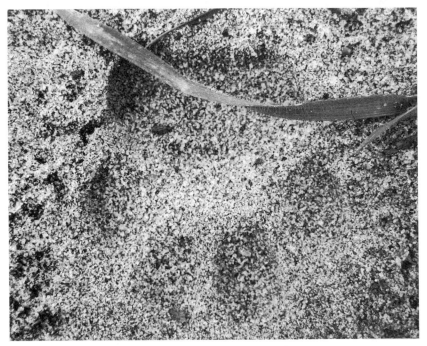

Bobcat tracks. After three hours, grass has sprung back out.

whether the bobcat had been crouching before it saw me; if it was already in a crouch, it might have been hunting the deer. (Later in the day, I came across the deer again and saw clearly that one was a yearling and the other an adult female. A bobcat would surely go after a fawn, but probably not a yearling.) Bobcats take down full adult deer—but often bedded.

The bobcat quickly regained its composure. Hidden behind a bush 15 feet from me, it proceeded to lick its paw. How typical of a cat, I thought, to act calm and collected even under pressure. I decided to take advantage of the opportunity and snap a shot of it with my digital camera. I picked my settings carefully and aimed, but the cat was too hidden. I had to move closer to jolt it out from behind the bush. There was a trail nearby, and I had a premonition that it would be the cat's route of choice. As I walked slowly toward the cat, I aimed the camera at this trail. When I intruded into the cat's comfort zone, it zipped out from behind the bush and onto the trail. Everything was going as planned, except that the camera took too long to focus, and all I got was the tail end of the cat. Despite missing the shot, I extracted from the experience valuable images of fresh animal tracks that were later confirmed with an actual sighting of the animal that made them. Two hours later, on my way out of the area, I passed that first fresh bobcat track I had seen on my way in. The blade of grass pressed into the heel pad had popped back out, and most of the sand had slipped into the floor of the track.

Depending on where you live, these experiences can be rare, but when they happen, they're well worth the effort. Aging tracks is a dynamic and challenging art, and you rarely receive affirmation from the animals themselves to support your speculations. The exercises in this chapter are designed to sidestep this limitation and provide you with an ample supply of aging experience, so that you can be reasonably certain of your observations. This requires an understanding of weather patterns, soils, and hydrology and how these contribute to the degradation of tracks and sign over time.

SETTING UP A WEATHER STATION

J.Y./T.M.

Knowing weather patterns is essential to aging tracks. Weather provides one of the best indicators of age, and knowledge of such things as wind direction and rain heightens your awareness of all things in nature, including but not limited to the age of a track, the behavior of an animal, the changing patterns of water sources, and plant growth and fruit production.

A weather station on your property is an ideal way to keep an accurate record of the weather in your area. News weather reports are often unreliable. For example, where we live, there are microclimates within the neighborhood; it can be raining three blocks from my house but not a drop on my street. Your weather station can be an electronic device or the combination of a thermometer, barometer, rain gauge, wind indicator (wind sock), and hygrometer (instrument for measuring humidity). The setup of your weather station is up to you, but when it's complete, you should be able to record these five things: temperature, wind direction, rainfall, barometric pressure, and humidity. If you regularly track at the beach or other tidal zone, be sure to include accurate tidal information in your weather journal.

To familiarize yourself with your station, record weather data once in the morning and again in the evening. Try placing the station in different locations around your house, but keep it convenient, or you might find yourself using it less than you had hoped. Check your data against local weather reports.

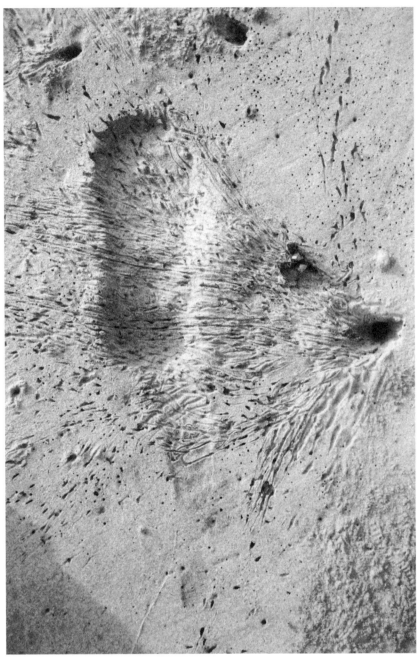

Ghost crab tracks on a beach in Saladita, Mexico, created below the high-tide mark in the evening after much human use during the afternoon.

Fresh snake track on a well-traveled dirt road. Notice the aged tracks of passing vehicles under the snake track.

{Weather Journal Entry}

Date: 5/29/02

Time: 8:45am Location: Raynes Neck, Maine

T: 55°   H: 100%

W-D: East   B: 30

W-mph: 5   L: ⬤ new moon

P: Rain last night with thunder and lightning. Today scattered showers

C: Complete

O: A raccoon ran off with the chicken feed in the middle of the night.

KEY TO ABBREVIATIONS:
- T=TEMPERATURE/TREND ❀ W-D=WIND DIRECTION
- W-MPH=WIND SPEED ❀ H=HUMIDITY
- B=BAROMETRIC PRESSURE ❀ L=LUNAR PHASE
- P=PRECIPITATION TREND ❀ C=CLOUD COVER DECRIPTION
- O=OBSERVATIONS OF WILDLIFE

To get you started, we've included a sample weather journal on page 287 that you can either photocopy or use as a reference to create your own weather journal template. The template we've created allows for three weather journal entries each day. Your skill in aging tracks will improve significantly if you journal the weather morning, noon, and night. Also provided is a sample of a single entry and a key to the abbreviations.

THE ART AND SCIENCE OF AGING TRACKS

When you consider all the aspects of tracking, determining when a track was made has to be the most challenging. Tracking involves the investigation of an infinite number of intersecting variables. As trackers, we comb through as many of the familiars as we can; then we isolate the unknowns and work at each until it becomes known to us or we give up trying. The study of track aging is tedious and requires a lot of work to limit the variables to a manageable number.

USE YOUR SIT SPOT AND STUDY AREA

Tracks in different substrates age differently. Substrates also vary widely and include everything from solid granite to frost on grass. In between are dry, damp, and wet sand; dry, damp, and wet garden soil; dry, damp, and wet clay; dry, damp, and wet oak leaves; dry, damp, and wet loam; and so on. What is a tracking student to do?

Since you're going to your sit spot every day or to your tracking areas on a rotating basis, you can take advantage of these routines, routes, and cycles by marking the ground with a stick in a variety of substrates. The strategy for learning differential aging rates is easy: make a track in dry sand and mark the time and date; make a track in clay and mark the time and date; journal the aging process of these two tracks over days, weeks, months, or years.

Don't mark too many places; ten to twenty different substrates will do. Then just watch how the marks degrade over time. Those in sun will degrade at different rates than those in shade. Wind, dampness, and slope also affect how tracks age, so integrate these variables in your study marks.

Journal each mark as you make it, indicating the date and time and numbering the stations so that you can remember where they are. The next time you pass a station, make another mark far enough away from the first so it isn't distorted, but close enough to get roughly the same substrate conditions. Journal the fresh mark and note the differences between them. You may even want to take a digital photo.

Do this each day you visit the place, and note how things change. After a while, you can make new marks less often, such as after rainstorms, before heavy frosts, or whenever an event dramatically affects the substrate and aging conditions.

AGING YOUR OWN TRACK

This exercise was developed in part by Paul Houghtling for the Shikari Tracker Training Program. Using your own track takes away the guesswork, because the footprint is easy to find, and you'll know exactly when it was made.

Morning Session

Put on your favorite pair of shoes and head out to a clear patch of soil. When you arrive at your destination, make some notes about the weather in your weather journal. Your observations here need not be too technical, so this should take only a couple of minutes.

Next, make a track in the clear soil. After you have removed your foot from the track, use a stick to mark both the toe and the heel so that you can find the edges of the track later on. Similarly, in an area where the ground doesn't show tracks as clearly, such as grass or forest debris, make another track. Mark the edge of your toe and heel for this track as well.

Study each of these tracks and make sketches of them. Spend only about five minutes looking at each track and ask yourself, What about this track tells me that it's fresh? Study how the grains of sand or mud are pressed together. Note how the edges of the track are piled up. What about moisture? What is the color of the track compared with that in the area around it? Note where the substrate is compressed and where it's not. What happened to any sticks, grasses, or leaves in the track? Are they crushed, broken, or bent?

Evening Session

In the evening, put on the same shoes you wore in the morning and head back to the tracking site. Once again, make some notes about the weather. Next to the track in the clear soil, make another track. Don't step on the track that you made this morning, though, because we are going to compare your newest track with the track from this morning. Taking only five minutes, study these two tracks and compare them. Make another sketch of your track from the morning. Consider the same questions and note what has changed in the older track. Is it still the same color? Are there raindrops in the track now? It's likely that some of the edges that piled up around the track have dried some and crumbled into the bottom of the track.

Repeat this process for the track in the less clear ground. Can you still find the track you made this morning? It may be hard to find, especially if the grass has sprung up again. What would happen to the ground here if people or animals continually stepped on it? Take five minutes for your study of this track, and then head home.

You can keep returning to this place indefinitely and adding new tracks for age comparison. Once you've practiced this with your own foot, it's time to find a fresh animal track. The best way to do this is to observe the animal making it. With a permanent pen, write the date on a Popsicle stick and place one stick in the back of the track and another in the front. Return to the marked track occasionally and journal the weather conditions and the changes you see in the track.

AGING TRACK AND SIGN

J.Y.

This exercise is designed to be done at your sit spot, at the tracking areas you've adopted, or at any other place you visit at least several times a week. The longer you can keep going to the same place, the better. Ideally, this kind of knowledge is accumulated over several years of living, tracking, and exploring in one area—like in the old days, when people tracked as part of their everyday lives and lived in one place for all or most of their lives. The ability to tell the age of track and sign accurately can be gained only through repetition and experience, especially in the same place.

When I arrive at a new location, or if I haven't been to a favorite spot in a while, my ability to age tracks and sign with any certainty is diminished. That is to be expected. The ability to age tracks and sign is related to seeing the same places every day—the same tracks, the same scat and other sign—along with noting local changes in vegetation and substrate, new growth, and the effects of weather on substrate and landscape.

For this exercise, be prepared to make a commitment of several months, concentrating on just a few species. This shouldn't take more than a few minutes of regular observation and journaling, however. Results are seen over months—not consecutive hours.

Here is a summary of the individual steps. An explanation of each follows.

1. Find the circuit
2. Set up the aging stations
3. Map the circuit and stations
4. Make baseline observations
5. Visit the circuit on a regular basis
6. Develop specific questions—focused on a few species
7. Journal the results

Finding the Circuit

Choose a route that you take all the time anyway. Include your yard, your neighborhood, and your place of work if you have too.

These should be places that you are already frequenting as part of your daily life, because if you set up a circuit just for this exercise, you will quickly grow bored.

Keep the circuit simple and not too long. You will be setting up a dozen or so stations along the way. The goal of the stations is to provide a wide variety of substrate study opportunities (different soil, clay, sand, gravel, leaf litter, and the like), as well as different slopes and aspects (for study of solar exposure) and different types of exposure to rain, wind, and other forces of erosion and degradation. Over time, you will develop little subcircuits that you visit sometimes but not on a daily basis. Don't be too strict with yourself, or the exercise won't be fun.

Here's a description of my circuit, as an example: My main circuit includes a quick visit to the creek in my backyard (about 20 yards from the door), then along a trail beside the creek, along the edge of the yard, across the street, and into the woods. This includes three stations so far. One is the muddy bank of the creek for a few yards; raccoons, rats, squirrels, and songbirds use this area regularly, so I watch their tracks and sign change. I also see human tracks in varying degrees of wetness in the mud and clay along the edge of the creek. In the woods, there is a station just at the entrance to the forest and another one just inside the edge along the trail. It is drier there and loamier. There are squirrel tracks and deer tracks, along with horseback riders and their dogs and sometimes bicycle tires. I watch all these in my three places.

The trail intersection is the next station. I have gone a total of 40 yards now. It takes only twenty minutes at most, even if I dawdle along the creek. My sit area is the next station, where I am the animal under study. As I sit, I also study the worm castings as they age. I look at the fresh ones. I consider the dew, the mist, the rain, the dampness of the soil. Here it is not as loamy as back at the edge of the forest. The soil is a bit denser here, darker, richer, yet more compact. I watch this soil and the leaf litter, as well as the little plants growing, but not too closely.

When I am up and walking again, I head down the old wagon road. The wagon road is similar to the rest of the circuit, although there is one stretch where the soil holds moisture longer because the hill tips to the north, away from solar exposure. The forest canopy is more complete here, too. The forest composition is changing slightly. Lessons in differential aging for the same bicycle tires, horse riders, and dogs are available here, as I have been following the same trail they did. I also watch my own tracks from previous days. Every once in a while, I make a new track to study against the older ones. I also have a good idea of when the squirrel tracks were made, and I watch these age over subsequent visits.

Generally, I'm not stopping, only slowing down and looking. Occasionally I stop, bend, and look more carefully, especially if something looks new or strange. I let my curiosity lead me, but I always have good questions in my mind to guide my inquiry.

I have been walking just thirty minutes total (not including the stopover at my sit spot). As I approach the locust grove area, the soil changes dramatically, with sandy places and red soil. There are just a few more stations I will visit today.

Setting Up Stations

What makes a good station? Stations should measure only a few square yards at most. Most important, there must be tracks or sign there that age. These can be tracks you make or tracks left by animals. Deer trails, where they cross our walking paths, make great stations. Sometimes a deer run crosses a human run in an obvious way, with daily traffic on both. These are great spots if you want to know how deer tracks age over time.

A mud puddle or creek bank can be a good station. Having regular visitors (besides you) is helpful. For instance, if there are no deer tracks along the puddle station on Monday but you return on Wednesday and find deer tracks there, you have to wonder whether they were made yesterday, the day before, or today. Now you have a question to guide you. You can experiment and see what changes in the deer trail over time. You can set up several deer track stations over a series of substrates along your favorite route.

If an animal leaves a scat along the trail and you notice that there are other scats of varying ages, make this a station. The first time you study this place, you will know for sure only that the fresh one is fresh and the rest of them are older. Over time (perhaps months), you will see the older ones disintegrate while new ones are deposited for your further study. Feeding sign also makes good station material.

Stations should also cover changes in soil; exposure to wind, rain, and sun; and other elements. Focus on just a few stations for the first few months. And you can look at everything at your stations, but focus on just a few species—ten or so. Don't overwhelm yourself with too much too soon.

Mapping the Circuit and Stations

Draw a map of your circuit, using symbols to represent the stations; include a key to explain symbols. Write questions in your journal, and index them to the map. Each time you visit a station, adjust the map. Your map will evolve as your understanding of the place grows, so you may want to redraw the map from time to time. If the circuit is in your sit area, you can include your observations in your field inventory map and journal.

Making Baseline Observations

Make sketches and write brief descriptions of the area. For example, describe the substrate, the moisture content, the clay versus sand content. Describe the animal track and sign present when you start, and try to count individuals. More than anything, this journaling process helps to ferret out questions and focus your initial observations.

Visiting on a Regular Basis, Developing Questions, and Journaling

Visit the circuit as often as possible, and journal your observations. Make sketches of changes and details from time to time, but keep it simple. Remember, you want to move along your circuit and not get caught up in too much detail. Don't keep adding questions; keep your initial deer track question alive over time. Test yourself. Are you getting better at telling the age of deer tracks? When you feel that you have exhausted this question, add another. When you have a few questions, drop the oldest one, but first journal what you learned from it.

Adjusting the Exercise for Long-term Observations

After working on a circuit for a few months, add some new animals; add a few new stations and remove one or two old ones; change the circuit a bit, but not too much. Then, revisit this exercise. When three months are up, you can decide whether you want to continue.

11

Bird Language

Birds, for the people of this great bush country, had many magical properties. For example, they were thought to know the secret of all living things, to have great foresight and to fill with wisdom the hearts of those who took the trouble to learn their language and listen.

—Laurens van der Post
A Story Like the Wind

J.Y.

The language of nature is told in stories. The land, the water, the weather, the plants, and the time of day form the context. Similarly, bird and animal stories fit together to tell a story that is surprisingly discernible by anyone who takes the time to watch and listen. The fascinating work of animal behaviorists concurs. Over the past twenty-five years, I have been helping others learn bird and animal language, thereby expanding their understanding of tracking.

Most of us think of good tracking substrate as moist sand, fresh mud, shallow snow, or deep dust. But I consider bird and animal voices a form of good substrate as well. The key to understanding this substrate is routine exposure to the same birds and animals, along with applied awareness. This can result in the ability to read this living substrate analogous to reading the detail in the best track substrates.

Bird owners tell stories of their pets recognizing the arrival of individual family members and announcing this in a way that others can understand. Field biologists and animal behaviorists are finding similar abilities. Prairie dogs have been proven to respond to individual coyotes in measurable and specific ways. They can recognize individuals among hawks, humans, and even nonpredatory species such as bison and cows, and they can remember an individual human for up to two months and still say that person's "name" in prairie dog

Identifying bird tracks and sign will show you whether a bird is in the area—understanding their language can help you discover who else is in the area.

Pellet of American Crow.

language. They can even say whether a person is carrying a gun, according to animal behaviorist Con Slobodchikoff of Northern Arizona University.

Learning to understand the basics of bird and animal language requires asking the right questions. All bird and animal language is a departure from what is normal, expected, or baseline. We need to experience baseline ourselves before we can learn bird and animal language well. To learn this language is to take the time to sit and watch and then share stories with others to expand beyond ingrained perceptions and beliefs. Not much has been published on learning bird language, so it takes persistence to master this skill.

The process of learning bird language requires specific routines: sitting in the same place, walking slowly and quietly, watching the animals and birds, asking many questions, reviewing observed events. Repeating these activities will help you to get to know a few birds very well. From direct observation, you will learn about their world, their food, their enemies, and their boundaries with others of their kind. You will learn how they relate to other creatures around them, including you. Start with birds close to your home and those that inhabit your favorite tracking haunts. Figure out which ones are likely to be most affected by the mammals you like to track, and learn their habits and calls well. Over time, this will add new dimensions to your tracking experience, and soon you'll be surprised by the accuracy of your theories about their language.

Science is just beginning to study some specific instances of bird and animal language, but the indigenous peoples of the world have long studied and passed on important and practical aspects of this communication system. Several of my mentors in tracking helped me decipher bird and animal language, which is a great substrate for studying the movement and passage of other creatures. Although this language is not limited to alarms indicating a predator's approach or presence, that type of bird or animal language is the easiest and most obvious place to start.

USING BIRD LANGUAGE TO WIN AT HIDE-AND-SEEK

In his writings, expert big-game tracker Jim Corbett wonders how people can be surprised by a tiger or a leopard in daylight when the whole forest knows its precise whereabouts based on the language of birds, deer, monkeys, and other creatures. No mammal larger than a squirrel or a rat—even nonpredators such as deer or wild pigs—can make a move without being "talked about." Crows, jays, ravens, hawks, and owls cannot move without someone saying something that can be understood by a listener and observer of nature. Even humans cause a reaction that can be understood to a surprisingly refined degree.

When I was in my teens, I had been tracking for several years and enjoyed the challenge of trailing deer. I liked to look for the freshest deer tracks in the damp soil of the creek banks or the bottomlands between streams. I would follow the trail left by a deer only hours or even minutes earlier until I got close enough to detect its motions by the sound of sticks breaking and the sight of bushes moving. My mentor encouraged me to learn the language of birds, squirrels, and chipmunks to enhance my ability to trail deer. Because I used a stealthy approach while tracking, initially, the deer weren't sure whether I was following them, so their first response to my quiet and slow approach was to sneak away with their tails held tight against their hindquarters. (I call this "ghosting," and it is very obvious in their tracks and trails.) Eastern forests have a good complement of sentinel species such as chipmunks and jays that are happy to tell everyone around about any suspicious behavior. So all I had to do was consider the shape of the basin the deer were in, the patterns I had seen them take in the past, their most recent trajectory, and the new data from the jays and chipmunks, and I could cut the deer's path at a good angle and actually ambush them as they passed.

The combination of trailing fresh sign and track on the ground and using bird language is an ancient and respected skill. With this method, I have successfully trailed weasels, minks, otters, raccoons, bears, rats, bobcats, domestic cats, wild cats, domestic dogs, gray and red foxes, cougars, elk, black-tailed deer, mule deer, moose, wolves, coyotes, and humans. The language of birds and animals offers many opportunities to expand our tracking horizons.

COOPERATIVE NEIGHBORS?

When learning both tracking and bird language, asking questions is key. Research based on the observation of patterns determines which questions are most relevant. The relentless pursuit of the answers to these questions, coupled with observations and testing, can unlock patterns in most aspects of the natural world. Following is a good story from my friend Scott that points out a potential pattern in bird and animal language. This story is interesting because the characters are all "invaders" from other lands and have not had very long to "evolve" their behaviors. It is astonishing how fast birds and animals learn things from one another and how well they retain that knowledge.

On the northern side of one of the Hawaiian Islands, there is a community of small farms that yield downslope to some impressive cliffs and the Pacific Ocean beyond. One day while Scott was out tending his small organic farm, he heard some enticing bird language. He had already learned some bird language basics and had been practicing his awareness by using the sit spot routine. He was aware of the normal, or baseline, patterns of the birds around his farm. He also knew which birds could be expected around his place, so he noticed when there was a break in this pattern.

Loud, incessant, staccato sounds were coming from a group of birds moving in a spherical pattern. This "ball of activity" was about 20 feet in diameter. The birds were moving up and down from the lower shrubs about 6 feet above the ground up to the telephone wires about 20 feet high. There were three species present at first: Mejiros (also called Japanese White-eyes), Northern Cardinals, and Mynahs. But their sounds and behaviors apparently drew a Northern Mockingbird from the valley to the south. It made a beeline toward the fray of bird sound and motion, to a place where Scott had never seen this species before.

Scott arrived on the scene at about the same time that another bird joined the ball of bird activity. This one came from the same road that the mockingbird had followed in, but the new arrival came from the north. It was a Barn Owl. In broad daylight, the owl flew straight to the center of the sphere of alarmed birds. It looked over both shoulders quickly but steadily, looked down to the ground in the middle of the ruckus, and plunged from a mango tree branch into the 4-foot-high California grass. Suddenly, the bird language changed from noisy and demonstrative to quiet, and all the birds flew off in different directions—not alarmed at all. It was as if the birds said, "Okay, it's handled. Let's get back to our lives."

Scott spent some time trying to approach the owl in the tall grass to get a look at the reason for the alarm, which the owl now seemed to have possession of. Although he tried to be as quiet as he could, the owl took off, flying more or less straight up from the grass, and made considerable noise doing so. The owl winged away down the valley, and Scott moved into its landing place, hoping for a warm track to study. What he found was even better. There on the ground was the largest male rat body Scott had ever seen. The corpse was headless, however, for the owl had decided to eat dessert first. Mystery solved.

The pattern Scott described in this story is a parabolic alarm—usually offered to nest robbers. This phenomenon is something you can see and hear on the mainland during nesting season in response to the arrival of a jay, squirrel, raven, or crow. I have seen this so many times that, at least in my own area, I can usually identify the nest robber by the bird language "signature." In other words, I can tell one nest robber from another by the combination of bird sound and motion, the size of the sphere, its height, its location, the time of day, and the season. It helps to spend a lot of time in one place observing the daily patterns throughout the seasons.

TELEMETRY AND BIRD LANGUAGE: SIDE-BY-SIDE TECHNOLOGIES

One afternoon, I received an emotional phone call: "My goat has been killed by a mountain lion. The man from the state wants to kill the lion. Please come over quickly. I don't want the lion harmed."

This was becoming a familiar story. I knew that the lion's life was probably nearing its end. As mountain lions were finding their way into neighborhoods that were once forest and meadow, interaction between people and their pets and these shy predators were on the rise in western Washington. Here, the foothills of the Cascades roll out into river valleys, carrying glacier melt across spawning beds for salmon and feeding zones for bears and eagles. People also find these lands attractive. The new neighborhoods and the slightly older farms have caused a new population dynamic in these second-growth forests of Douglas fir and western red cedar. The ground is densely carpeted with fern fronds and tangled with a variety of shrubs, salmonberries, and vine maples. This is not easy country to track in, and having bird language skills is an advantage when trying to determine the movements and whereabouts of bobcat, deer, bear, and coyote. And once in a while, a cougar story emerges.

When I arrived at the little farm, I went to the scene of the goat's struggle for survival. Upon investigating, I discovered that the original story related by the onlookers was a bit different from what I was seeing. I found the place where the goat had been jumped by the cougar. The goat then flailed around with the cat on its back; this slammed the full weight of the goat (a big one weighing well over 150 pounds) against a large fir tree that had metal-wire fencing around its base to keep horses and other livestock from damaging it. Quite a bit of lion fur got stuck on the sharp ends of the fence, leaving evidence to match the deeply dug-in hoof marks of the goat, slanting with great pressure toward the tree.

The goat then broke into a trot and moved away from the tree for a few sets of tracks. Suddenly, the cat's weight appeared again on its back. This time, the goat's feet splayed out to the left and right, and it faltered and fell. In this spot, it voided the contents of its lower intestines and left a scent that I think of as the "smell of death." I have found it where wolves brought down an elk or a deer, where lions made their kills, and where coyotes killed a yearling black-tailed deer. This was a clue I used to find the actual kill site versus the place where the carcass is found. These are often two different locations, especially with mountain lions. I once trailed a mountain lion dragging a black-tailed deer from such a scented place and found the carcass more than three-quarters of a mile up a steady grade rising a few feet every 10 yards.

This time, the lion had made its kill and then dragged the goat to where it was still lying, a distance of about 15 yards. There was no feeding sign on the limp carcass. The lion, apparently disturbed by the home owner, left the carcass and jumped to the top of an 8-inch fence post about 6 ½ feet high, where it paused. The lion stayed there for a second or so and then dropped down onto the forest side of the fence, leaving clear impressions in the soft, mossy earth of its four feet supporting its 135-pound body. From there, it seemed to move off to the south and east through the ferns. I didn't cross the fence to see where it went for two reasons: it was a tall wire fence, and I thought I might bend it, and there was some intense bird language issuing from beneath a large cedar tree, concentrated at the ground among the ferns. Winter Wrens were alarming, along with a robin and some other smaller birds—perhaps a White-crowned Sparrow. The alarm was similar in shape to the "sphere" or "ball of birds" described in Scott's story, but less intense. Nest robbers get more attention than mountain lions.

At this point, the biologist appeared at the scene, and I shared my interpretation of the lion's trail and the goat's demise. We both asked some open-ended questions and let some things just hang in the air— as all trackers, naturalists, and biologists like to do—and then we began to discuss lion behavior in situations like this. The biologist, who was very experienced with mountain lions in this area, had put a radio collar on this particular cat. It already had a short history of domestic animal depredation and was now on a careful monitoring program to determine whether it could get back on its normal diet of raccoons, deer, and the occasional coyote and stay away from dogs, cats, and other domestic animals. Up until now, it had gone for weeks without straying from its natural diet, but this large, fat goat may have been too tempting to resist.

The biologist had decades of experience tracking mountain lions with radiotelemetry. He explained that in many situations, lions lie quite still and hold cover until the last possible moment. I asked, "How close have you gotten to them before they bolt? Could one be as close as that cedar?" I pointed to the center of the bird alarm sphere there among the ferns. He assured me that this was highly possible and went to get his telemetry equipment. The bird alarm stayed active for the entire five minutes it took for him to go to his truck and back and continued while he set up his antenna and receiver. He pointed it at the cedar tree and got a very strong signal; he replaced the antenna with a smaller homemade one he used for close range and verified that the cougar was at the base of the cedar tree among the ferns.

When the houndsman arrived with his dogs to tree the cat for tranquilizing and potential relocation, the bird alarms took on a more frenzied tone. The lion was apparently getting nervous at the sounds of new voices, the whining dogs, and the impending chase. The tension in the air was palpable. One of my tracking associates, Alex, was now working with this team as a volunteer, and he directed the houndsman to the cedar tree. By the time the dogs arrived at the tree, the alarm had moved off to the right, followed by the birds. We never saw the cat, although we could clearly see the ferns where the dogs picked up the scent from its hiding bed. Song Sparrows joined the alarm a bit farther west, and a number of other birds added their voices as the cat moved at a brisk pace away from the approaching hounds.

When the dogs arrived at the base of the cedar tree, they began to bay loudly for the first time, breaking their previous pattern of whines and tentative barks. The houndsman worked toward the south, pulling against the dogs; I waved to Alex and pointed toward the bird alarms moving west. Convinced by Alex's urging, the dogs and men followed the lead of the alarming birds. Once on this trajectory, the hounds went into continuous baying until their voices disappeared in the distance.

Based on their direction and speed, I guessed that they might come out on the road on the other side of the forest. Getting into my car, I drove in that direction and arrived in time to see the biologist's graduate assistant carrying the anesthetized, unconscious cougar out of the forest slung over his shoulders. I followed the pickup truck back to where we had started. Once we arrived, the young male cat was weighed, measured, and given a general physical examination.

On this day, old and new technologies in tracking and fieldwork came together in the study of conservation in suburban corridors.

BASELINE BEHAVIOR VERSUS SHIFT OUT OF BASELINE

To understand patterns of disturbance, you must first understand what is usual. These are what I call baseline patterns in nature. Birds and animals that are not disturbed and not worried about predation are usually engaged in maintenance or resting behaviors. Get to know what these are for your sit spot. Baseline patterns include feeding, preening, dust bathing, water bathing, drinking, playing, and resting. Don't mistake sentinel behavior for resting. Birds on high alert in a position that gives them a view of the landscape are not resting. Actual resting is usually accompanied by fluffed up feathers (or fur in mammals), sunny or shady places, and napping.

All animals and birds would rather be in baseline—a state of rest and low energy output. Many behavior strategies and territory choices are a result of the need to conserve energy by feeling protected. When birds or animals shift out of baseline to avoid danger, they may lose some of their awareness powers because of anxiety and anticipation. In addition, the sounds they make when anxious seem to attract attention from predators and mobbing animals such as jays and squirrels. This puts the predators in a better position. Animals and birds avoid anxiety states if they can, so early detection of potential danger is important to them. Maintaining baseline is key to both early detection and energy conservation.

Baseline for birds can be surprisingly rare and short-lived, especially in a land rich in hawks and owls, bobcats and foxes, weasels and other nest robbers. A list of the possible predators that could disrupt songbird baseline would be quite long. In my area in California, there are more than a dozen constant threats in most songbird territories. And keep in mind that most predators in the bird world are much larger, stronger, and faster than their prey. It's a tough existence to be a songbird.

When you are studying bird language, analyze baseline patterns, areas of song, and baseline maintenance behaviors and make a mental map that you constantly update. These patterns will shift as predators and other threats move and as the time of day and time of year change.

THE FIVE VOICES OF THE BIRDS

There are generally four baseline voice patterns among songbirds that are heard during maintenance behaviors. The fifth voice is alarm. (My audio series, *Seeing through Native Eyes,* contains many more details about learning the five voices of birds and developing a list of bird species to study.) Although this is a simplification of bird vocalizations for the sake of field study, the five voices of birds are:

1. Song
2. Companion or contact call
3. Territorial aggression
4. Begging
5. Alarm

Song is the sound birds emit to establish territories and to attract and keep mates. The companion or contact call is given between members of the same species, or sometimes among a feeding guild; it keeps the birds in contact as they lose sight of one another in thickets while feeding.

Territorial aggression can sound like alarm, but generally when one bird is vocalizing or acting aggressively toward another member of its own species, the others ignore them. This situation is usually limited to males fighting for turf or one bird driving others off a feeder.

Begging calls are usually given during feeding forays. Sometimes, however, young, inexperienced birds continue to beg even when a real threat is near. In most cases, there will be no second chance to learn from this experience. Predators feed *their* young with inexperienced beggars.

Alarm can be anything from mild annoyance to extreme fright. It is vocalized as well as expressed behaviorally through position and body language. When a bird sounds a true alarm, the call can go across species and even from birds to mammals and back again, and it can extend over hundreds of yards. With enough experience, one can see the approach of danger over many miles, especially with a good view of the landscape. Because the sound and motion of the bird alarm call can tell a lot to a tracker who understands the language, the rest of this chapter is devoted to alarms.

THE ALARM ZONE

Alarms often take the shape of circles (spheres), with the source of danger at the center. The alarm zone always has a dynamic shape, size, and height. Start looking for these dimensions and plot them in your tracking journal.

Sometimes you will find an island of alarm in the midst of baseline (parabolic alarm, discussed later): birds singing and feeding as far as you can see in the treetops and middle canopy, but an intense bird alarm—measuring only 10 yards in diameter and 10 yards high—in the shrub layer from several songbird species.

The height of baseline and the height of alarm are revealing. If a predator is on the ground, bird language hovers near the ground. If the predator is in the air, the bird language originates in the air, dives for cover, and then maintains some degree of silence. Carefully analyze where the pressure seems to come from. In many cases, there may be a ground predator prowling about, but the treetop birds are singing and feeding without a care in the world. Likewise, birds on the ground may be in baseline when there is some disturbance up high that doesn't matter to the ground dwellers. Plot this from a side view in your journal, next to the maps showing the size and overall reach of baseline and alarm.

ALARM DYNAMICS
Speed of the Disturbance

For ground predators, it is relatively easy to figure out how fast the source of alarm is traveling; this may take a little more practice for fast-flying predators. Keep in mind that some birds have small territories and don't follow predators too far past their own boundaries. Others have large territories and seem to follow predators all day. For instance, you may be watching an alarm moving along a hedge at about the speed of a slow-walking cat. The Common Yellowthroat alarms at one edge of the hedge, moves about 10 yards, and then stops. The Song Sparrow picks up the alarm just before the yellowthroat stops. The jay follows all the way (a moving parabolic alarm, discussed later). This allows you to estimate the speed of the unseen predator beneath. If it's moving at the speed of a slow-walking cat, it may just be a slow-walking cat.

Fast-flying predatory birds tend to enter the scene like the break shot in a game of billiards. Birds scatter everywhere in a panic; there is a spray of birds at the end of the hawk's trajectory (a bird plow, discussed later).

Intensity of Body Language, Movement, and Vocalization

Watch for intense body language while listening to the sounds of alarm. In general, the intensity of behavior—measured by volume, phrasing, pitch, tempo, and motion—is directly proportional to the level of threat. This response intensity can also be overloaded to the point of sudden and complete silence (oppression, discussed later).

The "Shape" of Bird Alarm Behaviors

Notice the arrangement of alarming birds. This can be both static and dynamic. If there is a static nest robber in a tree, the birds tend to form a sphere, keeping a safe distance from the threat. These shapes can also move. In time, and with enough practice, alarm shapes will become "visible" to your ears as well as your eyes. You will even be able to tell the difference between crows mobbing a Great Horned Owl and the same crows mobbing a Red-tailed Hawk. The key is the subtlety of the dynamics and shape of the alarm.

Assessing All Possible Sources of Alarm

Knowing in advance what animals or birds cause which alarm shapes really pays off. So get out your field guides and study them to determine what predators are in the area where you'll be studying bird language. The sources of alarm create reactions that take certain patterns and fall into certain categories, based on the predator's hunting strategies.

Birds

Raptors that excel in chasing down songbirds (accipiters)
Raptors that catch birds opportunistically (harriers, Red-
    shouldered Hawks, kites)
Owls (some are bird eaters, such as Pygmy Owls)
Soaring raptors (eagles and buteos)
Falcons (wide variety of behaviors between kestrels and
    peregrines)
Corvids and nest robbers (jays, magpies, crows, ravens)

The more intense a bird's reputation with the local songbirds, the greater the alarm response. This can be based on species, but it can also be based on specific, localized behaviors of an individual. For instance, most Red-tailed Hawks don't worry local songbirds, but occasionally an individual hawk develops skill in hunting pigeons and doves, so in that territory, a redtail causes alarm among songbirds.

Mammals and Other Wildlife

Nest robbers (rat, opossum, skunk, raccoon, pig, bear, cat, squirrel, snake, lizard)

Dog family (fox, coyote, wolf, domestic dog)

Cat family (bobcat, lynx, cougar, feral cat, domestic cat)

Larger mammals (usually ungulates; can cause alarm when sneaking)

Snakes (specifically, those that eat birds and mammals)

Humans (many types of behavior)

In the case of mammals, as in the case of birds, individual reputations can vary within a species, even in a given backyard. For instance, some domestic cats are declawed or just not interested or not very good at hunting birds. Local birds know the difference. In contrast, feral cats have a much more intense reputation among songbirds.

As you begin to study the impact of humans, you will discover that different people cause different kinds of responses. For example, joggers cause different reactions than people dressed in full camouflage stalking deer.

HONING YOUR BIRD LANGUAGE SKILLS
Mapping

Map your observations from two points of view: top view and side view. Top view helps you see and hear bird language as it moves across the landscape and trains your senses to wake up. Side view helps you analyze the height of alarm and baseline, indicating likely sources of alarm.

Shared Observation and Corroboration

As in tracking, telling the story—that is, sharing your observations with others—helps you detect and recognize patterns. This process is critical. Some people even form practice groups, which can be very helpful. When I was learning tracking as a youngster, it was vital for me to have someone to share my observations with. With bird language, this is even more important, because you often need to have eyes in more places than is possible when you are alone.

When hearing, seeing, and otherwise sensing the language of nature, one is often left with a feeling of uncertainty in terms of possible interpretations. It is not always as easy as identifying an oak tree or recognizing the clear print of a dog in the mud. There may be no definitive answer for the tracker. However, there is still a need for corroboration—as there always is when adjusting our perceptions. Bird language is one of the most subtle aspects of tracking and therefore requires the greatest adherence to the scientific method. Group study and the corroboration afforded by many eyes and minds is the most helpful way to learn bird language. In hunter-gatherer societies, corroboration comes in the form of guiding questions from elders. Stories are shared by those who return from the field, and the group listens. Questions are asked; patterns are discovered and shared.

When you study on your own, it is important to record your observations of bird language, even if you don't know all the answers. Share these with others through storytelling or even e-mail. Our instincts to share and enjoy stories are part of our genetic makeup that enables us to learn valuable lessons that can potentially save our lives.

Repetition

It is important to return to the same sit area each time you exercise your bird language skills. That way, you will begin to see patterns emerge. For instance, you will notice bird territories and see that many of the same birds are present every time you go. You will note the territories of various species, how big they are, how many of each species are in the area, and other natural history features. You will develop a sense of familiarity with the landscape and its inhabitants that just isn't possible through reading and other forms of secondhand learning. Your tracking skills will be honed as you begin to detect track and sign of animals that you never see, and the bird and animal language will start to match that of the footprints, feeding sign, and scat left behind.

You receive important feedback from the animals and birds, from their behaviors and their tracks and sign, when you visit your spot on a daily basis, at all times of day and year, and in all kinds of weather. Patterns will emerge that reveal the regular habits and whereabouts of a variety of previously hidden forest creatures; track and sign help verify all this. Eventually, you will adjust your own way of moving and develop a low-impact strategy. You will become more attuned to the energy of life around you and how you contribute to that life. This is a valuable and enriching journey.

Research and Questions

When studying tracking and bird and animal language, there will often be times when you can't find the answers in any book, no matter how hard you look. Even Google will let you down. The questions that you ask and hold in your mind become like your best friends and mentors. These powerful vacuums of the senses drive your conscious and unconscious tracking until learning becomes a quest for knowledge and understanding.

THE SHAPES OF ALARM

The signature of alarm is the shape it takes with respect to how the species involved broadcasts the alarm and how the individuals behave when signaling one another. Each species of predatory bird, fish, reptile, and mammal—even swarms of bees or wasps—has a distinct alarm signature that can be detected, analyzed, and identified. Every person who moves about the landscape has a distinct alarm signature. When the moods of animals and people change, so does the alarm signature.

It is important to remember that not only reputation but also intent (indicated by body language and behavior) is key in causing an alarm response. For example, a well fed Cooper's Hawk with a full crop sitting on a telephone wire and preening causes little alarm. However, the same hawk hunting in the same territory can utterly silence the landscape for 100 yards or more. All the shapes listed below are the result of alarming intent and behavior, not resting or baseline behavior, of a species.

Bird Plow

When a great threat is sensed and it is approaching rapidly, birds move quickly and usually in the same direction. The bird plow is somewhat like the break in a game of pool, where one fast-moving ball strikes and scatters the others on the table. Analyze the shape and extent of this activity, and which animals and birds are involved, to determine the source. Possible sources are flying hawks (especially accipiters), charging dogs, and fast-walking people.

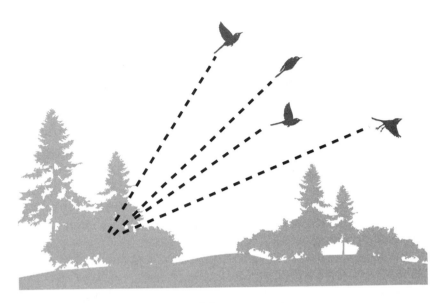

Bird plow: the shape and extent of the escape route.

Bullet

The bullet is a variation of the bird plow. The dynamics of this alarm shape indicate extreme danger to fleeing songbirds. This alarm shape usually represents the approach of a fast-flying bird hunter, such as a Sharp-shinned or Cooper's Hawk. It looks like a bullet moving through the landscape, scattering birds and animals along the way. When a bullet alarm is moving through suburbia, ditching behavior is the result.

Ditching

Ditching is often seen when a hawk approaches a backyard feeder, resulting in an explosive exit—the birds literally ditch themselves into bushes to hide. Ditching behavior often causes small birds to hit windows. When a Cooper's Hawk or a Sharp-shinned Hawk is in the neighborhood, small birds are usually hiding in the tightly branched shrubs along houses or between yards. During a visit from an accipiter, pigeons, blackbirds, robins, and other flocking songbirds may be seen flying in circles or in erratic patterns.

Sentinel

This is one of the most common patterns in bird language. Inexperienced observers often mistake sentinel behavior for resting. Birds are

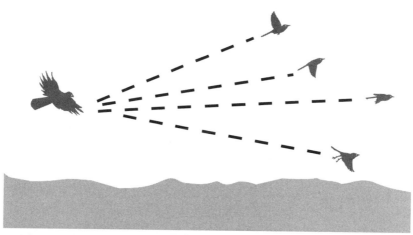

Bullet: shooting straight out like a bullet indicates extreme danger to the birds.

Ditching: birds take this evasive action in order to "ditch" themselves into hiding.

seen sitting very still, usually in high places where they can see danger or detect alarm signals that you may be unaware of. Sentinel is always a posture of alertness. Because many birds are in the same posture, there is usually a pronounced silence in the area. They are often all looking in the same direction as well.

Sentinel: not resting, but staying very alert to its surroundings.

Tunnel of Silence

Usually associated with a passing raptor, such as a Red-shouldered Hawk, or an accipiter, the tunnel of silence indicates the recent flight path (or trail) of a predator. It is an amazing phenomenon that is actually the wake of a flying bird-eating specialist. Birds remain hidden, unsure where the danger is; they slowly come out of hiding over time or if a bird they trust begins to sing nearby. During nesting season, when the landscape is full of singing birds, a predator flies through and causes a marked silence along its path. Suddenly, sounds can be heard that had previously been masked by all the birdsong and calling.

Oppression

Related to the tunnel of silence is oppression. This is usually caused by an accipiter or another serious threat, such as a raven quietly studying the landscape during nesting season. Oppression is characterized by a pronounced silence, usually circular in shape, that extends from the

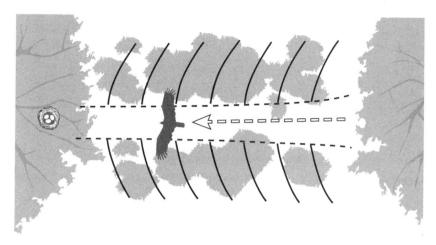

Tunnel of silence: predators employ this technique in order to listen for previously masked sounds.

ground to the canopy. This can last for a surprisingly long time, causing inexperienced observers to mistake oppression for baseline. On a sunny, calm morning, especially in spring, birds should be active, with lots of vocalizations and motion to be observed.

Where I live in California, I noted a marked oppression caused by nesting Cooper's Hawks three years ago, a Steller's Jay pair one year ago, and a raven's nest the next year. The Cooper's Hawk nest caused a very large area to be silent for most of the spring. I saw Black-headed Grosbeaks nesting but never heard them singing. I thought there was something wrong with the landscape until I discovered the nesting hawks—then it all clicked.

Oppression is not always associated with nesting predators; it is frequently caused simply by the appearance of a hawk that flies in to watch and wait for an opportunity. A hawk can sit patiently for many minutes even more than an hour—giving the impression that the silence is baseline when it is really an alarm. When the hawk moves, you can hear the "front" (see below) sound off.

Safety Barrier

This scenario involves unusually close encounters between humans and fleeing or even feeding songbirds, often when there is oppression from an accipiter—such as in the nesting territory of a Cooper's Hawk or when a bird plow occurs nearby, caused by a hawk. For example, if a sparrow is feeding very close to a person out working in the gar-

Safety barrier: songbirds may even use humans for cover when fleeing from predators.

den or in proximity to a tracker sitting at a sit spot, this may be safety barrier behavior. In other words, the sparrow is using the human for cover, because it seems to know that the hawk won't come too close to humans.

The Front
The front is a combination of dynamic calls and movement that denotes the location of the edge of a predator's path—usually many yards ahead of the predator's actual location. Just as an approaching storm causes winds to shift in a dynamic pattern, a moving predator causes alarms to shift dynamically. The silence of oppression is broken by calls and movement along the front as the predator begins to move again; this is often heralded by jays or crows. Baseline usually returns quickly in the wake of the predator's departure.

Parabolic Alarms
When a nest robber or ground predator is detected as a threat on the landscape, groups of birds mob the predator from a safe distance.

Parabolic alarm: birds group together to form a sphere of alarm sounds and motion.

Because the perceived safe distance is usually shared by all the individuals, the mobbing crowd maintains a consistent distance from the threat. Since there are many of them, they circle and form a sphere of alarm sounds and motion. Pay attention to the position of each alarming member of the mobbing group. This will help you determine the location of the threat, which is often hidden by camouflage coloration.

Moving Parabolic. Birds sound off and move with great intensity, often traveling along a hedgerow or other type of thicket or ravine.

This usually denotes an animal in a slow walk or a stalk—a signature of the cat family. It can also be caused by a stalking deer or other ungulate.

Static Parabolic. The mobbing group surrounds something unseen in the subcanopy or, less frequently, in a thicket near the ground. In most of the northern temperate climate, this almost always denotes the presence of a nest robber in the nesting season or an owl during the rest of the year. It could also be a snake moving slowly among the branches.

Popcorn

Sometimes birds literally "pop" out of cover; move in a short circular pattern; and dive back into the cover. They may or may not give off alarm calls. This alarm shape moves quickly in a linear pattern, following a hedge, thicket, or ravine. This is the signature of an animal in a trotting pattern, usually caused by a member of the dog family, but it can also be caused by "ghosting" deer, elk, wild pigs, or other ungulates.

Popcorn: "popping" in and out of cover.

Weasel Shape

This particular alarm shape is reserved for animals that appear for a moment, disappear into underground passages or tunnels in the brush, and then reappear. Birds alarm with great intensity when they can see the predator; then they change their cadence, frequency, and intensity when the predator disappears from view. Often they move their heads and bodies nervously as they search for the recently seen danger. This is most often the signature of a weasel, but it can also be caused by minks along streambanks or otters along the edge of a pond or marsh.

Hook

This behavior shows that the bird "knows" the limits of the approaching threat. It flies only high enough or far enough to get beyond the reach of the threat. Its retreat often follows a hooking path that allows it to get away from and then circle back toward the advancing danger, thus providing a strategic view.

Hook: movement away from danger while maintaining a strategic view.

12

Storytelling

*The telling of stories like singing and praying would seem
to be an almost ceremonial act, an ancient and necessary
mode of speech that tends the earthly rootedness of
language.*

—David Abram

J.Y.

It seems like our bodies are programmed for telling and listening to stories. Perhaps all humans once used storytelling as a primary means of learning and sharing. Storytelling is not just about passing on bits of hidden information, and it's not a replacement for reading. Storytelling can actually propel a tracker into an entirely different realm of skill and experience—one of intense observation, the synthesis of amazing detail and subtle awareness, and a deep understanding of and passion for living and learning.

Curiosity is contagious. Storytelling is also contagious, and I believe that these two are inextricably linked. Whenever I return from the field, I always tell a short story to whoever's around to get them caught up in the moment I just experienced with a wren, a raven, or a fox, with a slug, a group of gnats, or rabbit scat. Wondering out loud is my favorite thing to do. This gets the natural "expert" in others to come out. When I ask a question out loud that I can't answer, they simply must try to fill the void. Then I ask another question beyond their ability to answer, and we all start conjecturing like a bunch of chorusing frogs.

The fun of this is that the shared story, the shared curiosity, ignites the need to know in all my friends and family (and sometimes even strangers). Soon we're continuing the stories every chance we get—in the driveway, on the phone, while washing dishes over the sink. All these places are good ones for sharing the short stories of the day, spreading curiosity, and elucidating the edges of our experiences.

If you work this magic into your tracking journey, along with one more childhood passion—pretending—you will find that tracking is not only amazingly interesting but also a source of profound joy. Pretending, imitating, and storytelling all use the same parts of the brain. These acts, coupled with paying attention to detail and gathering detail through all the senses, can be some of the most powerful learning experiences life has to offer. Storytelling stimulates all these nodes of learning and more.

WISDOM AND STORIES

Wisdom, I was once told, is the ability to learn from other people's mistakes and hard lessons—not just from your own. The tracking skills of native cultures grew from the accumulation of hard-earned experience combined with the cultural wisdom and mentoring skills to pass it forward. This is also true today. Trackers would do well to learn from the wisdom of others.

Much of my skill in tracking, bird language and awareness, and cultural mentoring can be traced to the tips, stories, and lessons learned from many experienced individuals from various backgrounds: native culture, science, trapping, hunting, photography, and tracking. Through stories, this knowledge is passed along. When stories are written down, edited, illustrated, and published, we tend to call them field guides and books, but at their core, they are still stories.

An experience of wildlife tracker Paul Rezendes illustrates the passing on of wisdom. He had spent years trying to identify a certain sign left by beavers. He had found this sign on numerous occasions and did much research before he finally figured out that this mysterious sign was a beaver scent marking behavior. Later, he had mixed feelings about passing on this knowledge to others when he realized that what had taken five years to discover the hard way could be shared verbally in about five minutes. Of course, the hard lessons have a lasting impact, while we tend to quickly forget information that is easily obtained.

The art of storytelling, when refined, can also help the tellers "burn into" their minds certain images, experiences, and other nuggets of wisdom. Each time Paul, or anyone else, shares a tracking experience, it gets replayed, etched, and synthesized in the storyteller's mind in a way that isn't possible during the actual experience itself. Sometimes this is due to cross-fertilization and the catalyzing of ideas, theories, and experiences from a diverse group of listeners who also share their stories.

THE POWER OF STORYTELLING

Utilizing the ancient and effective pattern of storytelling unleashes the most powerful aspects of our abilities to perceive, to discern, to model, to link disparate concepts, to problem solve, to know our place, to know ourselves, to laugh, and, perhaps most important, to live fully in the moment. The power of storytelling cannot be underestimated as either a teaching aid or a learning aid. Most people think of story-telling as something that elders do for children, where the emphasis is placed on the teacher or storyteller and his or her skill. What I have learned through many mentoring situations over the past three decades is that the telling of one's "story of the day"—at the end of a hike, the end of the trail, or the end of any experience—is a critical element of learning.

Imagine a time long before the modern era. At the end of the day, the villagers return from a day afield spent hunting or gathering, wandering and exploring, or perhaps collecting items for healers or elders. The family members enter the home, sit by the fire, and begin to share, in turn, the stories of their journeys. The elders, uncles, aunts, siblings, and other relatives and friends are present and interested in every detail. Many questions are asked of the storyteller. The little children listen carefully and watch with admiration as each adventurer holds forth. Each person's story is equally important.

Since we all have the same ancient roots, we are all designed to respond to this universal model. Go into the field and explore, following your own curiosity and encountering your own edges. Nature speaks to us in different ways based on where we are on our individual journeys. Explore and try to pay attention to everything, because when you get back home, you'll be expected to remember the details. Today, I apply this pattern in every long-term program based on tracking or awareness. Whether through independent study or direct mentoring in the field, sharing stories is crucial to the learning process—tracking, in many aspects, *is* storytelling. Therefore, a tracker who avoids storytelling is avoiding the very thing he or she has set out to learn.

OVERCOMING LIMITED AWARENESS

Perceiving nature through the lens of holistic tracking requires a greater utilization of our senses than is commonly required in modern school settings. Although we gain many benefits from school-based studies, we can enhance our learning and experiences through the practices of wildlife tracking and awareness. We can add new habits to the patterns learned at school to augment our perceptual tools.

Storytelling is both a storage and a delivery vehicle for the collective tracking experience available to the next generation. It is an essential reinforcement technique and is at the center of an expansive learning process. When used effectively, storytelling is the best tool for learning many aspects of tracking; it can influence all aspects of the tracking experience—fieldwork, research, reading, journaling, and even dreaming. Storytelling activates our senses and utilizes many aspects of our human intelligence. Plus, it can be a lot of fun.

APPLYING STORYTELLING TO LEARNING

Consider this example of mentoring: A novice tracker returns from the field, and the elder asks about her day. The young one tells a story of cat tracks along a stream. The elder asks about the mice and the grasses along the river. The young tracker returns to the streambed the next day, determined to answer those questions and to look into places she was uninterested in before. Thus, the world becomes more alive as stories are shared with elders who possess a greater context. More questions are asked, and the cycle continues.

Inspired by this ancestral style of mentoring, today's mentors include many more aspects of the natural environment in the questioning process to broaden students' understanding of nature, including ecology, weather, and astronomy. Years afterward, students cite this kind of questioning as being a great influence on their observation skills, their sense of connection to the natural world, and their inner sense of well-being. The use of journaling is a reflection of this pattern of learning and mentoring.

When students return from the field, they do individual journaling and mapping. Then they meet in small groups, share their experiences, and map again, featuring more of the landscape and ecology and adding more details. Then the whole group meets and shares stories with experienced facilitators playing the role of elders—asking questions. Eventually, the students themselves learn how to ask good questions, and the group moves forward more independently. We often quiz the group on things the students don't see as "important"—especially after we learn their blind spots. For example, if I see that they aren't particularly interested in trees, I ask a lot of questions about trees.

An important aspect of the story of the day is describing the ecological zones experienced in the field, as well as the local and recent conditions of the life cycles of the various plant and animal communities, the water conditions, and the nature and condition of substrates. Synthesis of individual and group experiences causes all of us, including facilitators, to learn from the experiences and curiosities of others. Such a learning community can greatly enhance the learning journey and make it a lot more fun and interesting.

OLD STORIES OF PLACE

Nuggets of wisdom are often hidden in ancient stories of place. Sometimes the stories are about how animals or birds received the traits they have. Sometimes the stories have information about bird language or ecology. Sometimes they contain ancient wisdom that can save lives, such as how to survive tsunamis. Sometimes they seem to make little sense at all, but at least they get you thinking. Take some time to review storytelling resources from your favorite tracking regions, your current place of residence, or your ancestry.

Research the traditional stories that belong to your ancestors, whatever part of the world they come from. Over the past thirty years, I have learned from many native groups. I have learned tracking, cultural mentoring, and awareness techniques from European, Asian, African, Australian, North and South American, and Polynesian cultures. All these cultures have great respect for their traditional, ancestral stories. Learn some of the stories from your ancient past—this will influence your path in holistic tracking.

HEROES AND ROLE MODELS

One important genre of traditional storytelling is that of the hero culture. There are many amazing tales of great feats of tracking, hunting, gathering, and other important life skills. Usually these feats are represented by mythical, ancestral, or animal heroes. Through the stories of role models such as Jim Corbett and Tom Brown, people are motivated to learn tracking. There is also a body of literature that concentrates on detailed lives and personalities and vivid experiences with wildlife such as cougars (R. D. Lawrence), all sorts of backyard birds and mammals (Jean George), and ravens and owls (Berndt Heinrich). It's always a good idea to have an engrossing animal or tracker story for bedside reading to help you to your dreams.

THE STORYTELLER AND THE TRACKER

Can you tell the story of the forest today? Can you tell your own story? Are you able to journal at night and express what you truly felt and saw that day? Can you describe what you heard and what you were thinking? Can you write a coherent and compelling story from the events of the day's tracking? Can you tell it right when you get back to the "village"?

Learn to give voice to your true heart and self. Tell stories to friends when you return from the field, tell stories to tape recorders, or write stories down in your tracking journal. It's vital that you be able to tell the story of the day. And in the storytelling, in the retelling of and reflection on the actual event, you synthesize new information.

Ingwe, the late, great tracker and elder who learned tracking, survival, and awareness while living among the Akamba tribe of East Africa, was a profoundly gifted storyteller. When Ingwe told stories, you felt like you were in Africa, even if you had never been there. You could see the thorn trees in the distance; you could smell the scented grasses of Kenya. He used to tell us tricks to empower our storytelling. He spoke of not only telling the story but also seeing the forest, smelling the loam, hearing the rustle of leaves in the wind and the birdsong, and feeling the breeze on your face while telling a story, even if you were sitting in a room.

Ingwe would say that it's no good telling a story unless you've learned to truly pay attention when you're in the situation. Gathering sensory images, sounds, feelings, and smells is part of "harvesting" the story. When you're in the field, think of what you will say to bring people to that place. Gathering the sensations of a place develops good habits for both storytelling and tracking. Ingwe talked about storytelling as the weaving of dreams. He let his love of nature shine through his stories, and he always recommended that we do the same. Storyteller and tracker are often the same people, in both Ingwe's tribal experiences and throughout traditional hunter-gatherer societies worldwide.

IMITATING, ACTING, AND PRETENDING

Another tip for storytelling skill and empowerment comes from the field of drama. Today, only actors get to experience this powerful gift, but sharing tracking stories is probably where humans evolved the capacity to act in the first place. So, learn from the ancient and modern professionals of storytelling. Get your whole body involved when telling stories; use your hands to show the tracks on the ground when describing the trail of a coyote on the beach. In fact, relive the experience to the extent that you can actually see those tracks on the floor and vividly describe with your voice, body language, and hands the details of each track. Imagine the coyote making the tracks, and imitate the coyote making them. Become the coyote in your mind, but also in your eyes, head, and hands.

Suppose if you had to act out a part in a play, and the role was a particular animal. How could you become so much like that animal that the audience no longer saw a person but an animal? Learn all its natural history. Learn how it moves, how it uses its senses. Learn about its archetypal associations in native lore. Watch the animal in the wild if you can. Follow it for miles in the snow or on the sand. Watch videos of the animal. Read about its life in detail. Then, try becoming that animal through storytelling. This is related to what the Bushmen call putting on an animal's mind.

MAPPING AS STORYTELLING

The story of the day always includes a kind of "song line," which is a storytelling version of a map. From this, a listener can memorize a route and return the next day and follow the same route. In native cultures, when the story map is recited, the elders ask detailed questions to refine the landmarks, to add names to the story linked to the oral traditions and history of local people, and to check the sense of direction of the adventurer. Today, we substitute this part of the exercise with mapping routines: drawing a personal journal version of a map of the route of travel, referring to an actual topographic map of the area or better still, an aerial photograph. The map is drawn from memory; it is not recorded in the field. If more than one person participated in the outing, the individuals' maps are collated onto a larger map (usually a flip chart).

This is a good exercise to do every time a person returns from a tracking hike, regardless of how often he or she has visited a place.

This is one of the core routines of my Kamana Naturalist Training Program. For the first few years of training in tracking, an earnest student can benefit greatly by repeating this exercise for each journey taken. Some people actually benefit more from the exercise than they do from the actual field experience, especially if they are new to tracking. They realize that there were many things they overlooked in the field and therefore pay more attention the next time.

STORYTELLING TIPS

When in the field, notice things beyond the track and sign. Assume that someone will ask you questions about the trees, the weather, and the birds. This is how tracking becomes truly powerful.

Tell stories of the day in the evenings before going to sleep. If you don't have someone to share them with (my kids loved these stories at bedtime, whether the events were fresh from the field that day or from ten years ago), write them in your journal for the children of the future. It is the telling of stories that brings bird language alive for me and for others I know. Stories shared around the village fire or at the diner bring the lessons of nature into the realm of integral awareness. Write, draw, speak—document and relive your field time in whatever way is most comfortable for you.

HIKE AND TRACK

Take your usual tracking hike, but assume that when you get home you'll have to answer to the elders of map, ecology, and detail, so make good observations. Before logging and journaling your track and sign treasures, tell the story of the day.

STORY MAP

First, prepare a simple map of your route from memory. Next, compare your route map to a topographic or aerial photo map. Then correct your map by drawing it a second time—this time referring to the official map.

Write a paragraph or two describing the journey you took that day.

ECOLOGY AND SEASONS

Write a few paragraphs on the local seasonal events you witnessed. Use your Naturalist Inventory described in Chapter 7 as a reference, and write at least one or two observations for each category of nature.

DETAILS OF TRACK AND SIGN

After completing the preceding journaling assignments, get down to the usual business of track and sign. This time, link the activities of the creature you tracked to the map and the ecology in as many ways as possible, thinking of factors such as food, safety from enemies, water, shelter, shade, and other features of ecology.

13

Intuition

You have to leave the city of your comfort and go into the wilderness of your intuition. What you'll discover will be wonderful. What you'll discover is yourself.

—Alan Alda

SURPRISED BY A BOBCAT, CHASED BY A FOX

T.M.

I had been working at my desk all morning and was eager to get out into the riches and solitude of nature. One particular question had been burning in my mind: Could a bobcat and a gray fox be using the same trail, just moments apart, and if so, how could the fox live right under the bobcat's nose? I had read that gray foxes are prey for bobcats, but there was no literature about them living as neighbors. Being that their tracks are quite similar, especially when obscured in mud, I was struggling to determine whose tracks were whose, even with the help of field guides.

I took a back route to my sit spot, up a small redwood-lined ravine, and popped out into the oak meadow, which was drying out from the warmth of the past few days—a real contrast from the damp redwoods. The trail in question used by both bobcat and fox had deep wheel ruts from a rancher's four-wheeler. Water had collected in the ruts, but the puddles were now drying out, leaving perfect muddy substrate for tracks. The muddy pockets were usually filled with raccoon tracks; however, on this day they held a line of gray fox tracks headed north. I followed them until I could no longer make them out, then skipped ahead to the next good muddy patch. The familiar shape-shifting fox-bobcat track that had perplexed me so often was engraved in this next patch. I was leaning toward bobcat, but the track was in the exact same line of travel as the gray fox tracks. The two side toes registered perfectly—very round with tapered ends—but somehow the two front toes were smashed together and looked like one, and the heel pad was obscured by the bank of the depression.

Voices coming from the top of the hill to the west pulled my attention away. I was surprised to see two teenage boys I didn't recognize. It was unusual to encounter people in this area because it's private land and difficult to access unless you're familiar with the place. The sun was setting behind the hill, blinding my view of the boys. I looked for somewhere to hide, but I was cornered by a long stretch of cleared brush that runs from one end of the meadow to the other, with a healthy supply of poison oak guarding it on all sides. The closest escape route was a tiny hole in the brush that would require contorting my body to avoid thorny blackberry vines and poison oak. Somehow, deer manage to squeeze through this hole effortlessly; nothing in their tracks shows even the slightest struggle or hesitation.

It was too late; the boys were in view, just beginning their descent. The civilized side of me said stand up, present yourself, and greet them. But I sat still, watching them in a crouched position. When they were halfway down the hill, I stood up; they saw me immediately, but neither party acknowledged the other. They disappeared behind a brush pile and didn't resurface. I walked ahead a few paces to where I could see around the edge. Now the boys were crouched down, just out of shouting distance.

Rather than struggling with the blackberry thorns in the deer trail, I walked twenty paces farther to where the thicket consists of mostly ceanothus and there's a clear trail. I stepped into the shadows, crept away until I was out of sight, dropped down, and crawled back to the meadow's edge to wait and watch. The boys, thinking that I was gone, stood up and continued down the gradual slope, unaware that they were being watched. It occurred to me that this was exactly how I'd seen deer behave. They take off so fast that it seems they intend to put as much distance between us as possible. But when I take the time to investigate, I often find them just out of sight, hiding. My experience hiding from these kids added another piece of information: animals are conserving energy by hiding just out of sight, but they're also investigating; they want to know who is in their territory and why.

The boys eventually disappeared through another break in the thicket at the opposite end of the meadow, and my thoughts returned to the possible bobcat track. I cautiously poked out of the ceanothus and cruised back to the wheel rut trail. Coming from the opposite direction, I had a new perspective. The track that had seemed to be traveling south was actually traveling north—in the opposite direction of the fox. What I had thought were the front toes was actually the heel pad. The perfect registering lobes along the back of the heel pad had fooled me into thinking they were toes. It was clearly a bobcat track: two lobes on the front of the heel, three in back. The four toes formed an arch; the side toes lined up with the middle toes, rather than behind (as in canids). There was a space between toes and heel, without the little mound that occurred in the gray fox track. The mud in the tracks was mostly smooth, indicating a lack of hair covering the pads.

If the language of the birds changed from quiet feeding to alarm, I didn't notice, but for some reason, I had a strong sense that the creator of this track was watching me. I looked up, halfheartedly attempting to check whether my feeling was correct, but my eyes soon fell back to the tracks. The sun was sneaking behind the hills and out of the track folds. I stood up to leave but was held by the remaining light. The paling meadow was covered in an early-evening fog like a soft veil. Draped in the veil, just ahead of me on the same trail, was a figure I couldn't quite make out. The length of its body faced me while the head turned to view me, a body position that deer often hold when they first recognize my approach. I wondered why a lone deer would creep out into the meadow on a random trail I'd never seen one use. More importantly, why did this deer look like a miniature pony? Then I realized that the misty creature of the thicket was the bobcat. It seemed surprised to find me standing there, or perhaps it was surprised that I had noticed it. Our staring contest lasted for thirty seconds—the cat lost. It turned slowly and crawled away in a low crouch, as if to make its body smaller and less visible. It slipped back into the brush line, into the ceanothus thicket where it had come from, which happened to be the same trail I had escaped on just moments before. I wondered whether it might be hunkered down just out of view, but it was too dark to tell.

Early the next morning, parallel to the fox tracks was a clear trail of fresh bobcat tracks moving in the same direction, most likely the cat I had seen the previous day. Finally, I had clear trails from both the fox and the bobcat, side by side, so I could compare their signatures. What luck, I thought, this was the exact information I needed to solve my mystery. The gray fox tracks I recognized immediately; they were unmistakable. The fox's back toes almost formed triangles squished behind the front toes, whereas the bobcat's remained round, with a little tapering at the top of the toes. The tiny pyramid in the middle of the gray fox track was not visible in the bobcat's track, which had a narrow arch extending across the top of the heel pad from one outer rear toe to the other. I saturated my memory with the physical details of the tracks until I could hold no more. Now that I knew for sure that both bobcat and fox used this trail, my mind was flooded with other questions: What is the relationship between fox and cat? Do their core areas overlap? Is it a female or male cat? What other trails do they use?

The next morning, my burning questions were smoldering under the weight of unrelated thoughts and distractions. On such occasions, I climb an old oak tree—I call it my tree of perspective—to get above such extraneous thoughts. The oak grows just inside the ceanothus thicket where the bobcat had emerged and disappeared. I arrived at the base of the tree, and my thoughts dissolved as I planted myself on my old perch. No sooner had I sat down when my ears picked up a rustling sound on the forest floor. Looking down, my eyes locked with those of a gray fox. I was stunned—the fox seemed unreal, like a ghost of the forest. The fox's powder gray color, so different from the red-colored foxes I had seen, added to its mystical qualities. I can only wonder what the fox thought of me sitting up in that tree, staring down at it. Our gazes snapped apart like the breaking of a wishbone, and without hesitation, the fox scaled the trunk of a nearby slanted tree—something I had always hoped to see one do. Perhaps it wanted to be on equal footing with me or wanted to get a better view. Whatever the reason, it didn't hang around for long; it glided down the tree and continued to glide as it trotted out of sight. This was where I had found a huge bobcat latrine and also where I had seen the bobcat disappear. Now I had definite proof that the gray fox also utilized this corner of the forest. It seemed that their core areas did overlap, or at least I was getting a more complete picture of how they coexisted.

A few minutes passed, and my ponderings were interrupted by what sounded like a crazed banshee. I had never heard this sound in the woods before, but it somehow seemed to belong there. A few more raspy, guttural calls echoed through the trees. I thought it might be a raven call, but it was coming from an unlikely location on the forest floor. I squinted at the wall of green where the noise was coming from, which happened to be where the fox had exited the area. An almost undetectable sliver of gray hair peeked through the bushes. The realization overwhelmed me all at once like a pack of excited puppies. The fox was just out of sight, and that strange noise was the fox barking at me.

I had recently read *How to Spot a Fox* by J. David Henry (1993), which is about red foxes and explains how to see them in their natural state. I figured that the information could be applied to gray foxes and decided to do a little experiment. I just needed to run home, get some beef jerky, and rub my scent into it. Then I would return to this location and offer it to the fox so that it would connect delicious snacks with my presence. It was all a little absurd, but I didn't have much time to act.

My run back to the house created a huge bird-plow alarm well in advance of my approach. I stuffed a handful of jerky in my pocket and headed out the door with the same intensity. I slowed down only after realizing that the concentric rings of my approach could easily reach the fox, even though it was a quarter mile away. I placed one foot in front of the other with as much deliberation as I could muster, and it seemed that my body control paid off. Around a bend in the road, a fox was moving away swiftly. For a moment, I thought that I was Snow White attracting all the animals of the forest, but the powder gray color was unmistakable—it was the same fox I had just seen.

The lesson of the previous day (hiding from the boys in the meadow) came to mind. Animals, like humans, are curious; they want to know who's in their territory and why, but from a safe distance. The fox had followed me home. It was curious about who I was and what business I had in its territory. Little did the fox know that I would come charging out of the house and we would bump noses again.

My only thought was that this was my chance to befriend the fox. I made a noise to make it turn around and see me presenting the jerky, but its pace only quickened as it moved away. I rubbed the jerky in my hands to give it my scent and left a trail of tiny pieces as the fox disappeared over the rise. I followed and was led to the wheel rut trail, where I had been comparing the fox and bobcat tracks. With the fox nowhere in sight, I left a small offering of jerky next to the tracks and retired for the afternoon.

I returned home elated by these brief animal encounters. They were beginning to answer some of my more difficult questions—answers that I had been unable to find in any of my field guides. Hours later, while engrossed in office work, I had an intense premonition that

I should check the trail where I had left the jerky. I dropped everything and scrambled up a nearby hill to the edge of the meadow; there's a log there that provides a boost over the barbed-wire fence encircling the meadow. The wire makes a snapping sound when it springs back into place, which I was acutely aware of. I didn't want to set off the delicate alarms of the juncos feeding there. Each step had to be silent because I was nearly to the site, but I rushed despite my warnings to myself. Around the end of the brush pile, I had a clear view of where I had left the jerky; my eyes were immediately attracted to motion just south of the site, where a soft shape was moving away. The fox, I thought, had accepted my gift. Then I saw that the legs were too long for a fox, and the movements were wrong too. This animal was moving off like a rocking horse, the now-familiar motion of a bobcat. It squirted through the hole in the blackberry thicket and was gone. I was eager to investigate whether it had eaten the treat I had left, but I found no sign that the cat had been investigating the jerky. In fact, I found only one of the bobcat's fresh, clear prints on the entire stretch of trail, even though I had seen its exact route of travel. This showed me that even when I wasn't finding bobcat tracks on the trail, it didn't mean that the cat hadn't been there. Clearly, the fox and the bobcat both used this trail regularly and frequently—sometimes mere hours and likely just moments apart.

It occurred to me then that something more than luck was working in my favor. The coincidences of my questions being answered were remarkable. Trying to explain instances of synchronicity can be like telling a ghost story: your audience will be searching for holes in your story and left with a sense of disbelief. This may cause your own skepticism to grow, robbing your stories of their magic. This is not meant to discourage you from telling your stories or fully living your experiences. It's a word of advice that you may want to keep some of your encounters just for yourself, tucked away in a journal or in your memory.

I don't know the purpose of synchronicity on a universal level; I only know that it can be an incredible tracking tool for those who are open to and accepting of it. This chapter goes into detail about how to cultivate synchronicity in your learning of tracking. It's important to note, however, that synchronicity is not a substitute for research, journaling, and questioning. In fact, only when these tools are combined will you get the most benefit from synchronicity.

THE PHENOMENON SYNCHRONICITY

J.Y.

Synchronicity is the coincidence of events that seem related but are not obviously caused by each other. A coincidence is something that happens by chance in a surprising or remarkable way.

Perhaps our modern way of life and learning has caused our thinking and reasoning processes and our instinctive sensing processes to become separate. This chapter examines how an ancient and powerful learning journey (i.e., tracking) can cause events that are seemingly at odds with our worldview. Ultimately, this chapter is about healing the rift between our instinctive perceptions and our reasoning mind. They are both within us and can live in peace together.

Tracking synchronicity occurs when, through happenstance, you find yourself in the right place at the right time and suddenly, there is the answer to your question. Sometimes this results from such an amazing series of improbable coincidences that you feel the hair standing up on the back of your neck and say out loud, "What the heck is going on here? How did *that* happen?"

This is an interesting part of the tracking journey that I have been contemplating since I was a teenager—when I first noticed synchronicity and muttered in an amazed manner. Still, nearly thirty years later, I have no conclusions. I have, however, noticed some consistent patterns, and I have discussed these patterns with trackers and others interested in the subject. I have drawn some basic conclusions, yet I am always open to reexamining my ideas and changing them as needed. So, although I have some experience with tracking synchronicity, I am not convinced that I understand it any better than anyone else.

There is a pattern that emerges from exploration and observation, coupled with the asking of really good questions—especially those that extend past the edge of our knowledge and observation experience. Since I acknowledged the existence and persistence of synchronicity in my life thirty years ago, I have tracked such occurrences fairly consistently and carefully. I can actually backtrack my discovery of synchronicity to a specific time in my life, and it relates directly to a very grounded and practical routine: exploration and observation, coupled with questions and research. At first, Tom Brown was the one asking the questions and guiding the research, exploration, and observation; he was a consummate master of mentoring principles and helped me become self-sufficient and self-motivated rather quickly. For this, he deserves special mention and honor. Tom Brown's motto is: "Put the *quest* back in questions" and "put the *search* back in research."

Your patterns of synchronicity will be different from my experience. This seems to be the way synchronicity works—it's very individually based.

DISCOVERING INSPIRATION AND NATURAL CURIOSITY

First, undertake a basic exploration: go out the door to the nearest tree and look at a leaf. Second, ask a basic question: What kind of tree is that? Third, consult a tree guide and find your answer. This is basic research. Has synchronicity happened yet? Some would say no and others would say yes. For now, I would reserve my opinion.

Now, let's close the loop of this basic exploration-observation and question-research process and make it a cycle. You find the leaf in the book, you do all the right "key processes," and soon you're pretty sure that it's the leaf of an American holly tree. Good job. Next you say to yourself, "I wonder . . ." Stop here for a moment. This is the beginning of the *search* in research and the *quest* in question, because you're being driven by genuine curiosity and interest. The next question is about to emerge, and this could go in any direction, depending on the individual, his or her personal interests and abilities, perceptual background, and related complex of prejudices, projections, and filters. The loop closes with a question based on discovery through research, leading to the need for further observation and exploration. For example, "I wonder if there are any more holly trees around here."

This leads to another trip out the door, into the backyard and the forest beyond, and a new search that drives both observation and exploration. Your eyes are now trained on the pattern of holly leaves, which translates to holly trees and bark and maybe berries. You discover that there are more holly trees, including some big ones. You climb in the holly trees and discover vines hanging down among the older hollies, and back to the field guides you go, asking, "What kind of vines are these?" And on it goes.

FACILITATING SUCCESS
IN THE NATURAL LEARNING CYCLE

Attaining self-motivation and self-sufficiency in finding and using field guides and other resources in an effective and efficient manner should be your first goal. Once you encounter those little moments of discovery and wonder, you've begun to tap into a natural energy source that makes the whole tracking and nature learning journey possible and powerful. At this level, does synchronicity surface? Not in an obvious way (or not at all, depending on your point of view). Let's take this natural learning cycle one level deeper.

REACHING A MORE FOCUSED LEVEL

After a few months of visiting my tracking area, exploring and observing, asking good questions, and using my resources, I developed a natural, self-motivated affinity for my sit spot and the areas where I learned a lot of my tracking. What's great about this cycle is that the more you do it, the easier it gets and the more intense your need to know becomes. This may be the key to understanding where synchronicity comes from in the first place.

At this point on my journey, I began to move beyond the ability of my field guides to answer my questions. This is an important part of the journey, and this is where the whole idea of synchronicity kicks in, in a hard-to-ignore way. Tom still played an important role for me at this point. He knew the limitations of the field guides, so he knew that I was going to get frustrated when they couldn't answer my questions about the tracks and sign I was finding.

When I was about sixteen, I began to notice that there were a lot of coincidences surrounding my discovery of answers to some really important tracking questions. When I was eighteen, I had an experience that involved so many places and players and such an unlikely series of events that it caused me to examine the meaning of life itself. One day while exploring a woodlot, I discovered some raccoon scats near my apartment. There were some interesting seeds in the scats that I couldn't identify. I washed them and burnished them, and they had a wonderful shine and grain. I looked in every field guide I had and found no answers. I asked all the dendrology (tree study) students I knew, and none of them could identify the seeds. Then I went to the teaching assistant, and he didn't know. I showed them to the professor, and if he knew, he wouldn't tell me. I was used to that. He must have known about synchronicity too.

One morning soon after, my roommate said, "Hey Jon, I'm going to the dining hall for breakfast. Want to come?"

Normally, I would jump at the chance to do anything with anyone. It was the first month of my first year of college, and I wanted to make up for all the time I had spent alone in the woods. Now that there were other nature students around who loved this stuff as much as I did, I was starting to feel less lonely. But to my own surprise, I said, "No thanks." That was strange, I noted later, because I was hungry. This was a gut feeling acting on my behalf.

My roommate left, and a short while later there was a knock on the door. One of the "really cool" guys was there and invited me to go to breakfast with his group of friends. "No thanks," I said—again, to my own surprise. Who was running my body and mouth at the time? I wondered later. Was this my body wisdom acting through my gut feelings?

A few minutes later, Jennifer knocked on the door. "Hey Jon, do you want to go to the research forest and pick persimmons with me? They're ripe right now and really good."

"Sure!" I said, surprising myself again, because she was good-looking and I was shy. We crossed the busy highway on the overpass, climbed under a fence, and soon we were in the woods eating persimmons. I bit into one and hit the hard seed at the center. I spit the seed into my hand and looked down in stunned amazement. There was the seed I had been searching for. Ever since, I've been a big believer in trusting one's gut feelings.

Events like these are part of a natural and powerful cycle. They are part of our instinctive drive to know our place and a sign that we can still tap into primal forces that are conspiring—somehow—to connect us with nature. I believe that our bodies are wise and can know things before our minds are ready to acknowledge them. I think that our peripheral sensing mechanisms, however they work (and I don't pretend to know), kick in to aid our instincts. This leads us to the right place at the right time. The power behind this phenomenon comes from several sources that I have identified and explain below.

Passion to Know. A natural curiosity exists in all of us. By facilitating the natural learning cycle, this can grow into a passion to know and learn.

Abundant Curiosity. Each of us is born with an innate curiosity about everything in creation. In adulthood, it may take some work to rekindle this fire, but once it's lit again, this becomes a baseline condition, a natural state of living. And this fire will keep burning until your light goes out.

Strong Imaginal Resources. Things like storytelling and air sculpting awaken our mind's inner resources, which seem to be linked to the occurrence of synchronicity.

Trust in Gut Feelings. This is probably one of the most important elements. It can be developed by slowing down and practicing exercises such as owl vision and sense meditation. We need to relax enough to notice the little feelings in our gut that are hard to hear when we're busy.

Journaling. When I was young, Tom would ask me questions to help me notice when synchronicity had happened. It was usually while journaling the situation later that I would discover the unlikely congruence of events. To journal synchronicity, simply reflect on your recent observations and explorations. Think of the curiosity and passion that bubble up around certain questions, and examine your need to know the answers or to ask better questions. Then continue the search and quest part of the cycle through and beyond resources, and notice how people, books, and even the animals themselves sometimes come straight to you with the answers. I recommend that you keep a synchronicity journal and make notes each day or each week as you take this journey. When an interesting event occurs that answers an important question, jot it down. When you have a vivid dream related to a deep question, jot it down.

Just know that if you're trying to figure out how or why these things happen, you're in good company, and you may never know the answer. But that's just fine. Just be grateful and marvel at the mystery of this world that we still don't fully understand. Ingwe says, "Don't try to find a logical explanation for these things. You will take something beautiful and destroy it." Instead, Ingwe, myself, and many others suggest that you draw or paint, write songs or poems, or journal these things to celebrate them and to keep them for posterity. Synchronicity is enhanced by the creative arts in all forms, and it seems to pertain to who we are—our purpose in life. One thing that all natives do in situations like this is to give thanks. Perhaps that's the most important lesson of all.

CULTIVATING INSTINCTS

The following exercises are designed to slow down your body and mind so that you're more receptive to your senses, your natural rhythm, the pulse of nature, and ultimately synchronicity. Read through the exercises and then choose one or two to focus on until you achieve a noticeable shift in your perceptions and sensitivity. Don't fall into the trap of making this an analytical process; doing so will be counterproductive. There is no right or wrong way to practice these exercises; the important thing is that you try them and congratulate yourself on your successes—and only you know what those are.

THE TREE SIT

A good climbing tree can be a great mentor in tracking and awareness. Sitting up in a tree or on any high perch looking down at the forest below gives us a special perspective on the world. Old, comfortable trees that are easy to climb are not easy to come by, but this exercise can also be done with the aid of a tree stand; these are portable, safe, and relatively comfortable, and they're available in many outdoor or sporting goods catalogs.

The tree sit is, in many ways, a variation on the quiet sit. Any form of sit time opens the senses and creates the kind of oneness with nature that can't be achieved any other way. There is no shortcut or replacement.

The exercise is simple: Find a good climbing tree that you can stay up in all day. Pick a good time of year when the weather suits you and the mosquitoes aren't too bad. Choose a day that you can devote to the experience, and climb up in the tree to watch, listen, and otherwise experience the world from a bird's-eye view. If your health makes this a challenge, or if you are afraid of heights, choose a good view from at least 10 to 25 feet up a hill or a cliff, and use camouflage.

A full day is a long time, so you may have to do this in shifts. The most powerful part of a tree sit is arriving in the darkness a good half hour before first light, getting comfortable, gaining stillness, and then waiting in a sense meditation for the light to come from the east. Spend as long you possibly can—at least from dawn to late morning, when the birds quiet down and the forest becomes still again. If you can stay longer, do so. Bring your lunch up there, and go down only to use the bathroom or to stretch. Try to make it through a whole daylight period. If you can't do this in one sitting, break up the sessions, with a few overlaps to be sure that you're seeing all times of day. While you're in the tree, make mental notes of the patterns of awakening of the landscape. Watch, feel, listen, smell, and otherwise relate to the changes as darkness becomes daylight. Note how your body feels being in the tree. Note the birds and their routines, and any changes. Note the animal trails and how the animals use them. Notice who lives there and in what order they appear. Journal the experience, doing your best to re-create the events you observed.

BLINDFOLDED STRING WALK

This exercise was introduced to me when I was an instructor for Coyote Tracks, Tom Brown's program for children. It was one of the kids' favorite activities, and even the instructors would jump at the chance to try a new blindfolded string walk. A favorite was the blindfolded creek walk; the difficulty of this walk helped us surrender to our senses and pay close attention to the rocks under our feet, the cool water around our knees, and the birds chattering above our heads.

This activity requires kite string or any thin rope. Choose a wooded area with a diversity of sensory experiences; include a creek, river, or pond, if it's safe to do so. Tie one end of the string to a bush or tree at hip height, and then weave the string through the woods from tree to bush, over different substrates, through tall grasses, into dense forest, into a creek, out to a meadow—there are endless possibilities. You can make the string walk as long or as short as you choose, but remember that you'll be blindfolded, so it will take longer than normal to finish the course. Then blindfold yourself and hold on to the string with one hand. The string acts as a guide, allowing you to experience the woods through all your senses except for vision. Temporarily removing your sense of sight typically has the effect of bringing your other senses to peak performance. It's perfectly fine to take your time—this isn't a race—and feel the wind on your face and the ground beneath your feet. Let your skin, ears, and nose absorb all the nuances of the forest as you trustingly follow your string and your instincts on the blindfolded string walk.

If the string isn't too obtrusive—meaning that a deer isn't going to come along and get clotheslined—leave it up for a few days and walk the course blindfolded at different times of day, noticing the different smells and sounds. Try it in the early morning when the birds are just starting their chorus or in the evening when the crickets are coming to life.

RADAR WALKING

Often when we venture into the woods, we have a purpose or a destination in mind. For this exercise, your purpose is to follow your instincts, and your destination is wherever they lead you. This form of walking utilizes your subtle sense of perception. Your radar may lead you toward a foraging deer, a perched owl, or a rare wildflower. Just trust your feelings and have fun following your radar.

When you are walking to your sit spot or a tracking location, stop and imagine that you are a radar receiver. Turn slowly to the left and then to the right. Sweep back and forth in an arc, and pay attention to any subtle differences in energy or any unexplained differences in temperature that your body detects. You may be drawn to go in a certain direction that you haven't gone before. Trust that feeling and go with it. Walk in that direction, and when it feels right, stop and use your radar again. Sweep back and forth to see what your body detects. Perhaps this time you'll be drawn to a particular part of the landscape, such as a tree or a thicket. Again, trust that feeling and go with it. There is no rush. Keep at it until your radar detects that it's time to go to your sit spot or to go home.

GIVING THANKS

The first thing that's done is you give thanks to everything. You thank the waters beneath the Earth, the stones, the soil, all the way up to the stars. It's just a reminder of where we are, and who we are within that part of it, we should never forget that.

—Kahionhes John Fadden
Turtle Clan of the Mohawk Nation

We believe an essential part of studying tracking is the connection we develop in our hearts with what we track. If you have your own way of summoning a feeling of thanksgiving, feel free to use it; if not, we've provided an exercise to get you started. Each time you track, take a moment beforehand to give thanks. Honor and acknowledge each element and being of creation, which so generously gives of itself to the humans and the other beings around it, and recognize the utter dependence of each being on all others. Greet and end each day with a genuine sense of thankfulness, and you will be amazed at the difference it makes in your tracking experience and in the rest of your life. We are grateful to Mohawk elder Tekaronieneken Jake Swamp for his patience and willingness to share this important lesson with us.

Here is one way to give thanks: First, give thanks to all the people of the earth and for all the gifts attributed to the human family. Send your thanksgiving and greetings to the people of the earth.

Turn your thoughts to the Earth Mother, who, like our own mothers, continues to provide for our well-being. She continues to care for us and has not forgotten her instructions from the beginning of time. Send your thanksgiving and greetings to the earth.

Now turn your thoughts toward the waters of the earth, for they too have not forgotten their original instructions from the creator of life. The waters continue to flow beneath the ground, in little streams and rivers, in lakes and wetlands, and in the great seas. These waters quench our thirst and help us keep clean so that we can fulfill our duty to creation. Send your thanksgiving and greetings to the waters of the earth.

Address all the beings, both seen and unseen, that dwell in the water, for they too have not forgotten their original instructions from the creator of life. There are many life-forms in the waters, which provide for us in many ways. Send your thanksgiving and greetings to all the life-forms of the waters.

Direct your thoughts to the many kinds of plants that live upon the earth—the mosses, the many grasses, the herbs, the food plants, and the many other low-growing plants—for they too have not forgotten their original instructions. There are many members of this family who sustain those of us who walk on this earth, and there are many others who take away the sicknesses of the human family. Send your thanksgiving and greetings to all the plants.

Think of the animal life in the world, for the animals continue to instruct and teach us, even to this day. We are happy that many still walk with us on our journey, even though their natural world has changed and their lives have become difficult. Send your thanksgiving and greetings to all the animal life.

Think of the trees. According to their original instructions, the trees give us shelter, warmth, and food, and keep the air clean. The trees can make the earth a more suitable place for all life to dwell. When we see the trees, we are reminded of the beauty and power of the natural world. Send your thanksgiving and greetings to the trees.

Turn your mind to the birds. At the beginning of time, the birds were given a special duty to perform—they were instructed to help lift the troubled minds of the human family. During the day, their songs often lift our spirits. They too continue to fulfill their obligation to continued creation. Send your thanksgiving and greeting to the birds.

Give thanks for the four winds, which continue to blow and cleanse the air in accordance with their original instructions. When we listen to the wind, it is as if we are hearing the creator's breath, clear-

Origins of Giving Thanks

Jeff Lambe and Jake Swamp

The Mohawk people trace giving thanks back to the beginning of time. According to their origin story: In the beginning, before people knew about death, they just lived on and on without ever dying. At some point, death was introduced, and soon many people were dying. The people didn't know what to make of this. All the people had always been there, and they had assumed that they always would be. Now, people were getting sick, which was strange enough, but many would fall asleep and not awake. They would stop breathing and turn cold. The people did not know how to handle this.

One person known as One with a Bright Mind prayed for a long time about what was happening to his people. He learned that this strange thing was called death, and once death touched someone, that person would not start breathing again. The families of the dead would never again be able to talk with them or hold them in their arms. One with a Bright Mind found that all people would one day know death and that the total number of days of each person's earth walk would remain hidden. It was said that people would live in a humble way if they never knew when death might be coming for them.

ing our minds as it blows through the trees. Send your thanksgiving and greetings to the wind.

Turn your attention to the thunderbeings, for they too have not forgotten their original instructions and welcome the spring with their loud voice. Along with the lightning, they carry the waters of spring on their backs. Send your thanksgiving and greetings to the thunderbeings.

Turn your thoughts to the sun. Each day the sun continues to carry out its instructions from the creator of life, bringing the light of day, the energy source of all life on earth. Send your thanksgiving and greetings to the sun.

Gather your mind and give thanks to the moon. It too has not forgotten its original instructions, binding the rhythms and cycles of the waters so that we may continue to carry out our obligation to creation. Send your thanksgiving and greetings to the moon.

One with a Bright Mind shared this knowledge with the people, and with this knowledge came a great sadness. For the first time, they felt the loss that comes from realizing that someone they had known and loved forever, whose presence they had taken for granted, would not be coming back tomorrow or the next day or ever again.

A great sense of emptiness and loss filled the people's hearts. Their eyes were clouded with loneliness, and their ears were clogged with grief. They walked with their heads down and their minds unclear. The people no longer took notice of the beauty around them. No longer could they hear the music of the waterfall; no more did they see the beauty of the flowers and trees. Even the singing of the bird nations no longer lifted them out of their troubled minds. It was as if they were no longer fully alive.

One with a Bright Mind saw that the people had lost sight of the miracle of creation. But through thanksgiving, One with a Bright Mind found that he could again see clearly and feel thankful. He shared this feeling of thankfulness with all the people, encouraging them to uplift their minds and hearts. In time, the haze was lifted; the people cast off the clouds of death and learned to embrace the happiness of life, with thanksgiving as a constant reminder.

Finally, send your thoughts to the star nation, which continues to light our way in the dark to guide us home. It holds the secrets of many forgotten stories, and it is said that if we are thankful for the stars, perhaps one day we will learn these stories again. Send your thanksgiving and greetings to the star nation.

We encourage you to adapt this thanksgiving address to suit your needs. However you give thanks is personal, and we support whatever version of giving thanks you choose. We include the practice of giving thanks because we've observed its capacity to enrich one's experience of nature and to increase synchronicity. Giving thanks is a practice, so if you haven't done it in a while, you may be a little rusty. Remember to give thanks for and say kind words to yourself as well, and allow your version of giving thanks to mature at your own pace. Give thanks when you arrive at your sit spot or before you go into the field to track. Try this for at least three months, and write about your experiences along the way. If you think that it's a waste of time, write that down. If you find that you're more thankful for the plants you consume daily, that's important to note. If you find yourself struggling to practice giving thanks, it may help to write down your observations about the process.

The wonderfully strange happenstances of synchronicity connect us deeply with one another and with the earth. These happenings help us realize that we are on the right path in life. Jake Swamp tells us that this is nature giving us affirmation. No one can really explain how it works, but we honor the fact that it does exist.

I have trained hundreds of people over the years, and many have told stories of special experiences that led them to important events or affected vital aspects of their lives. We can learn to recognize these things by simply paying attention.

Think of the times in your life when following your instincts, gut feelings, guiding force, inner vision, luck, or whatever else you might call it has resulted in something positive. These can be major, significant events or seemingly minor, inconsequential ones. If you go with a feeling and it results in a positive outcome, write it down and honor it. Give thanks for this guidance in your life. Know that there are many people around the world who are attuned to these kinds of experiences. Some people call it the Holy Spirit, the Great Mystery, or grace. Whatever you call it, it is operating in the natural world. And the more you use your senses, the stronger these forces will become in your life.

14

Tracking Tools

As perhaps the oldest science, the art of tracking is not only
of academic interest, it may also be developed into a new
science with many practical applications.
　　　　　　　　—Louis Liebenberg
　　　　　　　　　　The Art of Tracking: The Origin of Science

Tracking and science have always worked hand in hand, yet tracking is rarely spoken about in academic arenas. Rather, data, statis-
tics, and models are common terms in scientific discussions. But if you
listen carefully and probe beneath the surface, you will find that a
tracking-based methodology is often the tool employed to gather data
for analysis. Thus, although science does not study tracking, tracking
is one of the tools utilized by wildlife researchers the world over.

This chapter introduces certain common practices in modern and
traditional wildlife research; both are useful to the student of tracking
as exercises in learning and in understanding how animal tracking is
used in modern science. They are also useful tools if you would like to
participate in research, create your own projects, or sell your services
through consulting.

CYBERTRACKER EVALUATION

The use of animal tracking in wildlife research is limited only by our
creativity and our understanding of what is possible. An exciting new
development is tracker evaluation. One system of tracker evaluation
originating from South Africa is the CyberTracker Evaluation system.
This exciting new certification system has the potential to create more
professions in animal tracking by creating a database of reputable trackers. For those who already consider themselves tracking professionals,

an evaluation can raise some red flags—perhaps with good reason. The CyberTracker evaluation covers a broad array of animal tracks and sign. If you are a tracker who specializes in cougars, for example, and don't know anything about the tracks and sign of shrews, coyotes, bobcats, or the multitude of other animals you might be tested on, you might have some misgivings about an evaluation. However, having been through the evaluation, it's clear to me that if you already have a foundation of tracking knowledge—even for just one species—you can quickly learn the others. And knowledge of the tracks and sign of all the species in your area will improve your understanding of your target species. If the opportunity presents itself, we highly recommend that you take part in one of these evaluations. More information on evaluations can be found at www.wildlifetrackers.com.

The Evaluation

T.M.

Tracking didn't have any meaning for me until I discovered that tracks are an animal's story, and these stories aren't locked away in a book or in a chance meeting with a wild animal. I gradually learned that tracks are everywhere one cares to look: mud puddles, dirt roads, dusty barns, grass, tree trunks. They are accessible, unlike the animals themselves. Although this information was valuable to me on a personal level, my interest in tracking was similar to the interest one might have in identifying wildflowers. There wasn't much purpose to my tracking, other than curiosity.

An actual application for tracking wasn't apparent to me until I was introduced to CyberTracker. My friend Matt Wild showed me a topographic map covered in colorful dots on a computer screen. He explained that a handheld computer equipped with CyberTracker software had created the dots, and each dot represented a track or animal sign that had been observed in the field. A global positioning system (GPS) unit attached to the handheld computer accurately pinpointed the tracker's location on a topographic map. Louis Liebenberg of South Africa had developed the CyberTracker software to collect the observations of Bushmen of the Kalahari.

My first thought was that CyberTracker could be extremely useful in conservation efforts, and I asked, "How can you trust that the data collected are accurate?" Matt responded, "Good question." Three years later, my tracking skills have greatly improved, and I'm more aware of the vast amount of misinformation about animal tracking. However,

I'm only beginning to understand how big my original question really was.

Louis had already developed one possible, but controversial, answer to the growing issue of how to determine a tracker's abilities. In conjunction with the software, he had developed a system to evaluate trackers who worked for the game lodges and national parks. Because of the skill level of these trackers, the system had earned a good reputation. A positive result was that trackers certified by the CyberTracker system were in demand by the most reputable lodges and were receiving higher-paying jobs. In working toward the implementation of an international tracking evaluation system, Louis's first stop was North America, where I was a participant.

Five of us participated in the first official North American evaluation using the CyberTracker system. Mark Elbroch, author of *Mammal Tracks and Sign* and *Birds Tracks and Sign,* was hosting us in Santa Barbara. He was going to be evaluated as an evaluator, and his hope was that Louis would appoint him the North American CyberTracker ambassador. Dr. Jane Packard, a visiting scholar at Stanford whose specialty was ethnology, attended as an observer to determine whether the evaluation system would prove useful for testing trackers on a Texas river otter project. She arrived with Nate Kempton, a Colorado trapper and tracker who trained the FBI in man tracking. Nate would be tested in both portions of the evaluation: track and sign interpretation, and trailing. Having been evaluated previously in a mock-evaluation and receiving the highest score, I was a good candidate for being evaluated in track and sign interpretation. The guest of honor, Louis Liebenberg, arrived and we packed up our cars and headed over the hills.

We would be spending the weekend in Cuyama, a desert area about two hours east of Santa Barbara. The area had been chosen because of its diverse wildlife, ranging from bears and cougars to tiny kangaroo rats. Cuyama also offered trackable substrate: a dusty pan with sparse brush, soft hills, and sandy gullies perfect for recording an animal's movements, no matter where it roamed. From prior experiences in Cuyama and other unfamiliar places, I knew that understanding an animal's environment is as important as understanding the animals themselves. I had studied a topographic map before the trip, but maps can't substitute for the intimate knowledge of a place that comes only with traversing the landscape to discover where water, food, and other important resources are found.

Not only is an animal an instrument played by the landscape, but the landscape is an instrument played by the animal. Thus the spheres of animal, plant, and land come together to form a whole. (Tom Brown Jr., 1999)

Before leaving, I had studied my notes from previous visits to Cuyama, run my fingertips across track casts from the area, and tried to envision the local animals slipping in and out of shadow across the landscape. I was eager to see my strengths and weakness and to gain a realistic perspective of my growth as a tracker. I didn't expect the evaluation to be one of the greatest learning tools I had yet encountered.

We began in the crisp, early-morning hours under a bridge where the Cuyama River usually runs as a thin ribbon of water, except right after rain or snow, when it swells to nearly 100 yards across. As the water recedes, stretches of mud parallel each side of the thinning river and trap the footprints of countless animals. The bridge provides further protection from the elements and attracts an impressive variety of small mammals; rats, mice, voles, gophers, squirrels, chipmunks, and shrews can be found at one time. These can be deciphered only by nearly imperceivable details that are often obscured by wind or other tracks. One must draw on knowledge of gait, relative size, habits, and biology. This is one example of how the evaluation goes well beyond mere search images and tests one's skills as a tracker.

A tracker is a detective, gleaning facts from minute details and assembling them into a cohesive picture of what went on before. (Len McDougall, 1997)

We started with the track and sign portion of the evaluation. The interpretation of track and sign tests one's ability to recognize and identify single tracks or groups of tracks and to interpret sign, such as stripped bark on trees where wood rats gathered nesting material, or animal behavior, such as how an animal was moving.

Nate approached the first tracks, eager to get started. I waited my turn as he deciphered the tiny marks (each tracker waits for the other to finish so they can't discuss their findings). Nate whispered his answer to Mark while Louis listened in. After two trips to Africa and two near-perfect scores on track and sign interpretation on an unfamiliar continent, Mark was beginning to earn Louis's trust. It was apparent that Louis was invested in the integrity of his evaluation and wanted to ensure that its North American implementation was put in the right hands. It seemed that he also wanted to find out how we Americans compared with South African trackers.

I approached the first tracks. The two hind feet of a small rodent had touched down nearly on top of each other; the front feet didn't register at all. I recognized this motion immediately as the bipedal hop of a kangaroo rat, but which one? My mind went back and forth between Heerman's and Merriam's kangaroo rat; they are similar, but one is smaller. Then I did a risky thing: I evaluated the evaluators. The Heerman's kangaroo rat is the more common, which would have made it a simple identification question. I therefore concluded that they had probably chosen the tracks of the less common Merriam's. I rushed through the next set of tracks because they appeared to be quite simple. It was the clear track of a cottontail, the toes stacked up in a triangular shape that I was familiar with. The second part of the question required me to identify which foot. I couldn't make out all four tracks in the group, which would have made the answer apparent, so I jumped to the conclusion that it was the right front foot.

> We must all be willing to let go of our hypotheses as quickly as we make them, for 15 feet down the trail, further evidence may disprove our current thinking. (Mark Elbroch, 2003)

For me, the most valuable aspect of the evaluation came next, when the evaluators gave the correct answer and a thorough explanation. When tracking is a hobby, as it is for most trackers in North America, one rarely receives affirmation or, for that matter, contention. It's easy to jump to conclusions when you're tracking unchecked, because your hungry family isn't at home depending on you to bring home dinner. The only thing you're likely to bring home these days is a good story; the survival of your community doesn't hinge on whether that story is accurate.

The kangaroo rat, Mark explained while we hunched over the minuscule prints, was an Heerman's, the most common type in the area. I reminded myself to depend on what I could see, not on what I assumed. We moved on to the cottontail tracks, and I saw my mistake before Mark even began. It was the left front foot and not the right. I had confused which side of the body the foot was on. I barely listened as he gave his explanation. Another lesson was resounding in my brain: exhaust your senses and all possibilities before giving a final answer.

Cottontail tracks: Hind feet at top of photo register ahead of front feet.

Thankfully, the next tracks were simple—the identification of a raccoon and a coyote. My confidence rebounded a little, only to be knocked down again by the next set of tracks. They were obscured in mud, which made them appear to shape-shift into the tracks of myriads of animals. I squatted down to get eye level with the tracks. When that didn't work, I paced around them a dozen times trying to gain different perspectives. Fine nail holes had registered in the mud about an inch in front of the toes, and the only animal I could think of with nails like that, used for digging, was a skunk. The problem was that the gait of this animal was unlike any skunk gait I had ever seen, in muddy substrate or otherwise. I saw no way out of my dilemma and gave my final answer.

When Mark began, "This was an interesting find by Louis," I immediately recognized the tracks. "A badger, it's a badger," I blurted out, but it was too late. "It *is* a badger," Mark retorted. The glitch was that I hadn't thought outside the box. In my three previous visits under the bridge, I had never seen badger tracks, so it seemed a logical conclusion that badgers didn't tread there. Louis, who had never been to the area, was accustomed to tracking a similar animal in South Africa:

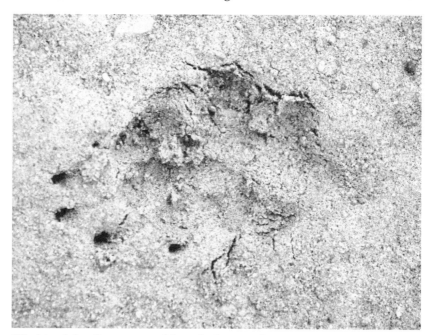

Hind track landing on top of front badger track.

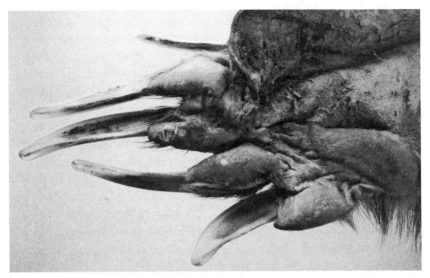

The front foot of the badger reveals the long nails that register well beyond the toes in the track. RANCHO DEL OSO NATURE AND HISTORY CENTER

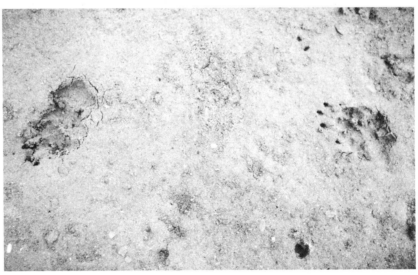

All four feet of a badger. Notice pigeon-toed walking pattern.

the honey badger. He was able to pick out the dependable arrangement of badger nails regardless of the continent or the species. His advantage, I realized, was that he had no expectation of what we would find.

Those first questions taught me some useful lessons for the remainder of the evaluation. Out of at least thirty-five more questions, I missed only two.

We left the area under the bridge to move upriver, where we were tested on the aged marks of leaves blowing across sand, the gender of a bobcat based on its tracks, and the tracks of five different birds (one that I didn't even know existed). Louis was careful to explain that the evaluator's role is to encourage the growth of the trackers and to support their learning process. The evaluator must have a precise clarification of the track in question, and he or she must be skillful enough to contest any arguments from those being evaluated. Arguments are allowed, and if they are sound, the question is thrown out.

Mark stopped suddenly. "You ready, Nate?" he asked, even though the trailing portion of the evaluation was scheduled for the following day. "We've got some bear tracks." Nate looked nervous and hesitant but eager to begin trailing. "They're recent tracks," Mark continued, as Nate made his way over to the track that Mark was holding with a fixed gaze. Nate took a deep breath, looked down the trail in the direction the bear had moved, and agreed: he was ready. Trailing animals is an art that requires patience, imagination, and innovation. I'm fascinated by the infinite details an animal sprinkles across the landscape as it passes. There are very few who can pick up these subtle clues to draw out the story. To these trackers, the animals speak volumes; to the majority of people, they remain silent. Nate was seeing and sensing things that were just beyond my reach. Apparently, they were well within the reach of Louis, who stopped Nate after a dozen tracks. "Nate," Louis began, practically pleading, "you don't have to see each individual track in order to continue on the trail." Nate had been hesitating at each track (more like scuff marks and shiny, flat patches of sand) until he found the next subtle clue. He looked up from the ground for the first time since he had started and met the frustrated eyes of Louis. "You must look ahead and predict, it doesn't matter that you see each track as long as you're still on the trail." Louis provided an example: "You see here where the bear has started to cross the dry riverbed? Now look across to that soft bank on the opposite side where you know this bear will climb up. Rather than looking for it here in the hardpan of the riverbed, you must predict and skip ahead to that soft bank for the next visible track."

We followed Nate 50 yards to the opposite bank, where there was evidence of the bear's crossing—a pile of dirt spilling out into the creek bed, marking where the bear had bounded up the edge. Nate explained that he had been trained never to leave the last known track. He added that in many North American tracking schools, a successful day of tracking was marked by how few tracks you had followed in the greatest amount of time. I agreed, as this had also been my experience in tracker training. Louis then pulled out a list of trailing skills that the evaluation tested. One of the first requirements for a high score was that the tracker's gaze be up and looking ahead on the trail. The farther out a tracker was able to predict, the greater the skill level. The lowest score was reserved for the tracker who looked directly at the ground, depending only on visible marks for trailing. Nate apparently took the lesson to heart. He skipped ahead, predicting where the bear would go next and looking down only occasionally to confirm that he was still on the trail. Daylight quickly waned, and we were forced to return to camp.

We awoke early the next morning for a full day on a fresh bear trail. Louis had never seen a bear, and his voice quickened with anticipation when we found the first track of a young animal. Even though it was nearly winter, the desert seemed far too hot for a black bear. I imagined the bear putting on its winter coat and unable to take it off; temperatures in the low eighties would make it miserable. "The bears in the region," Mark later explained, "don't hibernate in the winter, and their hair can reach a temperature of over 180 degrees at the tips when in direct sunlight, so they must find shady or damp places to rest during the middle of the day." This was encouraging news for Louis, who wanted to track a bear to its daybed; this would be commonplace in Africa, where they often track lions and leopards right to their locations.

Nate seemed more confident the second day, and we all followed him as he predicted the bear's movements based on the landscape. I was next to last in line, so it didn't take long for all the visible tracks to be obliterated by boots. Soon, I wasn't seeing tracks at all and was forced to take my clues from the landscape. We came to a grove of manzanita trees, and I wondered whether Nate had lost the trail. What I didn't realize was that the manzanita trees were fruiting, providing a larder for black bears. Our bear had taken a nap under one of the trees, leaving the round imprint of its body in the dust. Upon waking, the bear had defecated nearly on top of its bed, but the grass-filled mess slid down the hillside. Mark explained that because this was a young bear, perhaps two years old, this was his first season alone, and he was probably being pushed down to the valley floor by the other older, dominant bears. This explained why his scat was filled with grass rather than the energy-rich manzanita fruit.

The hill flattened out on top, and we stopped to catch our breath and study the three likely directions the bear might have taken. Nate investigated all three and found our bear's tracks heading straight across the plateau to a cliff on the other side. The cliff edge was menacing, and lucky for us, the bear seemed to think so too. He continued along the edge at a safe distance, and we followed. The bear walked back out to the edge several times and looked down and across, but it was still too steep. Mark hypothesized, "Because this is a young bear, he may not know the area and is searching for an easy trail."

The plateau sloped closer to the valley floor, and the first adequate trail appeared. Unfortunately, all the animals seemed to agree, and our bear's tracks were lost in the mix. Mark offered Nate another tip: "You know that the bear has gone down this trail into the valley, so just skip ahead to the valley floor and look for one of his fresh prints where it will be undisturbed." Nate welcomed the suggestion, and we all scrambled down the hillside after him. Down in the valley, the group split and went in opposite directions. Both groups called out at the same time that they had found a track. The tracks were headed in opposite directions, and it was up to Nate to decide which ones were the freshest and thus the ones we should follow. Nate paced up and down the valley looking for tracks on top of one another traveling in opposite directions. When none were found, Nate determined which were the freshest tracks by relative age, and we followed them.

Our bear reached the summit of another hill, where he mingled with dozens of other bears and it became increasingly difficult to decipher which bear was ours. The group dispersed as Nate searched for the next track. I saw a mossy area that looked cool and enticing in the heat. It occurred to me that a bear would feel the same way if it were standing there. All it took was a few steps in that direction, and I found the tracks of our bear in the damp moss. For the first time that day, I could see the soft, shiny, oval patches of a bear's foot without the disruption of our group's footprints. I called them over, and Louis reminded me to stay behind the tracker being evaluated. Somehow, that uninterrupted look opened my eyes to all the tracks that had previously been invisible to me. Even as we continued and the boot tracks

Mark Elbroch conducts a CyberTracker evaluation in Texas. J. E.

multiplied, I could see the distinct scuff marks of the bear's feet, which could scarcely be called tracks. For the remainder of the day, it was as though a curtain had been lifted and I could finally see what had always been there, just out of view.

Sadly, the day was nearly over, and it was decided that if the bear didn't go our way, toward the vehicles, we would have to call it a day. Of course, being a wild animal, he didn't go our way, and Louis would have to wait until his next visit to see a black bear. Nate could finally relax—he had scored a level three on his trailing. Mark would become a certified evaluator for track and sign interpretation (but he would have to return to Africa for a better score on trailing). Jane Packard and Mark would coauthor a proposal for the Texas river otter project. And I would become the first American to receive a level-three tracking certificate in track and sign interpretation.

CyberTracker Software

J.Y./T.M.

Many trackers ask how their experiences can contribute to the conservation of wildlife. Conservation issues are often complex, and people around the world are finding creative solutions that involve professional and amateur wildlife enthusiasts who believe in a future rich in wildlife opportunities. One of the most exciting new tools available is CyberTracker software. CyberTracker allows users to efficiently document their observations and share them with other people. Sightings are entered with pictures—called icons—into a small hand-held computer (also called a personal digital assistant [PDA] and sold under popular brands such as Palm and iPaq). A location from the GPS is attached to each entry, and the stored entries are later downloaded into a computer, where they can be transferred to a geographic information system (GIS) program. Although the acronyms can be confusing, the process for the user is simple. The software allows a single individual to record thousands of sightings between each download. Cyber-Tracker makes it possible to translate wildlife observations to maps, where wildlife activity can be studied alongside other data on water, human demographics and infrastructure, property ownership, and the like. CyberTracker is available for free online, and the equipment needed to support it costs only a couple hundred dollars.

CyberTracker software was created by CyberTracker International of Cape Town, South Africa. CyberTracker International was founded to advocate for the contribution to science of the ecological and wildlife knowledge possessed by the indigenous Bushmen of the Kalahari. Acknowledged by science as the ancestors of all people on earth, some Bushmen still live the traditional hunter-gatherer lifestyle. Contained in their culture is tens of thousands of years of experience living in the Kalahari; however, due to illiteracy and prejudice, their knowledge was not available to science until CyberTracker's icon-based technology allowed them to record their observations using pictures, which Cyber-Tracker's database later translated into scientific language. Cyber-Tracker International also initiated the world's first and most rigorous tracker evaluation and certification process (discussed earlier).

If you are interested in learning more about CyberTracker software, visit CyberTracker International's Web site at www.Cyber Tracker.org. To learn more about tracker evaluations in Africa and North America, visit www.CyberTracker.org and www.Wildlife Trackers.com, respectively.

COLLECTING TRACKS
Plaster Casts

Plaster casts are as close as you can get to bringing the actual tracks home without lugging the dirt, mud, or sand they were captured in. Plaster casts are light and relatively durable, making them the perfect record of tracks if you're looking for something three-dimensional. Plaster casts have the added sensory bonus of allowing you to feel the crests and valleys of the toes and heel pad. In fact, an excellent exercise is to close your eyes, feel your plaster casts, and guess what animals the tracks belong to. They are also one of the best teaching tools, especially when you're working with children. Some people like to place a hanger of some sort in the back of the cast before the plaster dries, so they can hang it on the wall after it hardens. How you display or store your plaster casts is up to you. The following instructions will get you started.

Supplies

- Plaster of paris (available at craft and hardware stores)
- Plastic container—an old yogurt container, a Ziploc bag, or a plastic bucket
- Clean, sturdy stick, spoon, ruler, or other mixing device
- Water—this can come from a creek or a pond, but if there's no water source, bring at least a liter of water in a bottle

Plaster cast supplies. D. F.

- Thin cardboard strips secured in a hoop shape with paper clips, plastic rings (cut from the tops of various sizes of plastic containers), or wooden embroidery hoops (optional)

Directions. First, find a track suitable for making a plaster cast. Here are some features to look for:

- Firm soil—wet sand, mud, or packed dirt
- Detailed track—showing at least an outline of all the toes and heel pad
- Clean surface—no debris or loose clumps of soil (some debris can be removed carefully by hand or by blowing it away)

If you're using a ring or other barrier, press it gently into the earth around the track before mixing the plaster. This ring can be removed and reused after the plaster has dried. If you're using an embroidery hoop, it can be left in place, providing a nice frame for the tracks. Containing the wet plaster keeps it from running too far, especially if the track is on an incline.

The trickiest part of this process is getting the right ratio of water to plaster. If the plaster is too thin, you'll have a brittle cast; too thick, and it will be soft and missing detail. Add water first, about the amount it would take to fill your track. Add the plaster until it has soaked up all the water—about two parts plaster to five parts water. Mix it with a stick or spoon, and add water until you get a smooth consistency free of clumps—like pancake batter. Pour the plaster into the track in a steady stream, making sure to fill in all the details of the nails and toes. Let the plaster run half an inch to an inch outside the track, or up to the edge of your framing device, so you get the entire print. This also adds to the thickness of the track, creating durability.

The plaster cast generally takes at least half an hour to dry. To check for dryness, knock on the back of the cast—it should make a ceramic-sounding ring if it's completely dry. If it's still mushy, allow it to dry longer. When it is thoroughly dry, scoop it up from underneath rather than pulling from the top. This can also be accomplished by carefully prying it up with a stick or a knife. Be careful not to crack it. Wrap finished casts in newspaper for safe transport and to soak up extra moisture from the track. Allow the plaster to dry overnight before removing the soil from its surface with water and a toothbrush. Leaving some soil in the cast creates contrast and a more dramatic track, so there's no need to make it sparkling white.

While the plaster is still wet, you may want to scratch the date, your initials, or some other reference into the back of the cast. This is best accomplished when the plaster has dried a bit. Another option is to write on it with a pencil when the track is safely home.

After you've had some practice, you may want to choose several tracks in the same area and fill them all with the same batch of plaster. Depending on the heat and humidity, the plaster can dry quickly in the mixing container, so you'll have to move fast if you do more than one track at a time.

Track Plates
Supplies
- Flat sheets of aluminum
- Acetylene torch

Optional Supplies
- Contact paper (white shelving paper)
- Plastic sheet
- Wooden box
- Bait (peanut butter, chicken, birdseed, cat food)

Directions. The first step is to acquire the materials. A scrap-metal yard is an ideal place to find inexpensive sheets of aluminum, or a hardware store may have them. Inquire about borrowing an acetylene torch from a local gas station or from a welder. If you can't find one, there is an alternative method that uses a gas and oil mixture, described in the sidebar. If you have a torch, burn one side of the aluminum sheet until you have a uniformly sooty surface. Be careful not to smudge the sooty side of this plate with your fingers or by rubbing it against other surfaces (this is where a box or carrying case comes in handy). Ken

Three track plate pieces. KEN CLARKSON

Track plate burn. K. C.

Finished plate. K. C.

Clarkson suggests using a plastic toolbox and creating slats to slip your plates into so that they don't rub against one another.

Place your soot tray in an area of concentrated animal activity—a location where you've seen either the actual animals or definite tracks and sign of the species you're interested in. This is a great way to learn which animals are present and how to identify their tracks (soot tracks take on a different appearance than tracks in natural substrates, but they're still an excellent reference). If you're baiting the tray, use only a small amount so the animal won't linger too long and smear the tracks. The tracks will appear as negative space where the soot has

---

How to Make a Soot Tray Without an Acetylene Torch

Karen Dvornich

Materials

- T-shirt or cotton rag—torn into strips 2 by 5 inches long
- Small saucepan or metal dish about 2 inches high
- Aluminum cooking pan (turkey size)
- 1 tablespoon gasoline-oil mixture—2 parts oil to 1 part gas
- 3 pieces of aluminum (sheet metal) large enough to fit over the cooking pan's width (about 10 by 12 inches)
- Pliers

Directions

- Pour 1 tablespoon of the gas mixture into the saucepan.
- Dip the cotton rag into the gas mixture.
- Put the saucepan into the cooking pan.
- Light the gas mixture, and put aluminum over the pan.
- Leave the aluminum on until most of it is coated with soot. (You can get three sheets done before the fire dies out.)
- Use pliers to lift the aluminum from the fire.

From this point, follow the same directions for using an acetylene torch, and by all means, be careful with either method. Don't touch the trays bare-handed until they've had a chance to cool down. Make sure there's nothing flammable nearby when burning the trays.

Ground squirrel track cluster on soot tray.

Gray fox on contact paper.

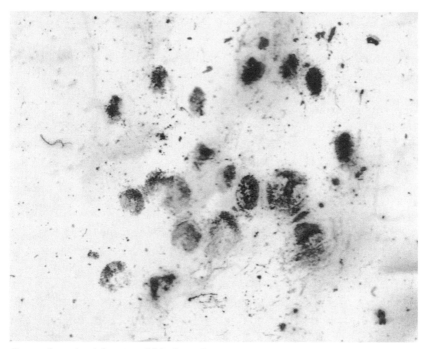

Ground squirrel front and hind tracks on contact paper.

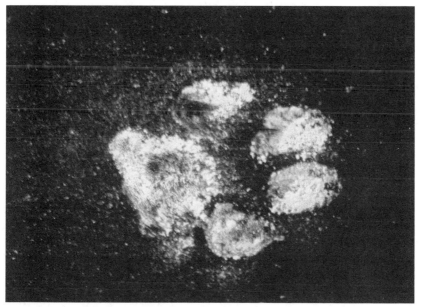

Fox track plate with use of flourescent powder. K. C.

been removed by the animal's feet. To keep the track for your records, take a wide piece of packing tape and place it on the track. When you lift up the tape, the track should appear as negative space on the tape; this can then be taped to a sheet of white paper and cataloged.

Another technique, which allows simple and clean record keeping, is to use contact paper. For this method, burn the sheet metal in sections, so that only part of the plate is covered in soot. Place the sticky side of the contact paper face up, and use tape to fix it to the tray where the soot is absent. When the animal steps from the soot to the contact paper, the tracks will be recorded on the sticky side of the paper. These can be kept in plastic file sheets and compared with others as you collect them.

Note: If it rains, you'll need a plastic sheet or some other device to repel water from the track plates.

TRAPPING SMALL MAMMALS BY TRAVIS BROWN

Near my current home in western Kentucky, there are at least fifteen species of small mammals that most people would call either mice or rats. These include animals that jump like kangaroos, some that remodel old bird nests to make their own homes, and others that have venom similar to a rattlesnake (but much weaker and no threat to humans), yet this group of animals receives little attention. One reason is that they are so hard to see, but naturalists have developed many means of learning about these small mammals.

Learning to track small mammals is a rewarding experience, and examining the tracks of a small mammal that you've captured yourself is one of the best ways to learn. Small mammals are often trapped to learn more about their abundance, life history, interaction with other species, and other aspects of ecology. Recently, they have been used as environmental indicator species, because habitat fragmentation and pollution can directly impact their population density, susceptibility to disease, and ability to reproduce.

Traps

Small mammal trapping can be an interesting endeavor, and if you're trying to catch a species that you've never seen before, checking your traps can be as exciting as Christmas morning. There are several types of commercially available small mammal traps, including Sherman box traps and Longworth traps. These are the most widely used small mammal traps and are available through several scientific supply companies. Other types of live traps are available at local stores.

When constructing your own live traps, the simplest is the pitfall trap. It consists of a coffee can or bucket buried about a quarter inch below ground level. Pitfalls are placed directly next to downed trees or any other sort of drift fence—a structure that small mammals perceive as a fence or a wall and tend to travel along. Other examples include rock faces, barn foundations, landscaping timbers, or commercially available drift fences made from thin sheets of aluminum. This type of trap is most useful for shrews because they can't jump out of even a shallow bucket. Other types of traps can be made from soup cans, pipe, or wood. One of the simplest is a homemade box trap with a lightweight, swinging door that only opens inward. You can find many live trap designs on the Internet.

Baits
One of the most widely used baits for rodents is birdseed. Like many birds, rodents prefer sunflower seeds and ignore millet and other grains. Peanut butter, oats, raisins, and fresh apple slices also make good additions to rodent baits. Shrews are insectivorous and are better attracted with meat such as canned cat food. One of the best ways to increase your capture success is to "prebait" your trapping stations for several days before actually setting the traps.

Animal Health
When trapping animals, it is your responsibility to prevent them from dying from hypothermia, lack of water or food, or capture stress. Shrews are especially sensitive animals and will die if left in a trap for more than two to four hours. They have an extremely fast metabolism, but capture death can be avoided by providing them with plenty of food in the trap. They can also drown in very little water, so you should prop up a shingle or piece of bark over pitfall traps. When the temperature drops below 40 degrees F, place several cotton balls in the traps to prevent hypothermia.

Human Health
Small mammals can carry several diseases and parasites. You should extensively research Hantavirus and plague before dealing with small mammals. I have handled at least a thousand small mammals in the

eastern United States without ill effects, but contact with feces, saliva, blood, or airborne feces particles can be extremely dangerous in certain areas. Washing your hands, wearing gloves, and wearing a facemask are simple precautions that can avoid infection.

Habitat

Learning to identify good small mammal habitat requires practice. Every species has specific habitat requirements that are described in regional mammal guides or in online species fact pages. For example, white-footed mice *(Peromyscus leucopus)* can be found in almost any wooded habitat in the eastern United States, whereas meadow jumping mice *(Zapus hudsonius)* are especially fond of moist, grassy, or shrubby meadows. Shrews need loamy soils such as those found near recently degraded woody material, and many small mammals can be trapped near dead trees or tangles of shrubs and vines.

Handling and Permits

Animals can be removed from traps by shaking them into a bag or by carefully taking them out with a gloved hand. Always wear leather gloves when handling larger species, and remember that a bite from the venomous shrew species can cause swelling and pain. Keep in mind that many states require educational permits for trapping small mammals, and several species are on federal or state endangered species lists. Check the regulations in your state.

Tracks

The most detailed small mammal tracks are often found in the shiny mud left when water drops a fine layer of sediment over an area. This substrate is often present after a stream floods or when a mud puddle begins to dry up. After capturing an animal, you can release it in one of these areas nearby, or you can prepare a container of wet sand to use. Small mammals can also be identified by the size and general pattern of tracks found in dry sand or snow (e.g., bounding, walking). An easy way to learn the tracks of small mammals is simply putting some flour on a surface for the animal to walk across.

Tracking tubes are a more elaborate option. They are made from short sections (about 12 to 14 inches) of tubing at least 1½ inches in diameter. Any sort of tubing will do, because its only purpose is to entice the animals into the small tunnel (which they have a natural tendency to explore) and protect the tracks from being ruined by rain.

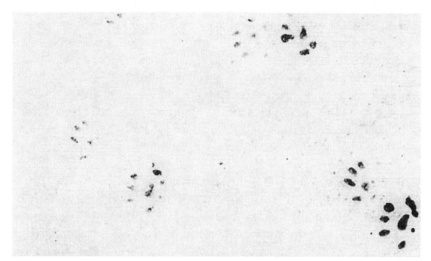

Southern short-tailed shrew (Blarina carolinensis*)*. TRAVIS BROWN

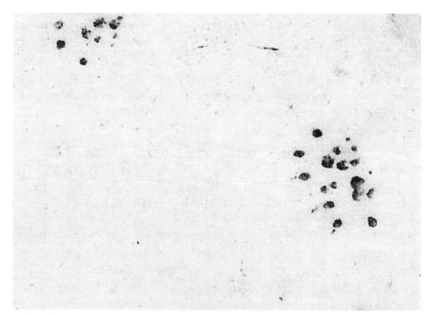

White-footed mouse (Peromyscus leucopus*)*. T. B.

Inside the tube, place a tracking paper; I use 1½-inch-diameter PVC pipe for the tube and a paper measuring 3½ by 8½ inches. Stick a 2-inch square piece of packing tape in the center of the paper, and smear the tape with "ink." I make ink by mixing 1 part graphite powder (available from scientific supply companies for about $10 per 500 grams) with 2 ½ parts mineral oil (baby oil). The ink should be slightly more liquid than pancake batter. Various nontoxic inks can also be used.

Set your tubes in locations where you would set small mammal traps (e.g., logs, trees). They can be baited or unbaited and can be left out as long as the ink remains moist. You can build a reference library of tracks from the animals you trap or use tracking guides to identify the tracks.

CAMERA TRAPS BY DONIGA MARKEGARD

Capturing the image of an animal in a photograph or on a video can both enhance one's tracking experience and provide a glimpse into the lives of animals unaffected by direct human presence. Your ability as a tracker is sometimes limited by terrain and substrate. At best, you can only speculate about the animals using an area. A camera trap can help you solve the mysteries eluding you. If you're fairly certain about an observation but need verification, a camera trap can confirm your theory. Capturing the image of an animal isn't a replacement for direct observation, but it allows you to determine where and when animals are moving on a landscape. For this reason, trackers with knowledge and experience using camera traps are a great asset to research projects.

When you set a camera trap for the first time, it is best to start on a main trail used by multiple species. This allows you to get acquainted with the camera system without having to deal with the problems of targeting a specific species in difficult terrain. Keep it simple to start; you don't want to burn out because of frustrating results, such as an entire roll of film showing a small twig blowing in the wind.

After the camera is set up, visit it about once a week. If you visit the camera too much, you'll influence the animals' patterns of movement. When the roll of film runs out, predict which animal images were captured based on the spoor in the area. Write these observations in a journal with as much detail as possible; you never know which details will be useful. After developing the film, compare the photos with your predictions. Sometimes your predictions will be close, and other times you'll have animals in your images that you didn't see any sign of. In my experience with camera traps, the latter included a gray fox carrying a rabbit to its den, foxes fighting, and a bobcat scent marking a bracken fern. In the case of the bobcat, I was able to go back to the site and pick out the scent on the fern because I knew where to look for it.

"Capturing" animals on camera can aid the tracker's research.

Once you get accustomed to the nuances of the camera equipment and have worked out the settings, you can target a specific animal on a less worn trail. After working with a camera trap for some time as an apprentice of the Shikari Tracking Guild, my goal was to get a picture of the elusive mountain lion. We had seen the tracks of three individual lions traveling in the Corte de Madera watershed on a handful of occasions over the years. The challenge was to find a route where I had seen mountain lion sign, set up a camera, and wait to see whether that lion would return on the same route. I found an area that was heavy with mountain lion sign, including scats of various ages, scrapes, and a log that had been scratched by a mountain lion. The trail that we chose was parallel to a creek, on a steep hill. This was also an area frequented by large bucks, the favorite prey of mountain lions in the coastal hills of California.

After what seemed like months of checking the camera, developing the film, and adjusting the settings, a large wounded mountain lion walked through the infrared beam. I had not predicted this and was amazed when it happened. A few months later, I got another picture of a mountain lion at that camera site, and half an hour later, that same mountain lion passed through another camera site set up with an active beam that works like a trip line. I was starting to get an idea of this animal's movement patterns. Without these pictures, I never would have been able to pick up this information by tracks alone.

In the next year, with support from the Shikari Tracking Guild team, the Riekes Center for Human Enhancement, and neighbors, we captured a total of six still images of the mountain lions of the Corte de Madera watershed and one video of a mountain lion. This piqued the interest of a local nonprofit land trust, which then hired the Shikari Tracking Guild to set up cameras on 4,000 acres of open space in the hope of capturing an image of a mountain lion. This project gave me the opportunity to experiment with various camera trap equipment in diverse locations, each posing its own special challenges.

The TrailMaster active monitor proved to be the most useful in situations of dense fog and high wind. It is triggered only by an animal tripping the laser beam. We used the Stealth Cam in areas of high human traffic; this unit is the most affordable and is easily concealed.

The TrailMaster infrared trail monitors are the cameras we used most often and had the most success with. You have to read the manuals thoroughly and test the camera before you set out on the trail.

Large cougar caught on camera. DONIGA MARKEGARD

There are active infrared monitors, video infrared monitors, and passive infrared monitors. The active infrared monitor uses an invisible infrared beam across the trail, in between the transmitter and the receiver. With the TM 1550 active infrared monitor, accessories such as cameras can be attached to it. I prefer this setup in areas of high wind for species-specific applications, and when the quality of the picture matters. Because there is a narrow beam, the monitor can be set to avoid the movements of small animals. When setting this monitor on a trail, it's important to set it at the correct height so that the largest mass of the animal's body passes through the beam. It may not trigger if it is set too low and only the animal's legs break the beam. It's also important to clear any brush or grass that may break the beam in the wind. A cable connects the monitor and the camera, which allows the camera to be set up at a good angle for taking pictures.

I prefer the TM 550 passive infrared monitor in less windy situations, in sparsely wooded or open areas, and when all species are targeted. With the passive infrared monitor, it takes a lot of initial setup time to get the target area established; once this is accomplished, the camera must be set and the target area adjusted based on the size of the camera frame. This is done by establishing where the animal is predicted to pass and allowing at least three animal body lengths for the triggering speed. This area is then marked on the ground so that the monitor can be set to trigger the camera in the correct location. Because the beam on the passive monitor is wider than necessary for most applications, it should be partially blocked with tape. There is a setup mode on the monitor, and a red light comes on when the monitor is being triggered by motion and heat. The beam continues in front of it, so it is best to have the passive monitor aimed toward a hill. To set the target area, walk in the area marked for the camera frame, and note when the red light comes on. If the area marked is smaller than the beam, add tape to the sides of the beam to narrow the target. All areas around the marked area should be tested and taped as necessary. The height should also be tested. If there is a large branch over the trail, the monitor can be strapped to this branch, aiming toward the ground. This stops the beam from reaching beyond the range of the camera frame.

When setting up a camera with either a passive or active monitor, there are a few things you can do to create quality pictures. It is important not to set the camera too close, which means you won't capture the entire animal, or too far, where the flash doesn't reach. The angle of the sun should also be taken into consideration, and ideally, the camera should be set up facing north, unless it would be in a completely shaded area. Because the camera is on automatic focus, it is important that nothing come between the camera and the target image; this can cause the target image to be out of focus. The angle at which you want to capture the image should also be taken into consideration. If animals travel in both directions on the trail, a side shot usually provides the best picture and the most information. If a front shot is preferred, keep in mind that the flash may affect the animal's movement patterns.

I had a camera set up along the travel route of a coyote and caught several pictures of it looking directly into the camera. I would also see the fresh tracks of the coyote traveling along the creek bank. During the first couple of weeks, I got several pictures of the same coyote. After that, I no longer saw its tracks and got no more pictures of the coyote. I searched for the tracks, wondering whether something had happened to the coyote. I found the tracks on the other side of the creek, avoiding the beam of the monitor. If the camera had been set to capture a side shot of the coyote, I may not have disturbed its movement pattern.

The video monitor, the TM 700v, is similar to the beam on the passive monitor. It is used with a video camera and a large light. When heat and motion trigger the monitor, the camera and light come on, allowing nighttime videos. When capturing video of an animal, it's a good idea to have something in the frame that keeps the animal in the area, such as scents or carcasses. Video is a great way to see how an animal is traveling through an area.

Another camera that I use in areas where theft is a concern is the Stealth Cam. This unit is easily concealed with its camouflage case and its small, self-contained camera and motion sensor. It costs less than $100. Another version of the Stealth Cam operates with digital cameras. The picture quality is good in ideal lighting circumstances. The setup for this camera is simple—the self-contained unit is just pointed at the target area.

Digital cameras can save a lot of money in the long run, considering the cost of getting film developed. The digital motion sensor camera that I recommend is the CamTrakker. It is an easy-to-use, self-contained system that works well in various situations but is not recommended in high wind. This unit can also be easily concealed and locked in place if theft is a concern.

As a tracker, I have been trained to ask all the possible questions about spoor before coming to any speculative conclusions. I have been taught to take in as many clues as possible, not to jump to a premature

Coyote captured on film. D. M.

conclusion. Sometimes a track mystery can be solved immediately upon observation; other times, it takes days, months, or years. Tracking is a series of mysteries that continue to unravel through time and experience. Remote sensing cameras can be a way to solve some of these mysteries as well as confirm speculations.

STILL IMAGE AND VIDEO RECORDING TECHNOLOGY

J.Y.

At Wildlife Associates, Steve Karlin (founder and director), and I worked with our staff to design, build, and load specially built viewing and teaching cages with the best substrate we could find at the Soil Farm in Half Moon Bay, California. In this tracker's-dream playground for learning, we place a gray fox or two and then watch from the comfort of folding chairs or hay bales. We let the foxes move around for a bit; then we remove them from the cage, and we go inside and study their trails. Sometimes we videotape them. We do this with all kinds of wild birds (hawks, owls, vultures), bobcats, servals, and opossums.

We also videotape dogs making trails and take sequential digital photos of the trail series under study. Then we go back to the beginning and try to "see" the dog doing its thing all over again. Later, we study the digital photos to see whether we can remember what the dog actually did. Next, we sit back and watch the video again. We keep going back and forth between the digital photos and the video. This is a way to make the tracks and trails last longer and use them as teaching tools again and again.

SAN DIEGO TRACKING TEAM BY BARRY MARTIN

One of the most satisfying aspects of tracking is the ability to apply the skill to practical situations. Whether you need it to find your next meal, assist in research projects, or for search and rescue, your competence as a tracker can be your key to success. I was interested in tracking from a young age, spending hours in the woods with visions of being an Indian scout trailing game (following deer or raccoon prints) or keeping tabs on the enemy (my sisters and their friends) via their tracks. I didn't begin to study tracking seriously until the late 1980s, when I moved to a neighborhood in San Diego that is right next to the Los Penasquitos Canyon open-space preserve. I quickly found myself involved in the preserve, initially as a volunteer patrol member working with the ranger staff—hiking, cycling, and even riding a horse on occasion around the preserve, ready to assist visitors. Soon the animal tracks and sign in this urban oasis made me curious about the wildlife using it. My childhood interest was rekindled, and I started studying tracking again. Eventually, I decided to do a wildlife survey; my intent was to cover the entire expanse of the nearly 3,000 acres of open space on a frequent basis and document what I saw. Since I was spending most of my spare time there anyway, I figured that it wouldn't require too much extra effort.

However, with family, job, and volunteer commitments, it quickly became apparent that this project was overambitious. I knew that I would need some help. By now, several questions were emerging in discussions with my ranger friends: What mammals do we have in the preserve, and at what population densities? Are there seasonal movement patterns, especially among deer? We also began thinking about how animals might be circulating into and out of the area as new development was planned around the perimeter of the preserve. There was some concern that our open space would eventually be cut off from other open-space areas. This would cause habitat fragmentation and eventual die-off of the trapped species as inbreeding occurred.

With support from the Friends of Los Penasquitos Canyon Preserve and the ranger staff, along with advice from the state Department of Fish and Game (DFG) and the *Wildlife Techniques Manual*, I devised a crude methodology for doing a track and sign survey. Then I wrote an article for the Friends' newsletter explaining the project and requesting volunteers with an interest in wildlife tracking to help collect data. I expected that maybe half a dozen folks would show up but was pleasantly surprised when nearly a roomful of enthusiastic people arrived that Saturday morning. With the help of a friend from the DFG, we held a basic track recognition workshop that day; gave each person a Peterson field guide, courtesy of the senior ranger; and assigned teams of two or three people to each of the many zones the preserve had been divided into. We began to survey these areas over the next few weeks, and the Los Penasquitos Canyon Preserve Tracking Team was born.

Whenever I accompanied the various volunteers in their search zones, I heard a common refrain: "We need more training!" I had been track aware for most of my life and took for granted seeing and recognizing common tracks. But for people who had grown up in cities and hadn't been exposed to wildlife tracking, it was like learning a new language. By this time, I had taken a few tracker school classes (the first of many) and was more than willing to pass some of that ancient knowledge along. I organized a class that went into more detail about track and sign recognition and interpretation.

Over time, the flaws in our first crude survey methodology became apparent, and we continued to seek advice from others, one of whom was Sue Morse of Keeping Track, based in Vermont. She gave us a lot of great ideas about running a survey transect, and we adapted those ideas to our unique situation. Eventually, we devised a simple, effective protocol for conducting a survey—described by one local DFG representative as the most effective field survey methodology he has seen.

Over the years, many dedicated volunteers have participated in many different ways in what has turned into a huge, ongoing tracking project. A certain spirit and imagination have infused this project. When people realize that they can take part in something that may help preserve open space and the corridors connecting large habitat areas, they feel empowered. When we point to the list of accomplishments due to the track and sign survey data we've collected over the years, many ask, "Where do I sign up?"

There is increased incentive to become a skilled tracker when you know that the data you collect may make the difference between a wildlife tunnel being installed or not. Accuracy and correctness are essential in any science-based pursuit, so we now require a comprehensive training program for each of our transect leaders (a transect is a length of trail, usually averaging a mile, that is surveyed for tracks and sign).

We've devised a curriculum that begins with a one-day introductory training session. Participants then sign up for one of our quarterly survey transects, where they can go out with one of the senior trackers and transect leaders to see what it's like. Essentially, we are responsible for documenting any tracks and sign from our list of focal species within 15 feet on either side of the center of the trail. Transects can be set up to sample large habitat areas, narrow corridors, under bridges, or through culverts or tunnels.

If a person's interest is still high after completing one or more transects, the new tracker candidate has an opportunity to attend the beginning tracker-naturalist class, which is a weekday evening and all-day Saturday event. After that, we have intermediate and advanced classes, with plenty of time between each to allow people to practice. Participating in quarterly transects gives new trackers lots of dirt time. New trackers have other opportunities to practice their skills at our monthly tracking hike, which is a low-key get-together conducted by a couple of senior trackers. These are our trackers with the most experience who have been with us the longest. They are not CyberTracker evaluated senior trackers. The transect leaders have the dual role of collecting data and acting as mentors to the up-and-coming trackers.

After completion of the advanced class, the tracker is encouraged to sign up for the apprentice program, which requires 100 hours of practice in various aspects of tracking. Upon completion of the apprentice program, and on the recommendation of two senior trackers, the new team member is invited to be a transect leader.

For those who persevere and would like to continue their path toward tracker perfection, we are also involved in the CyberTracker evaluation program originated by Louis Liebenberg of South Africa and administered in the United States by Mark Elbroch. This gives our trackers the chance to test their limits and aspire to new heights, and having certified trackers on our teams bolsters our credibility.

After a few years, word got out that we had a pretty good program up and running, and we got a call from an open-space advocacy group based in the hills east of us. We set up a series of classes for the group, and eventually some survey transects in the area. Soon that group had a tracking team, and we were helping the members run their transects until their own transect leaders were trained and ready. We got thinking, Why not set up teams all over San Diego County, affiliated with various open-space preserves? This would allow these areas to monitor the health of their ecosystems via track and sign surveys. Thus, the idea of the San Diego Tracking Team was born. It was plain to see that this practical approach was giving people an avenue by which they could reconnect with nature through tracking and naturalist skills. But it was also enabling them to contribute to the well-being of their communities.

We now have six teams in various locations around the county and several more in the formative stages operating under the San Diego Tracking Team network. We conduct transects every quarter; volunteers can choose from a list of more than 50 transects covering open-space areas and corridors throughout San Diego County. We now have a huge database, with well over ten years of data from some of our first transects, and more coming in each season.

The San Diego Tracking Team is a coalition of teams made up of people who are passionate about the outdoors, wildlife, preserving our natural heritage, and learning the ancient art and science of tracking.

We have a long list of success stories, including my favorite—not only because it was our first, but also because it had an unexpected impact later on. Here it is.

On the west end of the Penasquitos Preserve, the canyon is bridged by the confluence of two freeways—the I-5 and I-805 merge, as it is called. Underneath this mass of concrete bridges flows the Penasquitos Creek, winding its way into the Penasquitos Lagoon west of the merge and then out to the ocean. We started surveying under the merge back in the early days to see whether any animals were moving between the preserve and the lagoon. We discovered a tremendous volume of movement occurring through this long, narrow corridor, with ample evidence of deer, bobcats, coyotes, gray foxes, and the usual complement of raccoons, skunks, opossums, squirrels, and rodents.

During those days, a planning effort was under way by city authorities and many other concerned folks regarding the Multi-Species Conservation Plan (MSCP); this was mandated by the Natural Communities Conservation Plan (NCCP), which required each city in the state to come up with a plan for setting aside and preserving open space. We found that the merge link had been excluded from the original plan, even though it was a functioning corridor. We were able to get our data to the decision makers just in time for them to include this corridor as part of the MSCP. Later, when construction was begun on a multiyear road-widening project on the merge overpasses, authorities had to comply with provisions limiting nighttime work and lighting in the area to allow the flow of wildlife to continue. There will also be stringent habitat rehabilitation requirements upon completion of the project. These measures were facilitated by our data proving that the area is a viable wildlife corridor. What would have happened if we hadn't been there?

By far, the best assets the San Diego Tracking Teams have are the motivated and enthusiastic people. Each of our senior trackers is committed to becoming the best tracker-naturalist possible. In addition to relentless self-study, we have all attended many different tracking-related schools and workshops over the years in a quest for continual improvement. The Wilderness Awareness School programs; the Tracker School in New Jersey; Jim Lowery's Earth Skills programs in Frazier Park, California; weekends with Susan Morse in Vermont; James Halfpenny's A Naturalists' World in Montana; a class with Ab Taylor on human tracking; and participation in the CyberTracker evaluation program, to name a few, have all contributed significantly to the growth and skill levels of our tracking teams.

Learning to track is much easier when you have a group of like-minded people to do it with. I still enjoy those solitary times when I can experience the open spaces alone, but my tracking friends challenge me, keep me on my toes, and help me maintain my connection with humanity as well as with the wild. We help one another go beyond our limits in ways that we never imagined. So if you want to apply tracking to a project, gather a circle of tracker friends with a common purpose that goes beyond tracking but uses it to achieve the end result.

As your tracking skills improve and you can confidently identify the tracks in your area, it is time to expand your horizons. For our data collection surveys, we devised a simple form (found in the back of this book) that you can adapt to your own situation. Each form has twenty numbered observation columns across the top (see illustration). Down the left side of the form are several sections: "Species" (there are fifteen on our list); "Evidence"; "Presence of" (e.g., skunks, cottontails, ground squirrels, small rodents); "Age," with "Fresh" and "Historic" as choices; "Tracking Conditions"; "Topography"; and "Habitat." As you can see, that's a lot of information crammed into a small space.

Let's imagine that we're doing a data-collection hike, or transect. Choose a trail with a good representative sample of the tracks and sign in your area. Divide the trail into equal sections, if possible, using easily identifiable landmarks as section breaks. Don't try to cover too much ground—no more than a mile or a mile and a half

We start the transect by noting on the back of the first data sheet some general observations, such as current weather conditions, the last major precipitation event, any recent human events, such as trash dumping, development-related incidents, and the like. Then we begin in section 1. Put on your tracker eyes, and what do you see? Is that a coyote print? Get down for a closer look; check out the shape and size. Can you see any others to confirm it? Yes. The typical coyote trot pattern has the rear foot overstepping the front in a deliberate, purposeful track pattern down the side of the trail, unlike domestic dogs, which like to meander. On the data sheet, mark under observation 1 the number 1 for the section you're in; continue down the column and place a check mark adjacent to "coyote" in the "Species" section. In the "Evidence" section, check "Tracks." For the "Presence of" section, look around for any sign of skunks, cottontails, ground squirrels, or small rodents, and put a check by each one you see evidence of. This is important information in determining the overall health of the ecosystem. Next is the "Age" section. If these are fresh tracks, put a hash mark beside "Fresh." You can put up to five hash marks in one column, so if you continue down the trail and see another set of coyote tracks that are obviously not from the same coyote, you can put another hash mark beside "Fresh" or "Historic," appropriate. Then check the tracking conditions that apply, topography, and habitat, which can be useful in studying species frequency relationships. Now you're ready for the next observation.

Suppose your next observation is a fresh deer track just a few feet from the coyote print. Since you are still in section 1, all your marks on the data sheet will be the same, but in the next column over (under observation 2), and you will mark "mule deer" instead of "coyote" in the "Species" section.

You are looking for tracks and sign up to 15 feet on either side of the center of the trail. If you have a side trail that connects with the main trail, follow the side trail for about 15 feet from the center of the main trail, and see whether you can determine which animals are using it.

When you finish the data collection in the field, put the data sheets in a safe place. We do surveys every quarter, so they are filed by transect, with the season and year noted on each. We have a computer database into which all the data are loaded. If you are computer savvy, you can devise your own data management system to computerize your survey information. If not, you will still be in possession of an important body of work that, over time, can have wide implications for your area. At the very least, you will have an accurate record of the natural history of your place and will have learned much in the process. Perhaps most significantly, you will have connected with the natural world.

Whether you are a new tracker or have lots of experience, getting out and participating in this kind of data-collection effort will tax your tracking ability and improve your skills. It gets you out there with a purpose, forces you to answer questions that you may not have asked before, and, in the process, opens your mind.

15

The End of the Trail

Do not go where the path may lead, go instead where there
is no path and leave a trail.

—Ralph Waldo Emerson

T.M.

Early one morning at the field station, we received a call from a neighbor, a cattle rancher who lived less than a mile away. He knew that we were interested in wildlife and tracking and said, "Hey, I got a dead bobcat up here. It was chasing after my guinea hen and I had to shoot it. If you want it, I could bring it down while it's still fresh."

Mark Elbroch had answered the phone and responded, "Yeah, sure, bring it down. I'd like to take pictures of the feet for my records."

When our neighbor showed up with the cat in a garbage bag, I could feel the heat of its body radiating through the plastic. The rancher drove off on his four-wheeler, leaving Mark and me standing in the driveway with the carcass. Whenever I engage in the task of skinning, gutting, or otherwise handling dead animals, I always feel a little apprehensive, but you can't waste any time getting the job done, because the body will quickly decay and become rancid. We slid the cat out onto the driveway; it's body was still limber and fluid. I lifted up the feet with gloved hands, one at a time, so that Mark could get clear photos of the individual parts. When we moved on to the head, I lifted the lips to reveal old canines and missing incisors. Mark pointed out the various attributes of the teeth that identified this as an old bobcat. I hesitantly pried the teeth apart, feeling that the cat might spring to life at any moment. The coarse texture of the tongue reminded me of Velcro; I let the jaws snap back together. Out of curiosity, I opened up each eyelid. The first one was still clear and even vibrant looking. The second one was dark and swollen, and I immedi-

277

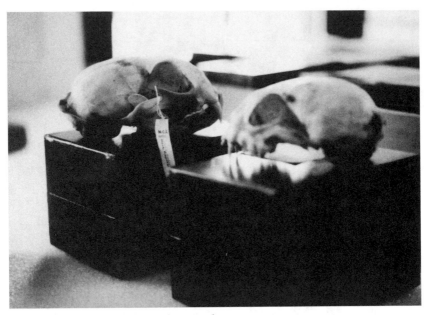

These animals still have much to teach us. MUSEUM OF COMPARATIVE ZOOL-
OGY, HARVARD UNIVERSITY

ately recognized it as the bluish purple orb of One-eye. As I sat in the
exact location where One-eye had killed Mathew, our goose, I was
struck by the irony of life and death.

It became apparent to me that the ostensible end of a trail is often
just the beginning. As soon as you think that you've reached the
conclusion, another chapter starts and the tale carries on. Even now,
through the telling of this story, the tracks and trails of One-eye and
Mathew continue. In the same way that the end of a trail is really just
another beginning, so it is with the end of this book.

Answer Key

HYPOTHESIS 1:
Bobcat walks and deposits scat in mud.

Track Identification: Tracks asymmetrical; heel pad appears large in comparison with toes, which are small, round, and tapered. Negative space in track forms an arch over the heel pad.

Scat: Smooth appearance or sheen on surface—filled with hair, mostly blunt ends.

Track Interpretation: Bobcat slows down at bottom of photo, stops to squat, defecates, and continues out of frame at top of photo.

HYPOTHESIS 2:
Coyote crouching, front legs outstretched, in sand.

Track Identification: The right front track (right side of photo) shows nails. The toes, especially the outer ones, are pulled in tight, behind the leading toes.

Track Interpretation: Front feet are pressed into the sand at left, and rear feet register at right. In the middle of these, the coyote's elbows are apparent where it rested on them while in a crouched position.

HYPOTHESIS 3:
Squirrel cache in cracked mud.

Track Identification: Front and rear tracks visible in upper left corner. The rear track, closest to the edge of the photo, has the telltale look of many rodent rear tracks—three middle toes pulled in tightly together, registering side by side in a row, with two outer toes jutting out. The front track is just behind the rear in the photo—three middle toes spread out. These characteristics may have given away the identification of this squirrel, but further information can be derived from the interpretation.

Track Interpretation: At the center of the photo is a patch of mud with obvious scratch marks radiating out from the edges. Being that squirrels typically cache acorns and other storable food items in the ground, it would be reasonable to assume that this track and sign were made by a squirrel. Thus, animal behavior is a key to track identification, and track identification can help you interpret behavior.

Tracking Forms

Many tracking methods and techniques have been discussed in this book. We wanted to be sure the reader was provided with the tools necessary to begin meaningful tracking explorations of their own. We have included in the following pages some of the most helpful forms to aid your tracking efforts.

The first set of forms are the templates to begin your own Orientation Tracking Journal as discussed in Chapter 3. Forms to begin your own Field Inventory and Field Inventory Map from Chapter 7 are included. The Weather Journal presented in Chapter 10 has also been added for your use. Finally, the SDT Wildlife Survey discussed in Chapter 14 is included as well. These same forms in downloadable format will be made available at www.animaltracking-basics.com.

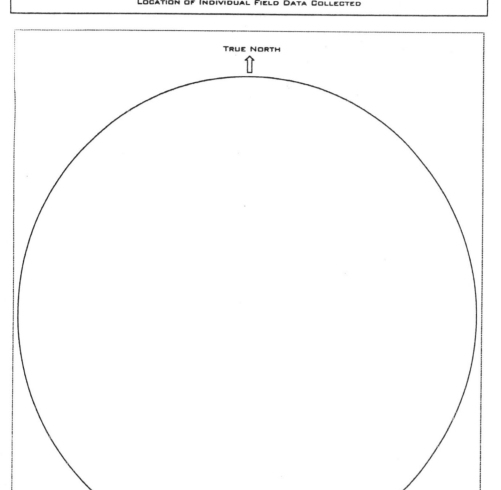

TRUE NORTH

NAME: DATE:

DIRECTIONS TO LOCATION:

LOCAL LANDSCAPE CONTEXT

APPROXIMATE SCALE

———— PACES X ———— PACES
———— FEET X ———— FEET

WEATHER

TIME: TEMP:

WIND DIRECTION: SPEED:

PRECIPITATION:

CLOUDS:

SUN RISE: SUN SET:

LUNAR PHASE: ◯

WEATHER TRENDS:
(WHAT WERE THE LAST FEW DAYS LIKE?)

OBSERVATIONS OF NATURE AND ECOLOGY

BIRDS:

INSECTS:

OTHER MAMMALS:

HUMAN INFLUENCE:

HUMAN ACTIVITY:

PLANTS:

TREES:

WATER:

OTHER:

NAME: DATE:

MASTER LIST OF POSSIBLE MAMMALS

_____

_____

_____

_____

_____

_____

_____

_____

_____

SKETCH GROUP OF FOUR TRACKS

SKETCH LARGER PRINT

SKETCH SMALLER PRINT

NAME: DATE:

THREE BEST POSSIBLE ANIMALS (USE MASTER LIST FROM PAGE 2)

1. NAME	WHY?	WHY NOT?
2. NAME	WHY?	WHY NOT?
3. NAME	WHY?	WHY NOT?

SURVIVAL

WHERE WERE THE TRACKS COMING FROM?

WHERE WERE THEY GOING TO?

WHERE DO YOU BELIEVE THE ANIMAL WAS DURING THE TIME THAT YOU WERE TRACKING IT?

WHAT WOULD YOU DO IF YOU WANTED TO SEE THE ANIMAL THAT MADE THESE TRACKS?

WHAT DO YOU BELIEVE THE STORY OF THESE TRACKS TO BE?

DRAW YOUR BEST MATCH FROM A FIELD GUIDE BELOW! (INCLUDE MEASUREMENTS)

NAME OF BEST MATCH: _____

SOURCE: _____   PAGE: _____

PERSPECTIVE

DESCRIBE OR DRAW WHAT YOU SAW FROM THE ANIMALS PERSPECTIVE:

NAME: _____   DATE: _____

DATE: TIME:

ECOLOGY/LINKING: WATER-SOIL-PLANTS-BIRDS-MAMMALS-PEOPLE-TREES-SUN-MOON-STARS

WEATHER NOTES:

NAME: WEEK DATES:

TITLE:

SOURCE:

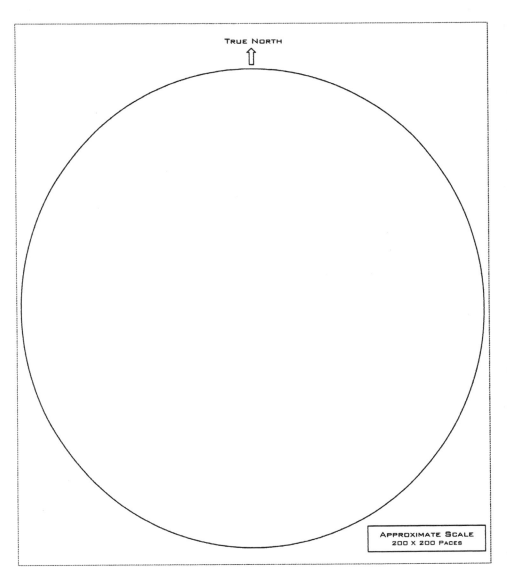

TRUE NORTH

APPROXIMATE SCALE
200 X 200 PACES

NAME: DATE(S):

TITLE:

SOURCE:

DATE:	DATE:

TIME: LOCATION:	TIME: LOCATION:

T: H:

W-D: B:

W-MPH: L: ◯

P:

C:

O:

T: H:

W-D: B:

W-MPH: L: ◯

P:

C:

O:

TIME: LOCATION:	TIME: LOCATION:

T: H:

W-D: B:

W-MPH: L: ◯

P:

C:

O:

T: H:

W-D: B:

W-MPH: L: ◯

P:

C:

O:

TIME: LOCATION:	TIME: LOCATION:

T: H:

W-D: B:

W-MPH: L: ◯

P:

C:

O:

T: H:

W-D: B:

W-MPH: L: ◯

P:

C:

O:

| SUNRISE: SET: | SUNRISE: SET: |
| MOONRISE   SET: | MOONRISE: SET: |

KEY TO ABBREVIATIONS:
✦ T=TEMPERATURE/TREND ✦ W-D=WIND DIRECTION ✦ W-MPH= WIND SPEED
✦ H=HUMIDITY ✦ B=BAROMETRIC PRESSURE ✦ L=LUNAR PHASE
✦ P=PRECIPITATION TREND ✦ C=CLOUD COVER DESCRIPTION ✦ O=OBSERVATIONS OF WILDLIFE

SDT WILDLIFE SURVEY Rev 10/04

Trackers: _____

Start Time: _____ Transect No: _____

End Time: _____ Date: _____

Total Roundtrip Miles _____ Page: _____ of _____

Observation Number	1	2	3	4	5	6	7	8	9	10	11	12	13	14	15	16	17	18	19	20
Section #																				
Photo?																				
Sample?																				
Comment																				
SPECIES Coyote																				
Mule deer																				
Bobcat																				
Gray fox																				
Raccoon																				
Opossum																				
Wood rat																				
Badger*																				
Black-tailed jack rabbit*																				
Cougar*																				
Black bear*																				
Spotted skunk*																				
Long-tailed weasel*																				
Ringtail*																				
Roadrunner*																				
EVIDENCE Tracks																				
Scat																				
Browse (name plant)																				
Claw marks																				
Rub																				
Den/bed/lay																				
Fur/hair/feathers																				
Evidence of predation																				
Cache of prey																				
Carcass																				
Sighting																				
PRESENCE OF Skunks																				
Cottontails																				
Ground squirrels																				
Small rodents																				
AGE Fresh																				
Historic																				
TRACKING Excellent																				
CONDITIONS Good																				
Poor																				
TOPOGRAPHY Flat																				
Moderate slope																				
Steep slope																				
East facing slope																				
West facing slope																				
North facing slope																				
South facing slope																				
Ridgeline																				

Observation Number	1	2	3	4	5	6	7	8	9	10	11	12	13	14	15	16	17	18	19	20
HABITAT Water present																				
Marsh																				
Wash																				
Transition area																				
Oak riparian																				
Willow riparian																				
Sycamore riparian																				
Grassland																				
Coastal sage scrub																				
Scrub oak chaparral																				
Chamise chaparral																				
Mixed chaparral																				
Oak woodland																				
Disturbed																				
Urban edge																				
Tunnel/underpass																				

COMMENTS PAGE:

Your general comments for the transect (including initial start comments) should note weather conditions and temperature for that day, plus any noteworthy weather conditions in the time period since the last survey. (Example: no rain for six weeks or rained two weeks ago.) Note also any particular disturbances on the transect. Comments about fire, off-road vehicular activity, construction, non-native invasive plants should be noted.

When writing up an **Observation** (does not include general comments) always reference the Observation Number from the top of the other side of the form. Please remember when indicating "browse," attempt to identify the plant.

_____

_____

_____

_____

_____

_____

_____

_____

_____

_____

_____

_____

_____

_____

_____

_____

_____

_____

_____

_____

Resources

SCHOOLS AND CLASSES

Boston Museum of Science
Contact: Maureen McConnell
Science Park
Boston, MA 02114
(617) 723-2500
www.mos.org

Designs by Doniga
Contact: Doniga Markegard
20080 Cabrillo Hwy S.
Half Moon Bay, CA 94019
(650) 670-7984
www.designsbydoniga.com

Earth-Heart
P.O. Box 926
Topanga, CA 90290
(310) 967-1336

Earth Skills
Contact: Jim Lowery
1113 Cougar Ct.
Frazier Park, CA 93225
(661) 245-0318
www.earthskills.com

The Institute of Nature Awareness
Contacts: Jon Young and Steve
    Carlin
P.O. Box 3098
Half Moon Bay, CA 94019
www.wildlifeassociates.org
www.jonyoung.info

Keeping Track
Contact: Sue Morse
P.O. Box 444
Huntington, VT 05462
(802) 434-7000
www.keepingtrack.org

A Naturalist's World
Contact: Dr. Jim Halfpenny
P.O. Box 989
Gardiner, MT 59030
(406) 848-9458
www.tracknature.com

NatureMapping
Contact: Karen Dvornich
University of Washington, Fish and
    Wildlife Research Unit
Attn: Karen Dvornich School of
    Fisheries
Box 357980
Seattle, WA 98195
(206) 543-6475
http://wdfw.wa.gov/outreach/
    education/naturmap.htm

Prescott College
220 Grove Ave.
Prescott, AZ 86301
(928) 350-1102
www.prescott.edu

Quail Springs
Contact: Warren Brush
P.O. Box 417
New Cuyama, CA 93245

Regenerative Design Institute
Integral Awareness Training Series
P.O. Box 923
Bolinas, CA 94924
(415) 868-9681
www.regenerativedesign.org

Riekes Center
Bay Area Tracking Club
Contact: Ken Clarkson
3455 Edison Way
Menlo Park, CA 94025
(650) 364-2509
www.riekes.com

San Diego Tracking Team
Contact: Barry Martin
P.O. Box 502345
San Diego, CA 92150-2345
(760) 715-4102
www.sdtt.org

Sense Shikari Training WildLore
6336 N. Oracle Rd., Ste. 326
    PMB #117
Tucson, AZ 85704
www.wildlore.com

The Shikari Tracking Guild
80 N. Cabrillo HWY
Box 150, Ste. 2
Half Moon Bay, CA 94019
www.shikari.org

Tatanka Mani Camp
Contact: Diane Marie
26971 SD HWY 89
Hot Springs, SD 57747
(605) 745-4119
www.tatankamani.org

Tom Brown's Tracking, Nature and
    Wilderness Survival School
Contact: Tom Brown Jr.
P.O. Box 927
Watertown, NJ 08758
(609) 242-0350
www.trackerschool.com

Tree of Peace Society
326 Cook Road
Hogansburg, NY 13655
(518) 358-2641
treeofpeace@earthlink.net

Vermont Wilderness School
3 University Way Suite 5
Brattleboro, VT 05301
(802) 257-8570
www.vermontwildernessschool.org

Victor Wooten
Bass/Nature Camp
Skyline Music
Lancaster, NH
(603) 586-7171
www.victorwooten.com

White Pine Programs
Contact: Dan Gardoqui
330 Mountain Road
Cape Neddick, ME 03902
(207) 361-1911
www.whitepineprograms.org

Wilderness Awareness School
P.O. Box 5000, PMB–137
Duvall, WA 98019
(425) 788-1301
www.natureoutlet.com

Wilderness Youth Project
5386 Hollister Suite D
Santa Barbara, CA 93111
(805) 964-8096
www.wyp.org

Wildlife Associates
Contact: Steve Carlin
P.O. Box 3098
Half Moon Bay, CA 94019
www.wildlifeassociates.org

Wildlife Trackers
Contact: Mark Elbroch
www.wildlifetrackers.com

ORGANIZATIONS

CyberTracker Conservation
Contact: Louis Leibenberg
P.O. Box 1211
Noordhoek, Cape Town 7985
Phone: +27 (0)21 949 2171
www.cybertracker.org

International Society of Professional
    Trackers
Contact: Del Morris
288 Brand Rd.
Santa Rosa, CA 95409
www.ispt.org

The National Wildlife Federation
11100 Wildlife Center Drive
Reston, VA 20190-5362
1-800-822-9919
www.nwf.org

Bibliography

Beier, Paul. "Determining Minimum Habitat Areas and Habitat Corridors for Cougars." *Conservation Biology* 7, no. 1 (March 1993): 94–108.

Bleich, Vernon C., Dorthy M. Fecske, Jonathan A. Jenks, Eric S. Long, Becky M. Pierce, and Richard A. Sweitzer. "Efficacy of Photographic Scent Stations to Detect Mountain Lions." *Western North American Naturalist* 63, no. 4 (2003): 529–32.

Brown Tom. *The Science and Art of Tracking*. New York: Berkeley, 1999.

———. *Tom Brown's Field Guide to Nature Observation and Tracking*. New York: Berkeley, 1983.

Burt, William H., and Richard P. Grossenheider. *A Field Guide to Mammals*. New York: Houghton Mifflin, 1976.

Carson, Rachel. *Silent Spring*. Boston: Houghton Mifflin, 1962.

Corbett, Jim. *Jungle Lore*. London: Oxford University Press, 1953.

Dillard, Annie. *Pilgrim at Tinker Creek*. New York: Harper Collins, 1974.

Diniz-Filho, Jose Alexandre F., Anah T. A. Jacomo, and Leandro Silveria. "Camera Trap, Line Transect Census and Track Surveys: A Comparative Evaluation." *Biological Conservation* 114 (2003): 351–55.

Edwards, Betty. *The New Drawing on the Right Side of the Brain: A course in enhancing creativity and artistic confidence*. New York, NY: Penguin Putnam, 1999.

Elbroch, Mark. *Mammal Tracks and Sign: A Guide to North American Species*. Mechanicsburg, PA: Stackpole Books, 2003.

Elbroch, Mark, with Eleanor Marks. *Bird Tracks and Sign: A Guide to North American Species*. Mechanicsburg, PA: Stackpole Books, 2001

Falkus, Hugh. *Nature Detective*. London: Victor Gollanz, 1978.

Franck, Fredrick. *The Zen of Seeing*. New York: Vintage Books, 1973.

Gibbons, Diane. *Mammal Tracks and Sign of the Northeast*. Lebanon, NH: University Press, 2003.

Halfpenny, James. *A Field Guide to Tracking in Western America*. Boulder, CO: Johnson Books, 1986.

Hanratty, Tom. *Tracking Man and Beast*. Milwaukee: Medicine Hawk Publications, 1997.

Haynes, Lisa, and Don Swann. *Suguaro National Park Results of the 2004 Mountain Lion Track Survey, March 8th–14th*. (March 2004) August 2004. *http://nps.gov/sagu/research/mtliontracksurveyresults.htm*

Heinrich, Bernd. *Why We Run*. New York: Harper Collins, 2001.

Hilty, Jodi A., and Adina M. Merenlender. "Use of Riparian Corridors and Vineyards by Mammalian Predators in Northern California." *Conservation Biology* 18, no. 1 (Feburary 2004): 126–35.

Hopkins, Rickey Alan. *Ecology of the Puma in the Diablo Range, California*. Diss: 1–246. Ph.D. dissertation, University of California, 1986.

Hornocker, Maurice G., Kenneth A. Logan, and Linda L. Sweanor. "Cougar Dispersal Patterns, Metapopulation Dynamics and Conservation." *Conservation Biology* 14, no. 3 (June 2000): 798–808.

Houghtaling, Paul D., Gabriel R. Spence, and Rocky D. Spencer. "Monitoring Strategy: Use of Motion-sensing Cameras to Document Wildlife Occurrence in Remnant Wildlife Habitats." *Draft* (2004): 1–18.

Jackson, Phil and Hugh Delehanty. *Sacred Hoops: Spiritual Lessons of a Hardwood Warrior.* New York, NY: Hyperion, 1995.

Jaeger, Ellsworth. *Tracks and Trailcraft.* New York: MacMillan, 1948.

Karanth, Ullas K. "Estimating Tiger *Panthera tigris* Populations From Camera-Trap Data Using Capture-Recapture Models." *Biological Conservation* 71 (1995): 333–38. *http://www.dfg.ca.gov/lion/outdoor.lion.html*

Kellert, Stephen R., and Edward O. Wilson, eds. *The Biophilia Hypothesis.* Washington D.C.: Island Press, 1993.

Leopold, Aldo. *A Sand County Almanac.* London: Oxford University Press, 1968.

Leslie, Clare Walker, and Charles E. Roth. *Keeping a Nature Journal.* North Adams, MA: Storey Books, 2000.

Liebenberg, Louis. *The Art of Tracking: The Origin of Science.* Cape Town, South Africa: David Philip, 1990.

Martin Alexander C., Herbert S. Zim, and Arnold L. Nelson. *American Wildlife and Plants: A Guide to Wildlife Food Habits.* New York: Dover, 1951.

McDougall, Len. *The Complete Tracker: Tracks, Signs and Habits of North American Wildlife.* New York, NY: The Lyons Press, 1997.

Murie, Olaus J. *A Field Guide to Animal Tracks.* New York: Houghton Mifflin, 1954.

Nyala, Hannah. *Point Last Seen.* Canada: Penguin Books, 1997.

Odum, Eugene. *Ecology: A Bridge Between Science and Society.* Sunderland, MA: Sinauer Assoc, 1997.

Rezendes, Paul. *Tracking and the Art of Seeing: How to Read Animal Tracks and Sign.* 2nd ed. New York: Harper Collins, 1999.

———. *The Wild Within: Adventures in Nature and Animal Teachings.* New York: Penguin Putnam, 1998.

Rue, Leonard Lee. *Sportsman's Guide to Game Animals.* New York: Outdoor Life Books, Harper & Row, 1968.

Schwartz, Charles and Elizabeth. *The Wild Mammals of Missouri.* Columbia, Missouri: University of Missouri Press, 2001.

Seton, E. T. *Animal Tracks and Hunter Signs.* New York: Doubleday, 1958.

Sibley, David Allen. *The Sibley Guide to Birds.* New York: National Audubon Society, Chanticleer Press, 2000.

Sobel, David. *Mapmaking with Children: Sense of Place Education for the Elementary Years.* Portsmouth, NH: Heinemann, 1998.

Stokes, D., and L. Stokes. *A Guide to Animal Tracking and Behavior.* Boston: Little Brown, 1968.

Van Der Post, Laurens. *A Story Like the Wind.* London: Hogarth Press, 1972.

Wessels, Tom. *Reading the Forested Landscape: A Natural History of New England.* Woodstock, VT: Countryman Press, 1997.

Wilson, D., and S. Ruff, eds. *The Smithsonian Book of North American Mammals.* Washington, D.C.: Smithsonian Institute Press, 1999.

Wilson, Edward O. *The Diversity of Life.* New York: W. W. Norton, 1992.

Index